Challenging Health Economics

Challenging Health Economics

Gavin Mooney

OXFORD

UNIVERSITY PRESS

RA
410
·M659
2009

OXFORD
UNIVERSITY PRESS

Great Clarendon Street, Oxford OX2 6DP

Oxford University Press is a department of the University of Oxford.
It furthers the University's objective of excellence in research, scholarship,
and education by publishing worldwide in

Oxford New York

Auckland Cape Town Dar es Salaam Hong Kong Karachi
Kuala Lumpur Madrid Melbourne Mexico City Nairobi
New Delhi Shanghai Taipei Toronto

With offices in

Argentina Austria Brazil Chile Czech Republic France Greece
Guatemala Hungary Italy Japan Poland Portugal Singapore
South Korea Switzerland Thailand Turkey Ukraine Vietnam

Oxford is a registered trade mark of Oxford University Press
in the UK and in certain other countries

Published in the United States
by Oxford University Press Inc., New York

© Oxford University Press 2009

The moral rights of the authors have been asserted
Database right Oxford University Press (maker)

First published 2009

British Library Cataloguing in Publication Data
Data available

Library of Congress Cataloging in Publication Data
Library of Congress Control Number: 2008942571

Typeset by SPI Publisher Services, Pondicherry, India
Printed in Great Britain
on acid-free paper by
the MPG Books Group

ISBN 978–0–19–923597–1

1 3 5 7 9 10 8 6 4 2

To Del

Contents

Contents

Acknowledgements

I am grateful to many people who have in many different ways supported this venture.

Especially helpful have been my 'backing group' who advised me on various aspects of the book (and to never to give up), all of whom read draft chapters. They didn't and don't agree with all of the content of the book (and some I suspect agree with very little of it!) but their comments, advice, and inspiration kept me going. They are: Amiya Bagchi, Steve Birch, Lucy Gilson, Steve Jan, Uffe Juul Jensen, Di McIntyre, Tom Rice, and Del Weston. The last, my wife, read the whole draft manuscript and we discussed various aspects of it many times. The book is dedicated to her and her love.

In addition to these people, I have learned so much from and been inspired by: David Coburn, Dennis Eggington, Bob Evans, Karen Gerard, Shane Houston, Ivar Sonbo Kristiansen, Miles Little, Maureen Mackintosh, Alan Maynard, Vicente Navarro, Jan Abel Olsen, Colin Penter, Mandy Ryan, Glenn Salkeld, Jes Sogaard, Ted Wilkes, Virginia Wiseman, and Alex Wodak. A big thanks to them all.

I also want to thank the many students who over several years have acted as guinea pigs for some of the ideas in this book and whose feedback has helped to shape my thinking.

Thanks to various reviewers whose comments have made this book so much better than it otherwise would have been and especially to the staff at OUP for their advice and guidance. Sarah Caro and Jennifer Wilkinson have been most helpful, patient, and understanding. Having had other less enjoyable experiences with other publishers, I know what a difference such support can make to an author. Thank you both.

Preface

This book is aimed first and foremost at my health economist colleagues. It will also be of interest to economists more generally, to social scientists with an interest in health and health care, to the various disciplines that make up public health, and to health service policy makers. The key intention, however, is to persuade my fellow health economists that there is a need to look at where health economics is and where it might be going. In researching for this book I have become aware that while health economics is changing, most health economists are stuck in the existing paradigm and those who recognise the need for change appear not to have in sight any new paradigm. This book seeks to put that right.

The book has emerged as a result of many diverse thoughts and impetuses. While working in Denmark, from 1985 to 1990, I became acquainted with communitarianism through Uffe Juul Jensen, the Professor of Philosophy at the University of Aarhus. Now a good friend, Uffe has had an enormous impact on my thinking. Also, having moved to Denmark from the UK and then later to Australia, I could not help but notice the differences in the health care systems of these societies and, perhaps more importantly in the context of this book, the difference in attitudes to their health care systems. This was especially noteworthy in relation to equity. It seemed that Denmark had the "strongest" equity principle. While the Danes seldom spoke about it, they were proud of their equitable system. It was a core part of their "Scandinavian solidarity". Private health care formed a small part of the overall health care system and was seen as some sort of aberration. The UK had perhaps the next strongest commitment to equity and the British were particularly keen to talk about it, almost as if it were unique in the world. The UK's National Health Service (NHS) was seen by them as being a world leader in terms of equity. Private health care was something that was largely to be frowned upon and relevant as a major player on the health care stage only in the rich and effete South East. The Australians were rather pleased with their equity principles, built into Medicare (the social insurance system), and saw the principle of equity as being very much linked to that of universality for certain services. They saw no apparent contradiction in there being a sizeable (in OECD terms) private sector. Indeed this was interpreted as forming a part of the equity idea, with the rich being expected to take out private health insurance, thereby leaving Medicare for those who were not so well off.

I suppose this is nothing more than a reflection of the fact that different societies design their health services differently, have different objectives for their health services, or have different cultural values which underlie their objectives and organisational arrangements. Yet the extent to which health economists take account of these differences in our analyses is minimal. We seem not to see the health care system as being a social institution, which might contribute to the welfare of a society. Value is placed solely on the outcomes of the individual services which that system provides. What is to be maximised is what individual consumers get out of it, i.e. usually better health. The structural or organisational aspects of the commodity health care at the level of health care systems are seen as purely instrumental. This results in health economists' missing out on certain key considerations in the economic analysis of health care.

Some of these concerns have been examined by Boswell in the context of economics more generally when he writes (Boswell 1990: 11):

I emphasize the motivational inadequacy of economic pragmatism or the idea that community and collaboration are good mainly because they help to solve specific economic problems... To regard public co-operation in the economy as [only] an instrument or mechanism produces... little support for it and even some confusion. Rather, the most effective cultural and attitudinal nurture for public co-operation comes from a deeper source. It springs from a conviction that public co-operation forms part of a wider search for community which has value in itself, indeed supreme value; from an assignation of top priority, in its own right, to the quality of interpersonal and intergroup relationships.

It is this idea of the social value of "public co-operation" that I would submit was embodied in a comment from Nye Bevan, the founder of the British NHS (Bevan 1952):

No society can legitimately call itself civilised if a sick person is denied medical aid because of lack of means... Society becomes more wholesome, more serene, and spiritually healthier, if it knows that its citizens have at the back of their consciousness the knowledge that not only themselves but all their fellows, have access, when ill, to the best that medical skill can provide.

There is however more to the genesis of this book than that. Conventional health economics has lost its way. There are various reasons for this that I will outline in more detail later. Importantly however the vast majority of what passes formally for health economics is by and large health *care* economics, and health care economics of the developed world, at that. Something like 70 percent of the world's health economists are based in the US. There is nothing either equitable or efficient about that distribution.

The literature on the social determinants of health (poverty, inequality, housing, education, etc.) has to too great an extent passed health economists by in the developed world—there's been more focus on that area in developing countries. The implications for health of gene patenting and the policies of global institutions such as the G8 and the WTO have been very much neglected by health economists. The fact that poverty is the world's biggest killer has failed to dislodge the hold that so many health economists have on economic evaluation of one pharmaceutical product over another, where the impact of the choice on human health and resource use is in most instances negligible. Estimating QALY gains, very largely from health *care* interventions, has become an obsession, while the world's poor have starved. The analogy of fiddling while Rome burns comes to mind. As Di McIntyre remarked at the world forum of health economists, the International Health Economics Association (iHEA) Conference, in 2005: 'Six sessions on obesity and none on hunger.' There is little recognition of the fact that QALYs are a western, primarily Anglo-Saxon, construct or that there may be some variation in what peoples of differing cultures want by way of both health and health services.

South African colleagues, Di and others, have opened my eyes to the narrowness of what so often passes for health economics, at least in 'the North'. Poverty remains by far the single greatest reason for ill health and early death on this planet. Yet reading most health economics texts one would never know that. I felt I had to try to address the issue in this book.

Another major influence on my thinking has been Miles Little, a giant of a man—not just physically—and something of a mentor to me. Some years ago Miles wrote the book *Humane Medicine* (Little 1995). He challenged me to write a book on "Humane Economics". I haven't as yet succeeded, but in these pages I've tried.

The writings of Amartya Sen and Vicente Navarro have become increasingly important to my thinking. I remember vividly reading Sen's *Inequality Re-examined*, where he writes (Sen 1992: 149): "an overdependence on what people 'manage to desire' is one of the limiting aspects of utilitarian ethics, which is particularly neglectful of the claims of those who are too subdued or broken to have the courage to desire much." That made me recognise the need to try to find a way of acknowledging the "claims of those who are too subdued or broken to have the courage to desire much". I have attempted to do that in this text.

From Vicente Navarro's research I have learned much, as is clear from the number of quotes in this book from his works. In particular, however, I have learned that, unless health economists examine the structural aspects of economies, we will fail to grapple with some of the most influential factors in national and global health. The influence on my thinking of his political economy approach to health issues (see for example Navarro 2002) is significant.

I have worked closely with Aboriginal colleagues in recent years and now have a better understanding of some of the cultural differences that Aboriginal people bring to the construct of health, to health services, and indeed to life in general. It is largely from these experiences that I have come to recognise the need for health economists to reflect much more on the diversity of culture and cultural values. Equally, the state of Aboriginal health cannot be understood without a recognition of the impact on these peoples' health of the dispossession of land, the destruction of culture, and the resultant loss of self-respect as individuals and as a society and culture. *Par excellence* these are examples of the negative impact of social determinants of health.

My experience in seeking to write this book came full circle when I realised that Aboriginal culture is communitarian. I recall a meeting in Skagen, in the far north of Denmark where, in a mixed disciplinary group chaired by Uffe Juul Jensen, I sought to defend my then still largely conventional approach to health economics. I was challenged to think non-consequentially and in particularly to see if I could gain some understanding of Aboriginal philosophy. I have had some limited success in that regard and there are echoes of that understanding in this book.

References

Bevan A. (1952) *In Place of Fear*. London: Heineman. Available at: www.sochealth. co.uk/history/placeofear.htm (accessed 20 Dec. 2007).

Boswell J. (1990) *Community and the Economy*. London: Routledge.

Little M. (1995) *Humane Medicine*. Cambridge: Cambridge University Press.

Navarro V. (2002) *The Political Economy of Social Inequalities*. New York: Baywood.

Sen A. (1992) *Inequality Reexamined*. Oxford: Clarendon Press.

Part I

Background and Critique

1

Why a New Paradigm?

1.1 Introduction

There is a need for change in health economics. Partly this is because there is too much emphasis on health care economics and too little on the social determinants of health. Partly there is a deeper malaise in that the existing paradigms of welfarism and extra-welfarism are inadequate for the tasks they seek to address. Partly the big issues of poverty and inequality, both at the level of the nation state and even more so globally, have been largely neglected in health economics. The value base of health economics continues to focus on the individualistic and the consequentialist, despite the fact that a greater focus on health care systems and public health as social institutions would merit more attention from health economists. The impact of the growth of neo-liberalism both in economies around the globe and in the global institutions of the World Bank, the WTO, and the IMF has, with few exceptions, been ignored in health economics.

There are areas where change is occurring and that is heartening but it is not based on any serious critique of conventional health economics. No new paradigm is apparent. The balance between health care economics and the economics of the social determinants of health has shifted a little over time. In 1992 for example, when the journal *Health Economics* was first published, while 18 articles could be classified as being about health care economics, only one can be identified as being about the social determinants of health. In 2007, in that same journal, 15 articles were on the social determinants of health and 56 on health care economics.

With respect to the two key social determinants of health however the situation is particularly worrying. In two major reviews of the literature on inequalities in income and health—one by epidemiologists (Wilkinson and Pickett 2006) with over 170 references and the other by a mainstream economist (Deaton 2003) with nearly 200 references—not one of these references is to an article in either of the two leading health economics journals, *Health Economics* and *The Journal of Health Economics*. Yet inequality in health and income ought to represent a major area of interest for these journals.

The mix of topics covered by the papers presented at the most recent International Health Economics Association (iHEA) Congress in Copenhagen in 2007 is also revealing. This congress is the "world meeting" of health economists. Out of 840 papers presented, there were at most 12 for which the title could be interpreted as possibly dealing with income inequality and health. The word "poverty" appears in the title of only three papers!

This book examines some of the problems in current health economics, proposes a new paradigm and indicates some of the differences the application of such a new paradigm might make.

1.2 Some problems with the current paradigm

Let me begin with a few examples of why I believe radical change is needed. First, there are the problems that arise from health economics not recognising that the hospital is a social institution. Second, the example of so-called "supplier induced demand", over which there has been much agonising by health economists, is shown to be largely a red herring in health care policy since it ignores the question of what society wants from its doctors. Third, there is the non-recognition by most health economists of the social nature of prevention and public health, and the need for such activities to be underpinned by community values rather than individual values. Fourth and relatedly, health economists have done too little to examine the impact of investing in society-wide social determinants of health as a means of explaining why some countries do so much better in health terms than others. Fifth, it is suggested that the idea current in health economics that health is a universalist construct needs to be challenged. Finally, in this introduction the acceptance of a need for community values to be represented in health care is shown to make a difference in health policy.

It becomes clear from these examples not only that a new paradigm is needed but also that such a new paradigm could make a difference to the nature of policy on health and health care.

The biggest spending in all health care systems is on hospitals. There is a very substantial literature on hospital reimbursement which in recent years has been dominated by the literature on diagnosis related groups (DRGs). While these were invented by non-economists, Fetter et al. (1976), they have been taken up enthusiastically by health economists, the latter seemingly being unable to come up with anything better. The DRG system is based on the idea that the goal of hospitals is to produce cases. Hospitals are then paid according to how many cases of different types they treat. So "cost weighted cases" become the measure of a hospital's output.

The assumed objective of the hospital is then to maximise cost weighted cases. The cost figure used to arrive at the weighting of cases in a DRG is an average cost across the relevant region or country and not a marginal cost. It is also usually based on past costings. Yet the raison d'etre for these DRGs is to improve efficiency. The cost data used to determine the cost weights are derived from inefficient practices from the past. So, the "pricing system" for the future is based on average costs, which are drawn from inefficient practices. If a hospital attracts additional cases, it will be rewarded according to some average cost for that type of case. Such a "pricing" mechanism is not based on any recognisable theory of pricing that would promote efficiency.

Only very occasionally are some efforts made in such hospital funding arrangements to measure differential quality. The DRG approach usually assumes that quality of output (which might best be measured by some assessment of the impact on health) is constant across different hospitals. At best when the question of differential quality is addressed it is with very poor proxies for such quality, such as re-admission rates or wound infections.

More fundamentally, it is to be noted that the measure of output is a measure of activity and not of output *per se*. Whatever the objective function of hospitals may be, in some broad sense they are about providing health, even if not that alone. Yet this variable is missing from DRGs. The weights applied to cases are cost weights not benefit weights. This means *inter alia* that if some specialty (such as dermatology) were on average not very efficient across the country, compared to other specialties, that specialty would get more money (based on average cost per case) than if it were relatively more efficient. Thus the DRG cost weighted indicator is not strictly about efficiency but rather about cost, since on the output side any variations in benefits or quality per case are seldom taken into account.

There is a need to take a new look at the hospital as an economic entity and ask most fundamentally the question that the DRG approach has failed to ask: what is the nature of the good (or benefit) of a hospital? In other words, what does society want from its hospitals? That question must surely be best answered by the (informed) citizens who are (potentially) served by that hospital. To adopt this position the hospital would then be seen first and foremost as a social institution. It would become the citizens' hospital or the community's hospital. This line of thinking immediately raises two more questions. How are we to get at community values as opposed to the individualistic values of most health economics? And second, what sort of new economics paradigm is required to support such a stance? Whatever the answer may be, that paradigm needs to be based on, first, community values, second, the treatment of the hospital as a social institution and, third, the idea that the hospital may be valued not only for its outputs but as an institution in its own right.

The way doctors behave is clearly important in any health care system. On the issue of supplier induced demand (SID) there has been a very substantial debate in the health economics literature regarding whether it exists. Yet whether it exists or not arguably does not in itself matter. What matters is whether what doctors are doing fits with society's wants and demands. What are the social objectives of general practice? Given the various influences on and incentives given to doctors, to what extent are these objectives currently being achieved? With few exceptions, however, the question of what society wants from its doctors is not addressed by health economists; indeed even its relevance is seldom acknowledged. Insofar as doctors are not currently meeting these social objectives, how can we get them to do better? This is a question of changing doctor behaviour, which is a legitimate area of analysis for economists. There are hypotheses here that can legitimately be tested by economic analysis. In considering doctor behaviour, health economists need to concentrate attention in future. There is then a need to establish what the social objectives are for our doctors, which means in turn abandoning the idea that, through the agency relationship (which in its conventional non-health-care setting is about helping the ill informed consumer to do better in the market place), simply patching up the paradigm and philosophy of the market is what is required. There is a need for a new approach, one that is not a proxy for the market, but one in which the socially defined good of health care forms the basis of health care policy. That points to a very different paradigm, where the community has a greater say, particularly with respect to the social institutions of, first, medicine and, second, health care.

With regards to prevention and public health, health economics has struggled to make much headway, and the literature on the social determinants of health has attracted much less attention from health economists than it merits. This, it is argued, will continue while we as health economists remain tied to the values of the individual and do not see prevention and public health as social phenomena. We too seldom recognise the power issues around health and health care such that the influences of national medical associations on resource allocation to tertiary hospitals goes almost unnoticed and certainly unanalysed by health economists. Public health and primary health care lose out, but where are the health economics analyses to show this? Of course, some of my colleagues might say that this is not health economics. For me such a response is a clear indication that there is a need for a new paradigm.

India has, as a population, very poor health, with an average expectation of life at birth of less than 62 years. Although it is still a poor country, it is currently under the influence of neo-liberal thinking in public policy, and as a result it is experiencing very rapid economic growth. A key question for health policy makers in India might be: how best in this time of boom might the Indian population, as a whole, achieve an improvement in their health status? This is the sort of question that health economists ought to be addressing too, but sadly there are few attempts to do so.

Relevant to this question is the experience of the Indian state of Kerala (Narayana 2007). If it were possible for the rest of India to "invest" in being like Kerala, this would lead to an estimated increase in years of life in India of approximately 11 billion. This is based on the simple calculation that there are 1.1 billion people in India and Kerala has an expectation of life at birth which is about ten years higher than the rest of India.

At least part of the reason for this difference in health between Kerala and the rest of India is historical and as such cannot be applied to other parts of India (Narayana 2007). It was, for example, the first state in the world to elect democratically a communist government. Land ownership is such that over 90 percent of Keralans own the land on which their home stands. Literacy among men is high compared to the rest of India (91 percent compared with 52 percent). For women the difference is yet greater: 86 percent and 19 percent respectively. But lessons can be learned from the approaches of Keralan society that have had a bearing on its good health status and which may be applicable elsewhere.

For example, Drèze and Sen (2002: 93–4) write:

the contrast between [the two Indian states of] Uttar Pradesh [with an expectation of life at birth below the Indian average] and Kerala...points to the special importance of a particular type of public action: the political organisation of deprived sections of the society. In Kerala, informed political activism, building partly on the achievement of mass literacy, has played a crucial role in the reduction of social inequalities based on caste, gender, and (to some extent) class. Political organisation has also been important in enabling disadvantaged groups to take an active part in the general processes of economic development, public action, and social change...the concentration of political power in the hands of privileged sections of the society has contributed, perhaps more than anything else, to a severe neglect of the basic needs of disadvantaged groups.

This emphasis on public participation leading to population health is again stressed by Sen (1999) in his *Development as Freedom*. He writes (p. 288):

the general enhancement of political and civil freedoms is central to the process of development itself. The relevant freedoms include the liberty of acting as citizens who matter and whose voices count, rather than living as well-fed, well-clothed and well-entertained vassals. The instrumental role of democracy and human rights, important as it undoubtedly is, has to be distinguished from its constitutive importance.

Kerala is not, however, unique in doing relatively well in achieving good population health despite severely limited resources. Cuba is another example.

A background paper prepared for the WHO Commission on Social Determinants of Health (WHO 2005) states:

Post-revolutionary Cuba constitute[s] an important example of "good health at low cost"...Cuba's population health profile more closely resembles wealthy countries...the socialist revolution of 1959...brought medical and public-health resources within the reach of formerly marginalized sectors of society. By redirecting national wealth towards the fulfilment of basic needs, the standard of living for the more disadvantaged social groups was improved despite the country's faltering economic performance in the 1960s and 1970s...The principles of universality, equitable access and governmental control guided post-revolutionary Cuban health policies, which focussed on achieving social equity through free provision of needed services, including medical care, diagnostic tests and vaccines for 13 preventable diseases. Cuba's public health policy prioritizes health promotion and disease prevention activities, decentralization, intersectoral action and community participation; it features a local primary care approach which exists within an organized system of consultation and referral for more specialized care. At local level, physicians and nurses live within the community they serve and provide not only clinical diagnosis and treatment, but also community education about general health issues and non-medical health determinants ... Cuba has made progress in addressing the social determinants of health, applying the same basic principles of universality, equitable access and government control. Education has been a national priority. The government launched massive literacy campaigns shortly after the revolution, nationalizing all private schools and making education free and universal. Subsequently, programmes to ensure that every adult obtained at least a sixth grade education were put in place. Cuba's literacy rate is 96.7 percent, remarkable considering that before the revolution, one quarter of Cubans were illiterate and another tenth were semiliterate. The post-revolutionary period also saw campaigns to improve standards of hygiene and sanitation in urban areas by increasing access to potable water through expansion of the network of aqueducts.

Thus Kerala and Cuba represent societies which have chosen the egalitarian and "cheap" route to good health. They have embraced key features of the social determinants of health and shown that success in terms of good population health indicators can be achieved in practical ways. The extent to which health economists have been active in analysing these case studies and establishing what health economics lessons can be learned from them is all too limited. The egalitarianism of both Cuba and Kerala, the active participation of the community in health planning, and the potential impact of the social determinants of health more generally are all features of the new paradigm developed in this book. Current health economists' unwillingness to analyse these factors to the extent that they merit is yet another reason for arguing for the need for reform in health economics.

In the West too there is evidence that social cohesion and a sense of sharing in a community can have a positive impact on health. Sen (2001) shows that in Britain in both the First and Second World Wars mortality (except, of course, war mortality) fell markedly. Sen puts this down to what he calls "the extent of social sharing and the sharp increases in public support for social services (including nutritional support and health care) that went with this" (2001: 343).

The literature on health status measurement in health economics, which has been dominated by QALYs (Quality Adjusted Life Years), has a number of problems. Here, however, I want to draw attention to one that has not been given the attention it deserves. Questions surrounding culture and health, as in, for example, the destruction of Indigenous culture, have not been seen as relevant territory for health economics research. Yet it is clear that the relationship between land rights and Indigenous health, and the resource issues surrounding such matters would benefit from being looked at through economists' eyes. More fundamentally, as Adams (2004: 283) indicates: "Health is a product of social, economic, political, and religious social structures that are themselves shaped and constituted culturally and in contested political terrain." Health economists have ignored this cultural dimension and assumed that the construct of health is constant across all cultures. The idea that health might be constructed differently by different nations and different cultures is missing from health economics. It is absent from the QALY debate.

Health economics currently uses the values of the individual in most evaluations and indeed it assumes most often that all that is valued in health care is health. That assumption does not stand up to examination. Citizens' juries (see Chapter 9), bringing together randomly selected citizens who have been given good, relevant information and time to reflect, have indicated clearly that as citizens representing their community they want more than health from their health services—they also want good information and to be treated with respect, they want fairness, and they value universality as features of the health care system. They want something different from what they are currently getting from their health service. For example, they are far more concerned about fairness than than the provision of more hospital beds.

These are some preliminary thoughts on why we need a new paradigm. These and other arguments will be examined in more detail in subsequent chapters of this book.

What has been difficult in the journey involved in writing this book has been to decide in my critique of health economics what constitutes health economics. By and large I have adopted the stance that health economics is what health economists do,while being flexible as to who health economists are. Although the book does wander into mainstream economics on occasion, I have resisted the temptation to go further into international health or international geopolitics and the work of other disciplines in health and health care. Drawing a dividing line between health policy and health economics has been particularly difficult.

An earlier draft of this text was written while looking over my shoulder for possible criticisms of my coverage. This version tries to be true to what I term "health economics", recognising that not all readers will agree with my definition of it. Where I have been critical of my sub-discipline and my fellow health economists, I have tried to be fair, but once again I am confident that not all readers will agree that I have. However, in seeking to tread carefully, I have also been mindful that too many caveats would make the book unreadable.

1.3 A path through the book

The book is in four parts. Part I is a critique of certain aspects of conventional health economics. It lays the foundations for a new paradigm that I have sought to build in Part II, while Part III indicates how the new paradigm might work in certain areas of health economics. Part IV provides a brief conclusion.

Chapter 2 expands on the examples above demonstrating how health economics has had only limited success in policy and in practice. Debates about choices of health care systems, priorities for resource use, alternative funding mechanisms, how to pay hospitals and general practitioners, how to price pharmaceuticals, etc., are all issues on which health economics ought to be making a significant impact. Where there have been contributions, they have been more limited than might have been hoped or expected.

In Chapter 3 there is an examination of how health economists have responded to the recognition that the market for health care fails. It looks at the reasons for this failure and suggests that too little attention has been given to the formulation of values, with issues around asymmetry of information perhaps excessively dominating the thinking on market failure. The blind alley of supplier induced demand is also discussed in more detail. The chapter ends by looking at two other key issues around market failure, namely externalities and public goods.

The need for a shift in the health economics paradigm is the subject of Chapter 4. That need arises for a number of reasons, but perhaps most fundamentally because of the desire to integrate more explicitly the three issues of institutions, power, and values into resource allocation, both in health care and in public health more generally. (Population health is used in this book to describe the health of a population; the population health "movement" that is the often rather loose arrangement that constitutes the organisation or institution that seeks to influence population health is called public health.) With respect to institutions, attention is drawn to the fact that health care systems as represented by organisations are, in conventional health economics, treated as purely instrumental and the value of health care is measured solely by its outcomes. Institutional economics treats institutions not only as organisations but also as a set of rules. The idea of public health as a social institution in the sense of both an organisation and a set of rules is missing from the health economics literature.

The question of power, which is essentially a political economy characteristic of health care, is absent from most health economics analyses. This is particularly important in analyses of equity. Related to that issue, the other main area where a shift is needed in the health economics paradigm is in the area of values. There is a need to examine resource allocation in health care and society more generally with respect to health by considering the health care system and public health as being first and foremost social institutions.

There is a change of focus in Chapter 5 to the more ideological and value issues that might underlie health economics. The chapter accepts that both public health and health care are politically and ideologically driven, and sets these in a political economy context. Ignoring these issues, as does most current health economics, means that our efforts as health economists are reduced in their effectiveness.

The chapter argues that neo-liberalism, the form of free market economic philosophy and ideology that has increasingly pervaded the globe in the last 30 years, is bad for the health of the people of those nations that embrace it. It also suggests that global institutions such as the World Bank and the International Monetary Fund (IMF) further the hegemony of neo-liberalism, and that, with few exceptions, these issues have been ignored by health economists.

Chapter 6 begins to build the new paradigm of Part II of the book. First, it sets the stage by introducing the "expressive theory" of Elizabeth Anderson (1993). This involves a number of features including being "intentional, backward looking, distributive, and non-instrumental" (p. 33). More fundamentally it rejects consequentialism and especially the context-free monistic value systems of both welfarism and extra-welfarism. It seeks to incorporate a form of democracy that embodies some form of collective decision making. Given these facets of Anderson's expressive theory, from my perspective (but I suspect not necessarily from hers) it can provide a base on which to build a new health economics paradigm.

The philosophy of communitarianism is outlined in Chapter 7. This can be used as a basis for the values on which to build the proposed new paradigm for health economics. (It is accepted, however, that this may not be the only way to address the problems highlighted in Part I of the book.) The chapter points to the emphasis that communitarians place on public life and community in general and the fact that people are not free floating atoms but members of communities, citizens with identities that are in part composed by their social setting. A definition of what in this text is meant by "a citizen" is set out, and a distinction is made between descriptive and normative communitarianism. The paradigm is firmly based on the latter. Community can involve such values as mutuality, reciprocity, sharing, and caring among a group of people as a community. "Communities" can be represented by small groups; they can encompass nations, as in the Australian society or community; or they can be worldwide or global.

In Chapter 8 it is acknowledged that, while there is a need to change the focus of much of the work of the various disciplines that come under the umbrella of health sciences, the key focus of this book is on the discipline of health economics. The question of a different paradigm for health economics is at the centre of this project. What is critical in this new paradigm is in a sense old. It is the specification of a relevant social welfare function for health services and public health. Against this background a central role for what are termed "communitarian claims" is set out.

The chapter builds on the previous two chapters using the idea of communitarianism of Chapter 9 and the expressive theory of Anderson from Chapter 8. Reflective and group preferences are used to provide a base for communitarian claims.

Part III of the book exemplifies some of the areas where the new paradigm might be applied to advantage, in health policy in general (Chapter 9), in priority setting (Chapter 10), in equity in Chapter 11, and then in a range of other areas in both health economics and the economics of health policy (Chapter 12).

In the wake of the new paradigm developed in Chapters 6, 7, and 8, Chapter 9 examines how population health and health care might be delivered better. The key to making progress here is to see health care, public health, and health policy as by social institutions in the sense not just of being organisations but also as institutions that are valued in themselves and that also provide a set of rules to assist in the process of resource allocation.

If the citizens are in a position to determine the criteria for allocating resources to different groups—according to, for example, ill health, risk, capacity to benefit, etc.—and to state their strengths of preferences for allocating resources to one group over another, according to their degrees of compassion for different vulnerabilities or disadvantages, then the prospects for analysing equity as a genuinely social phenomenon are greatly enhanced. Communitarian claims allow for this.

The chapter also looks at health policy globally going beyond consider-ations of formal health *care* policy. It examines how to overcome some of the problems created or exacerbated by neo-liberalism using the model of a national health policy as developed by Navarro (2007), but extending and modifying this to a more global level. This is based on an interpret-ation of Hegel's ideas of institutions (Muller 2003). It also argues for eschewing not just neo-liberalism but any hegemonic system, suggesting that the links between culture and health point to the need to preserve the diversity of cultures across the globe. This is best achieved by allowing different cultures to be supported by appropriate, and consequently differ-ing, economic structures.

The new paradigm has the merit of reflecting the concept from Sen (1992) of capabilities (but extending that to a community level); it avoids the consequentialist basis of conventional welfarist and extra-welfarist frameworks; and it allows community values as opposed to individual values to come to the fore. These issues are highlighted in Chapter 10. It is shown how the new paradigm provides a more acceptable value base for both the public and the health policy makers, alters the distribution of property rights, and increases the probability that recommendations from priority setting exercises, such as with programme budgeting and mar-ginal analysis (PBMA), might be implemented. Chapter 10 also demon-strates that the problems of lack of "credible commitment" can be overcome by bringing in players who do have an interest in organisational efficiency and who are likely to be present for the long term. The most obvious group that meets these characteristics is the community that is to be served by the organisation.

Chapter 11 examines equity in different conceptual and policy settings, arguing for the abandonment of a universal construct of access, and with it of a universal construct of equity more generally. The need for culturally particular constructs is emphasised and exemplified in the specific context of Aboriginal access to health care, where cultural barriers including insti-tutional racism and lack of cultural security/safety are major impediments to access for this minority group.

Thereafter certain cultural (ethnic) issues related to equity are set out, first, in a case study for Aboriginal people, and then more generally. Using the new paradigm, a way forward to pursuing equity when dealing with access as a cultural concept is outlined.

Chapter 12 continues the theme of addressing the question of what differences the new paradigm might make. Issues covered include economic evaluation in both health care and public health; the economics of health care financing and of primary care; and the economics of public health more generally.

In Part IV, Chapter 13 provides a brief conclusion.

References

Adams, V. (2004) Equity of the ineffable: cultural and political constraints on ethnomedicine as a health problem in contemporary Tibet, in S. A. Anand, F. Peter and A. Sen (eds.), *Public Health, Ethics and Equity*. Oxford: Oxford University Press.

Anderson, E. (1993) *Value in Ethics and Economics*. Cambridge, MA: Harvard University Press.

Deaton, A. (2003) Health, inequality and economic development, *Journal of Economic Literature*, 41: 113–58.

Drèze, J. and Sen, A. (2002) *India: Development and Participation*. Oxford: Oxford University Press.

Fetter, R. B., Thompson, J. D. and Mills, R. E. (1976) A system for cost and reimbursement control in hospitals, *Yale Journal of Biological Medicine*, 49: 123–36.

Muller, J. Z. (2003) *The Mind and the Market, Capitalism in Western Thought*. New York: Anchor Books.

Narayana, D. (2007) Adjustment and health sector reforms: the solution to low public spending on health care in India? in S. Haddad, E. Baris and D. Narayana (eds.), *Safeguarding the Health System in Times of Macroeconomic Instability: Policy Lessons for Low- and Middle-Income Countries*. New York: Africa World Press/IDRC.

Navarro, V. (2007) What is a national health policy? *International Journal of Health Services*, 37(1): 1–14.

Sen, A. (1992) *Inequality Re-examined*. Oxford: Clarendon Press.

——(1999) *Development as Freedom*. Oxford: Oxford University Press.

——(2001) Economic progress and health, in D. Leon and G. Walt (eds.), *Poverty Inequality and Health*. Oxford: Oxford University Press.

WHO (2005) Action on the social determinants of health: learning from previous experiences. A background paper prepared for the Commission on Social Determinants of Health. Available at: www.who.int/social_determinants/resources/action_sd.pdf (accessed 12 Apr. 2008).

Wilkinson, R. and Pickett, K. (2006) Income inequality and population health: a review and explanation of the evidence, *Social Science and Medicine*, 62: 1768–84.

2

Some Problems in Existing Health Economics

2.1 Introduction

Since the 1970s and in the wake of Grossman's (1972) seminal work on the demand for health, the emphasis in health economics has been almost exclusively on health. At the same time, however, but in another sense, the focus has been on health *care*. This seeming paradox is easily described even if not explained. Within the sub-set of health economics that is health *care* economics, other than health, the contenders to be included as a benefit—patient dignity, access, reassurance, information—have been ignored. Process variables such as decision making *per se*, which might have value in themselves, have been neglected. At the same time, when considering the producers of health, health economists have focused very much on health care services. This has meant that the literature on, for example, the economics of the social determinants of health is rather thin in health economics.

2.2 Health economics in health care

In considering the emphasis on health within health care, the starting point is the analysis of the demand for health in the early 1970s by Grossman (1972). He moved the debate away from the commodity of health care, where it had previously lain and placed the focus on health. This tied in with the messages of Arrow's (1963) classic piece on the nature of the commodity. Health economists quickly saw the relevance of the principal agent relationship from standard micro-economics, and adopted a revised version for health economics. Uncertainty and particularly the related conceptualisation in health economics of information asymmetry shifted the focus away from the commodity to health *per se*.

Grossman argued that individuals do not demand health care for its own sake but because they have a demand for health. Selma Mushkin's (1962) human capital approach had been endorsed but, in the wake of Grossman (1972), came to be questioned. However, the human capital approach was not questioned not too much; health remained the sole output, although it was seen as being not just about the ability to add labour value to GDP. The Lancastrian characteristics approach to commodities (Lancaster 1966) was adopted, but still with only one characteristic being taken into account, namely health.

Later in the 1970s in the research of George Torrance (1976) and again from the mid-1980s in the work of Alan Williams (1985) and others, this emphasis on health as opposed to the commodity health care was strengthened by the apparent ability of health economists to measure health. Quality adjusted life years (QALYs) held out the prospect that the way was open to provide the measure for addressing the problems surrounding efficiency, both technical and allocative, in health care. (Lying behind QALYs is "extra-welfarism" which is discussed in the next chapter.)

While this prospect was appealing and seemingly attainable, the same optimism to resolve equity issues was not apparent. In an editorial in *Health Economics* in the early 1990s, Alan Williams (1993) pointed to the need for economists to grapple better with equity concerns. Today it remains the case that the distance between where we are and where we want to get to with equity is much greater than that between where we are and where we want to be with respect to efficiency.

This may be because there is still a debate about what constitutes equity in health care, whereas the efficiency debate has an air of having been resolved—or perhaps more accurately, this *seemed* to be the case at the height of the popularity of QALY league tables in the 1990s. Given the decrease in the popularity of these, however, there has been some limited questioning of precisely in what terms efficiency in heath care is to be defined.

The other area of health economics that I want to touch on at this point is the nature of the underlying implicit welfare function with which health economists are operating. As Mishan (1971: 690) has argued: "In determining whether a potential Pareto improvement has been met economists are generally agreed—either as a canon of faith, as a political tenet, or as an act of expediency—to accept the dictum that each person knows his own interest best." In health economics, at least in the QALY world, that position is not accepted. All QALYs are normally treated as equal no matter who gets them. If one person values health more highly than another then that is not accounted for. This ignoring of individuals' preferences was possibly an intellectually lazy way of trying to build equity into our analyses.

There is a need for us as economists to think through just how best to represent the commodity of health care, and at at least two levels. There is, first, the level of what the prime concern is with treatment for an individual. Second, there is the community level where the concern is with the health care system as a social institution. (There is detailed discussion of the issue of institutions in Chapters 4 and 9.) In the health economics literature, the emphasis has been very much on the individual level.

There are few examples in the health economics literature of considerations of the value of health systems. One is by Mackintosh and Koivusalo (2005: 6). In defining health systems they argue that "health services must aim for universality of access according to need, and solidarity in provision and financing, and that health systems should be judged against these objectives. Solidarity here is about robust redistribution and cross-subsidy to sustain access on the basis of need." They go on to argue: "This implies that health system performance should not be exclusively defined in terms of health outcomes."

Typically, however, the health economics community has been obsessed with health and in many ways to the neglect of health care, particularly of health care systems and their value *qua* systems. This has repercussions for equity both in delivery and financing; financing more generally; remuneration, especially remuneration systems for doctors; the balance between institutional and community care, and the distribution of the costs of care between the formal health care sector and so-called "informal carers"; and the value basis for allocative efficiency in health care.

Listing these issues immediately suggests that there could be so much more to health care economics than we have been witnessing in the revealed preferences of health economics research in the last 30 years. Some of this can be taken care of by adopting a wider view of the arguments in the patient's utility function, and by allowing a broader set of consequences than just health. Processes as well as outcomes might be seen as being utility bearing. We can extend our view yet more by looking at the *citizen's* utility function (although some economists might baulk at the notion of a citizen having a utility function).

These issues of the good of health care and who is to define that form the basis of the critique of health care economics in this book. Methodologically too, this is where the real challenge lies, because it is difficult to see how we can retain a utility basis for the work at this level, where there are concerns that in conventional welfare terms are not utility bearing. Further, the issue of valuation becomes difficult when we are dealing with individuals who in many health care situations are able to desire only inadequately, to paraphrase, albeit in a different context, the words of Sen (1992). When set out in these terms, it is clear that transferring the standard micro theory of the principal agent relationship to health care needs to go beyond uncertainty and information asymmetry. There is a fuzziness with respect to the valuation of health and health care, which is not just information-based but value-based, and which relates to deficiencies in ability to desire. Further, the problem is about an inability not just to express preferences but also to formulate preferences.

Health economists have become obsessed with the maximisation of individuals' preferences, and we have not taken the trouble to question whether this is optimal, irrespective of how the preferences are formulated. We have not researched much at all on the question in health care of preferences *for what*. We do argue that preferences for roses can be equated through expected utility theory with preferences for life (Broome 1978), or at least for reductions in risks of mortality. But preferences based on envy we seek to ignore or argue are illegitimate.

There is, however, at least one reasoned health economist voice on this issue. Uwe Reinhardt (1998: 28) argues: "Normative economic analysis that abstracts from this common human trait [envy], because it is deemed unsavoury, might be useful on other planets. It misses the core of human experiences on planet Earth." Normally, however, preferences are in or out, and we do not weight them differentially except by 1 or zero. Why reject envy and not greed? And do we reject envy when it may be part of the incentive system as exhibited through, for example, relative income (Alpizar et al. 2005)?

2.3 Health economics in health

Turning to the social determinants of health, what is immediately striking is how comparatively little research has been done by health economists on this area. There is some on, for example, road safety (see for example Jones-Lee 2002) and quite a lot on smoking (see for example Parrott and

Godfrey 2008), but little on housing or on the key social determinants of inequality and poverty; almost nothing on the impact of the World Trade Organisation (WTO) on world health; or on the effect of patenting regimes on income distribution between developed and developing worlds and thereby on health. Fortunately research in this area appears to be increasing. The research here has been led by social epidemiologists like Marmot and Wilkinson (1999). Certainly Vicente Navarro (2002) has done some important work on inequalities and health, but overall there is a considerable lack of health economist work here.

A major exception is the work of the mainstream economist Angus Deaton who has conducted various studies into the relationship between inequalities in income and inequalities in health (see for example Deaton 2003). Conventional health economists have been slow to follow. The extent to which economists have analysed the impact on health of investing in housing, access to clean water, education, and social structures more generally on health is disappointing. Questions surrounding culture as a social determinant of health have not been seen as relevant territory for health economics research.

At the still broader level of social institutions and ideologies in a comparative international framework, looking at the WTO, for example, and the impact of its policies on health globally, health economists have been largely absent from the scene. The work of Navarro (2002) and that of a few others such as Gwatkin (2001) are immediately noteworthy in terms of their quality but also their rarity. David Coburn (2000), a sociologist, has done more work on health economics on this front than any health economist. There is evidence that neo-liberalism is bad for income distribution (Navarro 2002) and in turn for health, but again beyond the few names mentioned where is the health economics research? Tax policy and its impact on health (except in goods taxes on alcohol and tobacco) through changes in income distribution is not something to which health economists have devoted much of our attention. Yet there is little doubt that there is a health effect from, for example, altering the level or the progressivity of taxation.

World governments signed up to an agreement at a meeting of the WTO at Doha in 2001 (Hertel and Winters 2006). This was aimed firmly at poverty reduction. To what extent it is succeeding in that goal is questionable. Modelling has looked at the impact on poverty, which as it happens turns out to be small (Hertel and Winters 2006). Where are the follow up studies on health? The US Australia Free Trade Agreement occurred with few efforts on the part of health economists to model the health effects, not even of the most explicit impact of that agreement, i.e. that on the Australian Pharmaceutical Benefits Scheme, which provides government subsidies to more efficient pharmaceutical products.

The roads to economic growth and good population health are similarly neglected in conventional health economics. Yet they do matter, as Sen indicates in his comparison between growth mediated and support-led progress (2001). The former (p. 338):

works through fast economic growth and its success depends on the growth process being wide-based and economically broad...and also on the utilization of the enhanced economic prosperity to expand the relevant social services, including health care, education and social security. In contrast...the "support-led" process does not operate through fast economic growth but works through a programme of skilful social support of health care, education, and other relevant social arrangements.

Sen (p. 388) quotes the examples of "the experiences of economies such as Sri Lanka, pre-reform China, Costa Rica, or the Indian state of Kerala, which have had very rapid reductions in mortality rates and enhancement of living conditions, without much economic growth."

There has also been little interest by health economists in the Cuban health and health services. Yet as Aviva Chomsky (2000: 333) notes:

The Cuban revolution's commitment to the health of the country's population is notable in several respects. First, the government understands health to be the responsibility of the state. Second, the government approaches health as a social issue that includes health-care delivery but is far from limited to it. Thus, the state is responsible not only for building. maintaining and ensuring universal access to doctors, clinics and hospitals, but also for guaranteeing and sustaining the social conditions necessary for health: universal access to education, food, and employment.

There are macro messages here for health economics, even global ones.

The point is thus clear that, in the context of health care services, health economists have been obsessed with health; outside of health services we have researched too little on what contributes to or damages health.

2.4 The commodity health care

There is a problem with the way in which health economists have been wont to consider the nature of the commodity health care. This lies with the assumed nature of the social welfare function in health care and the form of aggregation from individuals' utility functions to the social welfare function. In conventional health economics there is no allowance for what Sen (1977) calls "commitment", i.e. the notion that one individual might act in such a way towards another individual that the latter's utility is increased but the actor's is decreased, even after allowing for some "caring externality". This Sen calls "counter preferential". The inhibiting feature of the health economics analysis here lies not in the concept of utility *per se* but the notion that each individual is maximising his or her *own* utility and that the social welfare function is a simple aggregation of individuals' utilities.

This problem can be overcome very simply by considering the issue in terms of some common project. We can then assume a social welfare function that is to be maximised independently of the maximisation of individuals' utility functions—*provided* that the individuals involved are committed to the maximisation of that social welfare function. The concepts of caring for and of being cared for, for example, then become easier to handle than in the standard externalities argument, which does not allow (indeed cannot allow) for Sen's counterpreferential commitment. This form of maximand can include commitment, where someone who cares for another can be committed to that other, can be acting counterpreferentially in terms of him/herself, but can still be concerned to maximise, jointly, the aggregate utility of the cared for and the carer. Thus individual utility maximisation is no longer the objective, and the social welfare function is no longer the aggregation of individuals' utility functions. Rather, the goal of all is the direct maximisation of the social welfare function.

It is this concept of a common project that is missing from the analysis of health care as a commodity. The conventional caring externality can handle Sen's sympathy (your pleasure is my pleasure) but not Sen's commitment (Sen 1977).

Relevant here is Wright's (1987) concept of a "moral community". He states (pp. 131–2):

Recognition of other persons and the relationship of caring are both important for the development of a moral perspective. Yet neither can be achieved without a sense of community, for a community gives context to the caring relationship of persons and substance to the moral imperative...The community is...a primary condition for the relationships and moral responsibilities of persons. Despite all else they might be, persons are part of a community...If nothing else, the community serves as a constant reminder of our relations to others and the fact that, to be moral, we must interact with others.

Also pertinent is the way in which preferences are expressed in Australian Aboriginal culture (Coombs 1994: 222):

Aboriginal decisions about their preferred lifestyles are, in part, based in the Aboriginal ethic of accountability to others. Social accountability is required by their commitment that autonomy, at a personal and a group level, will be exercised so as to ensure that what is done contributes to the care and nurture of others with whom they are related; so that personal behaviour becomes socially grounded ... [Their] sense of mutual obligation is not due to an external agent, like that sought by white authority, but to the group as a whole.

It is this sense of community, this context of caring *in a community* that health economists have ignored. This book argues that we should devote more of our research efforts in the coming years to these concerns.

What issues, then, need to be considered with respect to the *community* commodity of health care? The list here could be very long as it ideally has to cover all characteristics of the commodity in which individuals *as citizens* might have preferences. (The concept of "a citizen" is discussed in more detail in Chapter 7.) The sorts of characteristics however that might become relevant here are:

- equity and access
- agency
- weighting of health gains
- funding mechanisms
- the balance between community care and institutional care
- patient payments.

At the most macro level with respect to health services, Culyer et al. (1981), writing on the ideological underpinnings of different health care systems, lay out two possibilities that are at either end of a spectrum. For the first, they argue that health care is like any other commodity and hence financing through the private sector is to be preferred. For the second, they argue for a needs-based approach, which then is best supported by a public, more equity focused system. I would suggest that the former cannot be community focused as it is market driven. What is needed beyond the second is some mechanism for allowing this option for health care systems to be appraised by the community, asking the members of the community to choose or at least to express their preferences.

In this context it is useful to quote from Tony Culyer's (1988) *Inequality of Health Services is, in General, Desirable*. Culyer suggested the following as possible objectives of health services: "to maximise freedom of choice in sickness, to maximise utility, to maximise consumers' sovereignty". He went on to argue that there is an advantage (p. 34) "in choosing an objective that is... *likely* to command a consensus, which is not particularly quirky nor merely the idiosyncratic view of a particular pressure group or the tenet of a major but controversial political and social ideology" (p. 34). He proposed that the notion that "health services exist to promote health [is likely to] command a consensus".

Culyer (1988) sought to pin this down further by suggesting that there is a need for "something for which to strive and that can (at least in principle) yield indicators as to whether it is being attained". What he proposed was (p. 35): "given the resources available to the health services, the health of the community should be maximised".

Culyer went on to argue that in the debate in health care about equality versus maximisation (p. 46) "egalitarians in health policy are closet 'national health maximisers'". He might be right in this respect, although much depends on how egality is interpreted and what health maximisation is to mean.

The reason for quoting Culyer at such length is not to agree or disagree with him, but to draw attention to the point that he has to conjecture what the objective of health services is. Seldom is this objective stated very precisely. Even less often have attempts been made to find out what the community view is. What do people as citizens want from their health services?

As an alternative measure of what health services are about we can look more specifically to the QALY literature. Erik Nord et al. (1992), discussing the question of a social welfare function in welfare economics, claim that there is disagreement about both what to measure and the ethical basis for any measurement process. They go on to suggest that the ethical system underpinning the use of QALYs is that "social welfare is equal to a weighted average of individually determined utilities in which the weights ensure that each person's life-year is equally important, irrespective of the individual's personal characteristics or capacity to appreciate life-years". These authors continue: "The rule is almost certainly defective, as it ignores distributional considerations and issues of entitlement that are known to be important in decision making, especially in the health sector." We thus have health economists conjecturing again!

The normal assumption (but one that is increasingly challenged—see for example Mooney et al. 1995) in health economics is that health gains are to be valued equally no matter who gets them. The questioning of that represents one way of addressing vertical equity (see Chapter 11).

Nord et al. (1995), through a self-administered postal questionnaire to members of the Australian public, examined whether the public subscribed to the view that the objective of health services is "the maximisation of the QALYs gained, irrespective of how the gains are distributed" (p. 1429). They found that in a number of circumstances there was little support for such a policy, for example "when health benefits to young people compete with health benefits to the elderly" (p. 1435).

There is thus some research that has been carried out by health economists on the community commodity of health care. It is, however, very limited, surprisingly so since the question of the objective function of health care is so central to the work of health economists. How can we address efficiency of health care if we do not know what is to be maximised? For heath economists to conjecture about or, worse, to assume the objective is even less appropriate. Quite why this happens can be debated (and will be debated in the next chapter). What seems most likely is that health economists have accepted the medical/epidemiology model which makes the assumption, for example in clinical trials, that health is all that is there.

2.5 Two other issues

On equity there has been considerable debate about the nature of the objectives within health care systems. (See for example Culyer et al. 1992a, b; and Mooney et al. 1991, 1992.) Certainly many countries do make explicit statements about what the equity objectives are, at least in principle, that they want their health services to pursue (Donaldson et al. 2005). Little research has been undertaken to determine what citizens want from their health services in this respect (but see the Appendix to Chapter 9 on citizens' juries).

The debate within health economics has proved somewhat sterile, at least with respect to resolving what the appropriate dimension of equity is to be. This is because it has been conducted in a largely data free world. There is a need to ask the community what they want with respect to an equity goal of their health care system.

The majority of health economics research on equity has, in Bob Evans' phrase "moved the target to hit the bullet". It often subscribes in principle to "equal access for equal need" as a definition of equity, but then uses "use" as the variable for measuring access. Much of this research turns out to be useless because it is "access–less"!

The field of equity at an international level has thrown up a related but different problem. Work by Wagstaff and van Doorslaer (2000) defines access according to use. Further, they assume that their chosen definition is constant across different countries and cultures, thereby endorsing the notion of universality and denying the cultural basis of and significance of equity. This is tantamount to cultural imperialism. We see the same thing happening at a yet more crucial level when health is defined universally, especially in QALYs. Such QALYs are moved across countries and cultures with little thought as to whether an Italian QALY might be different from an Iranian QALY. This raises another problem that health economists have ignored. How, in examining equal access for equal need across two different cultures, can we construct health need that is equal? It is not possible logically to have two groups with "equal access" when one seeks access to oranges and the other to apples.

There is a need to find a paradigm which moves away from this universal culturalism with respect to, first, health and, second, equity. It may be useful to be able to identify whether the Irish have a more equitable health service than the Iranians, but to assume, without checking, that the Irish and Iranians have the same goal of equity and place the same weight on achieving that goal is at best inappropriate. Equity needs to be defined and prioritised according to local cultural values. Any new paradigm for health economics has to recognise that. That is attempted in Chapter 11.

Turning to another key feature of health economics, the agency relationship between health care professional (usually doctor) and patient, has been debated in the context of what the perfect agent is attempting to maximise, but with little resolution. As I identified some years ago together with Mandy Ryan (Mooney and Ryan 1993) there is less than agreement in the literature as to what agency is about, i.e. what the objectives are that agency seeks to achieve. The possibilities here are maximum health, information leading to better health, informed choice with respect to health, and maximising patient utility—whatever arguments the patient has in the utility function. There is also less than agreement under conditions of perfect agency, as to who it is, within the doctor–patient relationship, who makes the decision or whether decision making in this context is potentially utility- or disutility-bearing for the patient and/or the doctor.

Here the intention is not to address these questions, but rather to point to the fact that health economists have not adequately resolved them. We seem, by and large, still stuck in a quasi neo-classical world, or a health world where no other arguments than those regarding health appear in the utility function. What communities want from their doctors is a question that few health economists have sought to address.

2.6 Health economics and health policy

Turning, albeit briefly for now (this is followed up in more detail later), to the contribution of health economics to health policy, as someone who has worked in health economics for over 30 years, I am struck by how little our sub-discipline has contributed.

The example of hospital financing was raised in the opening chapter and some of the problems of DRGs exposed. The fact that DRG costing treats the hospital maximand as cost-weighted cases was challenged, especially as the costs used are average, old and based on inefficient practices.

There is thus a need to take a new look at the hospital as an economic entity and ask: what is the nature of the good (or benefit) of a hospital? That question is best answered by the citizens who are (potentially) served by that hospital. The hospital needs to be seen as a community commodity, as a social institution.

DRGs are just one example of the problems of conventional health economics. Staying with the hospital, however, there is much research on this institution as a production process that draws on various conventional economic theories of the firm. The extent to which these are valid then depends on the degree to which hospitals fit into any of these conventional theories. The lack of success by and large of such models as applied to hospitals (McGuire 1985) places a question mark over their validity.

Research 30 years ago from Harris (1977), who was both medically and economically trained, suggests that there may be two "maximands" in the hospital "firm", the maximand of health or cases, and the minimand of cost containment. The former is the property of the doctors, the latter of the administrators and managers. It is disappointing that health economists have grasped Harris' idea of a dual maximand so little, at least as far as can be observed from the subsequent health economics research on the hospital. It does not fit the conventional economic theories of the firm and thus seems destined to be ignored by health economists.

We need to look to an economics paradigm that analyses the hospital in terms that are recognisable to those familiar with the behaviour of hospitals, i.e. health service staff and doctors. Additionally however, we need to see the hospital through the eyes of the patients and the potential patients, i.e. the citizenry. Noteworthy here are two points. First, individual patients are less likely to see the hospital as an entity. They are more likely to focus on a ward or department such as surgery or dermatology. Citizens, on the other hand, are more likely to be interested in wider issues such as equity and option values: the hospital is there for me should I fall sick, or the social option value—the hospital is there should anyone fall sick.

The contribution to priority setting in policy by conventional health economics has been disappointing. There has been a great deal of work done on economic evaluation, but the extent to which that has affected health policy is all too limited, especially on technical efficiency. There are exceptions, such as some countries' policies on pharmaceuticals (Australia is a case in point). The impact of health economics on allocative efficiency, where it might well be argued that it ought to be felt most, is very limited. In, for example, programme budgeting and marginal analysis (PBMA) (Mitton and Donaldson 2001) we have the tools, but their impact has been minimal.

The explanation for this lack of impact on priority setting is multi-faceted. Perhaps most important is the invalid methodology in practice that conventional health economics has adopted. While PBMA as a methodology is sound in principle, it can be problematical in practice. The key difficulty is that it is dependent on what Steve Jan (2003) has called "credible commitment"—the idea that the relevant decision makers must commit to some longer term and wider goals than they would in their standard routine decision making. There is then a need to commit to goals such as population health, which are an aggregate of the various care areas or specialties in health care.

Just as important, however, is the fact that PBMA has tended to take place in a policy vacuum. Decision makers in health care do not think readily or immediately in terms of marginal analysis and opportunity cost. They are more focused on resolving big problems as thrown up by the discipline of epidemiology and then think in terms of needs assessment or the burden of disease—see below (and Murray and Lopez 1996).

Thus the problems of implementing the findings of PBMA are large, and conventional health economists have not adequately grappled with the institutional arrangements involved or hindrances to such implementation. This highlights the fact that conventional health economics has been slow to recognise the potential value of institutional economics and political economy. (An exception is the work of Steve Jan which is discussed in Chapter 4.)

More fundamentally problematic is the use by health economists of needs assessment, cost of illness, and the burden of disease methodologies for determining priorities. There is a substantial literature on these. For example, needs assessment is "a systematic method for reviewing the health issues facing a population, leading to agreed priorities and re-source allocation that will improve health and reduce inequalities" (NICE 2005). It involves an attempt to assess the needs for health care in some defined population, often a geographical population. The assumption is that it is possible to identify and quantify such needs. Having done so, such estimates can then be used, it is assumed, to help to assess priorities: the greater the need, the higher the priority. The economic logic of such needs assessment is, however, poor as it says nothing about the impact of allocating resources to reduce the need or about the benefit of doing so. The idea seems to be to prioritise according to the size of the problem.

Byford et al. (2000) state: "The aim of a cost of illness study is to identify and measure all the costs of a particular disease, including the direct, indirect, and intangible dimensions. The output, expressed in monetary terms, is an estimate of the total burden of a particular disease to society." A major part of the defence for doing these studies is normally that they can be used as a basis for setting priorities. Cost of illness usually covers the cost of treating the illness, together with the costs (for example, from absence from work) arising as a result of the illness. The logic appears to be that if the costs of a particular illness are high as compared with another illness, then the higher cost illness should get higher priority. To this extent they are an extension of the needs assessment approach. They also cover "burden of disease" (BOD) studies, which have been popular-ised and indeed promoted by economists at WHO and the World Bank (Murray and Lopez 1996). That is at best unfortunate. The fact that WHO has encouraged analysts in developing countries and some developed countries to estimate national burdens of disease is worrying. Analytical skills in developing countries are very scarce and if they are employed in low value activities then the opportunity costs may be very high. Further, it is possible that the results of BOD exercises may be used to set priorities in resource allocation erroneously.

What can explain their popularity? This question is difficult to answer. There is a superficial attraction, somewhat similar to that in the needs assessment approach, of allocating resources to "big problems", but that is so shallow an explanation, it is difficult to see that it is adequate. Partly too, it could be that big numbers look impressive. It may be for this reason that the pharmaceutical industry is so keen to fund cost of illness studies. If the industry can show that a particular disease is very costly and that they have a product which will reduce that cost, then this may be a useful marketing weapon. Policy makers, however, ought not to succumb to such an argument.

The use of cost of illness and burden of disease studies as a basis for priority setting in health care will not lead to an efficient allocation of resources (Wiseman and Mooney 1998), neither is this a way of getting to something approximating to efficiency. As Davey and Leeder (1993: 584) remark, in a neat, dismissive, and accurate phrase: "To know the cost of illness is to know nothing of real importance in deciding what we should do about the illness."

There is also a problem not recognised by conventional health economists, which is that the consideration of distribution of property rights in health service decision making results in it being very difficult to make much progress with allocative efficiency. First, this is because there is too little encouragement by health economists to stimulate debate about the nature of the objective function in health care that is to be maximised. As indicated, it is too often assumed or conjectured to be about health only. Yet if we do not know what the decision makers seek to maximise, how well can we pursue allocative efficiency? Second and relatedly, there is the issue of the uncertainty over where the responsibility for overall health system allocative efficiency lies. Oddly, that is often not clear in heath systems governance.

2.7 Conclusion

Why do we have this health economics heritage? I think there are primarily three reasons. First, health economists have concentrated on health to the exclusion of other arguments in the utility, interests, or welfare functions surrounding health care. We have tended to forget that there is a commodity, health care, both at the level of the patient and at the level of the citizen, which has attributes that go beyond health. Second, we have not broken sufficiently from the neo-classical mould or seized on the fact that in health care, having largely rejected the invisible hand, we have not tumbled to the fact that there is a need for this hand to be made visible. There is a need for health economists to be part of the process of making it visible. Third, the idea of health care systems (and public health) being social institutions has not been adequately accepted by health economists.

There are complexities beyond this and these are worth debating; that will happen later in this book. For the moment however, it is enough to recognise that, for whatever reasons, there has been too narrow a view of health provision by health economists and too narrow a view of what health care provides. There is a need to seek to rectify these issues in the future. This book begins that attempt.

References

Alpizar, F., Carlsson, F. and Johansson-Stenman, O. (2005) How much do we care about absolute versus relative income and consumption? *Journal of Economic Behavior and Organization*, 56: 405–21.

Arrow, K. (1963) Uncertainty and the welfare economics of medical care, *American Economic Review*, 5: 941–67.

Broome, J. (1978) Trying to value a life, *Journal of Public Economics*, 9: 91–100.

Byford, S., Torgerson, D. and Raftery, J. (2000) Economics note: cost of illness studies, *British Medical Journal*, 320: 1335.

Chomsky, A. (2000) "The threat of a good example": health and revolution in Cuba, in J. Y. Kim, J. V. Millen, A. Irwin and J. Gershman (eds.), *Dying for Growth*. Monroe, ME: Common Courage Press.

Coburn, D. (2000) Income inequality, social cohesion and the health status of populations: the role of neo-liberalism, *Social Science and Medicine*, 51: 135–46.

Coombs, H. C. (1994) *Aboriginal Autonomy*. Cambridge: Cambridge University Press.

Culyer, A. J. (1988) Inequality of health services is, in general, desirable, in D. Green (ed.) *Acceptable Inequalities*. London: IEA Health Unit.

——Maynard, A. and Williams, A. (1981) Alternative systems of heath care provision: an essay on motes and beams, in M. Olson (ed.) *A New Approach to the Economics of Health Care*. Washington, DC: American Enterprise Institute for Public Policy Research.

——van Doorslaer, E. and Wagstaff, A. (1992a) Utilisation as a measure of equity, *Journal of Health Economics*, 11(1): 93–8.

————(1992b) Access, utilisation and equity, *Journal of Health Economics*, 11(2): 207–10.

Davey, J. and Leeder, S. (1993) The cost of cost of illness studies, *Medical Journal of Australia*, 158: 583–4.

Deaton, A. (2003) Health, inequality, and economic development, *Journal of Economic Literature*, 41: 113–58.

Donaldson, C., Gerard, K., Jan, S., Mitton, C. and Wiseman, V. (2005) *Economics of Health Care Financing*. Basingstoke: Palgrave Macmillan.

Grossman, M. (1972) On the concept of health capital and the demand for health, *Journal of Political Economy*, 80: 223–55.

Gwatkin, D. (2001) Poverty and inequalities in health within developing countries: filling the information gap, in D. Leon and G. Walt (eds.), *Poverty Inequality and Health*. Oxford: Oxford University Press.

Harris, J. (1977) The internal organisation of the hospital: some economic implications, *Bell Journal of Economics*, 8: 467–82.

Hertel, T. and Winters, L. (2006) *Poverty and the WTO*. Washington, DC: Palgrave Macmillan and the World Bank.

Jan, S. (2003) A perspective on the analysis of credible commitment and myopia in health sector decision making, *Health Policy*, 63(3): 269–78.

Jones-Lee, M. (2002) Valuing safety in road project appraisal, *Applied Health Economics and Health Policy*, 1(3): 115–17.

Lancaster, K. (1966) A new approach to consumer theory, *Journal of Political Economy*, 74: 134–57.

Marmot, M. and Wilkinson, R. G. (eds.) (1999) *Social Determinants of Health*. Oxford: Oxford University Press.

Mackintosh, M. and Koivusalo, M. (2005) *Commercialisation of Health Care*. Basingstoke: Palgrave Macmillan.

McGuire, A. (1985) The theory of the hospital: a review of the models, *Social Science and Medicine*, 20(11): 1177–84.

Mishan, E. J. (1971) Evaluation of life and limb: a theoretical approach, *The Journal of Political Economy*, 79(4): 687–705.

Mitton, C. and Donaldson, C. (2001) Twenty five years of PBMA in the health sector, *Journal of Health Services Research and Policy*, 6(4): 239–48.

Mooney, G. and Ryan, M. (1993) Agency in health care: getting beyond first principles, *Journal of Health Economics*, 12(2): 125–35.

—— Hall, J., Donaldson, C. and Gerard, K. (1991) Utilisation as a measure of equity: weighing heat? *Journal of Health Economics*, 10(4): 465–70.

—— —— —— —— (1992) Re-weighing heat: a comment on Culyer, van Doorslaer and Wagstaff, *Journal of Health Economics*, 11: 199–205.

—— Jan, S. and Wiseman, V. (1995) Examining preferences for allocating health care gains, *Health Care Analysis*, 3(138): 231–4.

Murray, C. and Lopez, A. (1996) *The Global Burden of Disease*. Cambridge, MA: Harvard University Press.

Mushkin, S. (1962) Health as an investment, *Journal of Political Economy*, 70(5): 132–3.

Navarro, V. (2002) *The Political Economy of Social Inequalities*. New York: Baywood.

NICE (2005) Health needs assessment: a practical guide. Available at: www.nice.org.uk/aboutnice/whoweare/aboutthehda/hdapublications/health_needs_assessment_a_practical_guide.jsp (accessed 9 Apr. 2008).

Nord, E., Richardson, J. and Macarounas-Kirchmann, K. (1992) Social evaluation of health care versus personal evaluation of health states: evidence on the validity of four health state scaling instruments using Norwegian and Australian survey data. Melbourne: Monash University, Centre for Health Program Evaluation. Available at: www.buseco.monash.edu.au/centres/che/pubs/wp23.pdf

—— ——Street, A., Kuhse, H. and Singe, P. (1995) Maximising health benefits vs egalitarianism: an Australian survey of health issues, *Social Science and Medicine*, 41: 1429–37.

Parrott, S. and Godfrey, C. (2004) Economics of smoking cessation, *British Medcuak Journal*, 328: 947–9.

Reinhardt, U. (1998) Abstracting from distributional effects, this policy is efficient, in M. Barer, T. Getzen and G. Stoddart (eds.), *Health, Health Care and Health Economics*. Chichester: Wiley.

Sen, A. (1977) Rational fools, *Philosophy and Public Affairs*, 6: 317–44.

—— (1992) *Inequality Re-examined*. Oxford: Clarendon Press.

—— (2001) Economic progress and health, in D. Leon and G. Walt (eds.), *Poverty Inequality and Health*. Oxford: Oxford University Press.

Torrance, G. W. (1976) Social preferences for health states, *Socioeconomic Planning Science*, 10: 129–36.

Wagstaff, A. and van Doorslaer, E. (2000) Equity in health care finance and delivery, in A. J. Culyer and J. P. Newhouse (eds) Handbook of Health Economics. Elsevier: Netherlands.

Williams, A. (1985) The economics of coronary artery bypass grafting, *British Medical Journal*, 291: 326–9.

—— (1993) Priorities and research strategy in health economics for the 1990s, *Health Economics*, 2(4): 295–302.

Wiseman, V. and Mooney, G. (1998) Burden of disease estimates for priority setting, *Health Policy*, 43(3): 243–51.

Wright, R. A. (1987) *Human Values in Health Care: The Practice of Ethics*. New York: McGraw-Hill.

3

The Lack of a Comprehensive Paradigm

3.1 Introduction

This chapter examines how health economists have dealt with the recognition that the market for health care fails. It examines the reasons for such failure and suggests that too little attention has been given to the formulation of values, with issues around asymmetry of information overly dominating the thinking on market failure. That has meant that the theory of the agency relationship has not been followed through to make it the major influence that it should be. There remains in conventional health economics uncertainty as to who the decision maker is and also what he or she is seeking to maximise. The blind alley of supplier induced demand (SID), introduced in Chapter 1, is discussed in more detail.

The chapter also looks at two other key issues around market failure, namely externalities and public goods. These are perhaps less important in the market failure debate in the developed world and more important in the developing world.

Extra-welfarism as the main contender to welfarism is outlined. It is seen to be less an alternative theory and more an attempt to justify health maximisation and in turn QALY maximisation in the health care objective function. That leads into a discussion of some of the problems of QALYs, QALY league tables, and cost–utility analysis.

Welfarism is "the framework for normative economic analysis that has developed within the neo classical tradition" (Hurley 1998: 375). It is familiar to all economists; extra-welfarism is less commonly understood or used. According to Hurley (1998: 375) it "refers to frameworks for normative economic analysis that reject the conceptual foundations of the neo-classical welfare framework, particularly the exclusive focus on utility-based notions of welfare". This chapter highlights the problems in conventional health economics in restricting itself to using the values of individuals *qua* individuals and in being consequentialist; both of these restrictions being true of welfarism as well as of extra-welfarism. The chapter concludes that there has been no real attempt to date to provide a comprehensive alternative health economics paradigm in the wake of market failure.

3.2 Market failure, but then what?

There is nearly universal agreement, excepting most US health economists, that the market for health care fails, and Tom Rice's book in the late 1990s (Rice 1998) represented a major critique of that market. No alternative comprehensive paradigm has emerged. Certainly others have concerns for current health economics—see for example Coast (1999); Richardson (2001); and Anand (2003). Instead, in the main, we have attempted to patch things up. We have been slow to accept the problems associated with contingent valuation (willingness to pay) in health care and hung on to elements of welfarism in a way that seeks to keep the market alive in health care. We have invented QALYs within a new "paradigm" of extra–welfarism, which has been used by health economists to ease their analytical tasks but which represents by and large another example of Bob Evans' "moving the target to hit the bullet". The idea that health services are only about health has no evidence in practice to support it, and indeed there is growing evidence that it is quite seriously deficient. Attempts to place extra-welfarism in the Sen (1985) corner of functionings and capabilities do not stand up to investigation.

There is too little recognition that the maximands of both welfarism (conventional utility) and extra-welfarism (health) are inadequate. Patients cannot maximise utility in the conventional sense as they are not adequately informed to do so, and their values are formed by the process of illness and health care consumption and as such are not stable. Equity has been largely ignored in health care. It has been neglected almost totally at a societal level, despite the evidence that the social determinants of health matter and that these in turn equate in the main to poverty and inequality. Further, the implications of the separation of what is in the "evaluative space" (Sen 1992) for efficiency and what is there for equity have not been adequately addressed in health economics. The health economics research on globalisation and neo-liberalism has been paltry, even if Coburn (2000) and Navarro (2002) have to a limited extent come to the rescue on this front. All too little effort has been made to look at the implications for health service labour flows from poor to rich countries, and the impact of patents on medicines and genetic technologies for capital flows again from poor to rich countries. The macro economic *theory* of health economics is very much missing, with the few exceptions of, for example, the work of Sen (1992) and Navarro (2002). The macro *policy* end has fared little better, with especially the WHO Macroeconmic Commission on Health (of which more later) being so very disappointing. The emphasis has been very much at the micro end and then largely on clinical medicine, especially pharmaceuticals. Our desire to emulate the (seeming) scientific rigour of evidence-based medicine has made us forget our social science and philosophical roots.

3.3 Market failure—yes, but...

3.3.1 *Agency and uncertainty on the demand side*

There is much agreement in health economics that the market fails. This occurs largely because of the lack of information available to patients and potential patients who then have to rely on the knowledge and expertise of their agents (the doctors) who are trained to be better informed. This "agency relationship" (borrowed from standard micro theory) can allow the patient to be better placed in maximising his or her utility in health care.

A second related factor is at work, which Weisbrod (1978: 52) refers to as the counter-factual. He writes:

What a buyer wants to know is the difference between his state of well-being with and without the commodity being considered. For ordinary goods, the buyer has little difficulty in evaluating the counter-factual—that is what the situation will be if the good is not obtained. Not so for the bulk of health care...The noteworthy point is not simply that it is difficult for the consumer to judge quality before the purchase...but that it is difficult even after.

Patients are not well placed to judge what would have happened if they had not consumed health care.

There are a number of reasons for this. Sometimes the human body and/ or mind gets better on its own or as a result of some other non-health-care intervention, such as exercise or fresh air. The impact of health care is thus sometimes uncertain *ex ante*; and sometimes unknown *ex post*.

Beyond that there is a lack of agreement in the health economics literature about the decision making process and more specifically who makes the decision about treatment. For example, Alan Williams has argued that it is the doctor who makes this decision; Tony Culyer, the patient and Bob Evans, either (see Mooney and Ryan 1993 for a review).

There is also some doubt as to what the objective function is that the decision maker is attempting to maximise. It may be patient health or patient utility or something else that the patient wants maximised (and this in turn may be something else). There is no discussion of how that objective function might vary from society to society.

Related to the question of agency is the much debated issue of supplier induced demand. Do doctors induce demand in their patients? If they do, is this a good or a bad thing? The literature for several years debated this matter without coming to any very definite conclusion, especially on the latter question.

Now demand in any conventional sense is a function of, *inter alia*, the information that the consumer has about the product to be purchased. Since doctors are often sought out by patients to give them information as well as for potential treatment, there is a sense in which doctors inevitably influence demand. The amount of health care demanded is likely to be different after a patient has seen a doctor than before.

The concept of SID becomes complicated as the definition of what constitutes inducement gets debated. The most common view and one that is certainly defensible is that inducement only occurs when the amount demanded is different from that which the patient would have demanded had he or she possessed the same level of knowledge as the doctor. The perfect agent is one who succeeds in understanding the patient well enough to be able to get the patient to consume what is optimal for that patient. Most of the literature on SID concentrates on the potential benefits to the patient of the doctor's intervention altering their perception of benefits through the provision of better information for the patient.

Two issues arise from this. First, demand is about both information and values. Nothing has been said as yet about values and how these might be affected by the doctor. Second, the decision to consume is a function of the weighing up of not only the benefits but also the costs of the purchase of some good or service.

Economics in general—and this is also true in the debate about SID—assumes that values are a given. As economists we do not normally concern ourselves with how they are formulated, they are simply there. The idea that doctors might affect the values that patients have is not countenanced since economic theory tells us that this cannot happen. The idea that doctors might induce demand through influencing values is not considered.

More worrying, however, is that the emphasis in the SID literature is almost wholly on the benefit side. Judgements are made about whether SID exists by examining levels of consumption of health care when only the demand side of the equation has been considered. Yet, clearly, consumption is a function of both costs and benefits. Can the doctor influence the patient's perception of the costs that fall on the patient? The answer is surely, yes. If the doctor can get the patient to underperceive the costs, then the patient will "overconsume". This can occur at a number of levels and with respect to various facets of costs. A GP may understate the time costs involved in consulting a specialist or the anxiety costs in having or waiting for the results of a screening test. He or she may underplay the difficulties involved for the patient in getting child care while attending a clinic. While a doctor may be capable of being a relatively good agent with respect to estimates of health benefits, success in estimating the costs of attending for care and other costs falling on the patient is harder. The doctor at least has some training in estimating the former, but not the latter. Yet the health economics literature is strangely silent on the cost side (although, see Artells-Herrero 1981).

Relatedly but separate, it is also odd that the question of using consumption as a measure of demand has not been challenged. Perfect agency is about achieving consumption in some relevantly optimal sense. While consumption is what is used to measure agency success, the debate in health economics about how doctors influence such consumption is wholly on the demand side. On SID we do not discuss supplier induced *consumption* but only supplier induced *demand*.

Part of the problem here is that SID is seen as a litmus test by many health economists in the debate about whether the market can work in health care. Pro marketeers (largely US health economists) argue that SID does not exist and that the evidence SID proponents put forward is simply the result of normal market forces. Those who argue that the market in health care fails suggest that doctors do take advantage of the existence of agency to create higher incomes for themselves by stimulating demand.

There is a growing recognition that the debate about SID is one that simply cannot be resolved through empirical evidence. At a macro level the fact that the supply of more doctors in a geographical area results in more consultations may be SID, but it may also be simply the result of lower costs to the patient of access. At the micro level doctors' responding to raised fees may be simply the normal response to market prices. It may be supplier induction.

The more fundamental problem here is that inducement is about motivation and economists are not good at dealing with motivation. Ours is a behavioural science—we need to remind ourselves of that more often. While efforts have been made to try to keep the moral overtones out of SID, often there is an incorporation of the idea of unethical medicine being practised when SID is debated. Of course, it could be argued that SID is unethical if patients are being induced to consume health care for reasons that are not related to what patients want and or demand and more to do with doctors maximising their utility and/or incomes. Doing the best for patients is something of a mantra in medicine. The questions are then: what is best? And according to whose values is this judged? More crucially, trying to sort out motivations is not the province of economists. So SID, whether it exists or not, may well be something that economists should not have delved into.

As indicated in the introduction, the stance adopted in this book is that the question of whether SID exists or not does not in itself matter. What needs to be considered is whether doctors are doing what society wants. There needs to be a consideration of the social objectives of medicine. Seldom in health economics is that question addressed. However, it needs to be addressed, and only then can we consider the question of what doctors are doing and how we might influence them to do what society wants of them. We know that paying doctors in different ways, for example a fee for a service or capitation, affects what they then do. Unless we know what society wants from their doctors we cannot judge what is better.

3.3.2 Externalities and public goods

Externalities in health care are substantial, with communicable disease and caring being the two key considerations here. Where communicable disease exists, if left to individual consumers in the market place, there will be underconsumption in terms of what is optimal for a society as a whole. The caring externality exists where it is argued that people have a concern for the ill health of others or lack of access to health care of others. Again consumption in the market will be below the optimal level if such externalities are ignored. Each can lead to a form of market failure.

There was something of a belief until relatively recently that in the developed world communicable disease was by and large no longer a problem. Much of health economics has been predicated on this assumption. With the advent of AIDS, SARS, and bird flu that assumption, if it ever were valid, no longer holds good. The market is thus subject to failure more or less everywhere as a result of its inability to cope adequately with such externalities.

On the caring externality, Reinhardt (1998 p. 30) writes: "Most ordinary citizens in any country profess to derive positive utility from knowing that suffering fellow human beings receive appropriate health care, even if that care must be collectively financed." This positive externality is difficult to incorporate in the market place.

Some aspects of health care represent public goods, such as environmental spraying to reduce malaria transmission. Markets cannot deal with public goods. These are goods such as lighthouses, which classically are non-excludable and non-rival. When a good like a lighthouse is available it is not possible, or at least it would be very expensive, to stop someone using it even when they refuse to pay. Spraying fields to kill off mosquitoes provides health benefits from reducing malaria, and the resultant benefits are to all. No pricing system in the market can be used to exclude some individuals who might not be willing to pay the market price for such a service.

Many public health messages have the characteristics of public goods. Potentially everyone benefits from adverts on bill boards to stop smoking or to use condoms. Pricing cannot exclude some people. There is no method of establishing meaningfully people's willingness to pay and then using this to exclude those with low levels of willingness.

The other side of this is that these same messages cannot be avoided, at least not easily. This raises important issues regarding whose values determine whether these messages go on the bill boards or not; and this question is not addressed by current health economics. It can be addressed, however, in the new paradigm developed in Part II of this book.

3.4 Extra-welfarism's health maximand

Where has that led health economics? To date there has been little attempt to grapple with these issues in any way other than a piecemeal fashion. An important exception is extra–welfarism, which is both the most comprehensive and the most serious attempt that has been made to deal with market failure. It is different from other efforts to deal with market failure, which are more about trying to prop up a quasi neo-classical view of the market. Even if the extra-welfarist approach were valid as some alternative paradigm (and it will be shown not to be), it falls well short of being comprehensive.

The key impact of what has been labelled "extra-welfarism" has been to allow health economics to move away from welfarism and to agree, seemingly, that all that needs to be included in the individual patient's welfare function or utility function is health. This led not so much to the birth of the Quality Adjusted Life Year (QALY)—these had already existed since the late 1960s (see Klarman et al. 1968), most notably in the work of George Torrance in the 1970s (see Torrance 1986)—but rather to an attempted justification of the QALY in quasi-theoretical terms. Although useful up to a point (but see Gafni and Birch 1993), there is a substantial literature debating the pros and cons of QALYs.

QALYs are measures of health that have two dimensions, length of life and quality of life. These can be traded off one with one another in a quasi-utilitarian way. One QALY is a year of life in good or perfect health, and QALYs can be summed over a life time in such a way that, for example, a life with some health care intervention, at time t, can be compared with a life without that intervention to establish the difference in health produced by the intervention, i.e. its effectiveness in terms of health gains.

Culyer (1990) argued that his extra-welfarism was based on Sen (1985) and his capabilities. The extent of this influence (or it may be the interpretation that Culyer placed on Sen's work) is limited, at least for those who agree with Sen's capabilities as providing a basis for analysing health and health care. Yet Culyer (1990) writes of "two rather distinctive strands" in health economics in the previous 30 years, which he labels "welfarist" and "extra-welfarist", the latter of which he says is "heavily dependent on Sen".

Culyer suggests that for "health economists it is natural to focus on the 'health' of individuals as one of the 'characteristics' (Culyer 1990) or 'basic capabilities'... [see Sen 1992] of interest". He indicates that: "The distinctive feature of the extra-welfarist approach lies partly in identifying a personal characteristic, like health... as being relevant in comparing social states... and partly (and more significantly) in emphasising an objective—or at least less subjective—measure of health." It is further suggested by Culyer that, with respect to QALYs, while the "particular contexts [of the work on QALYs] vary greatly... [a]ll seem to imply, though in various degrees, the compromising of consumer sovereignty."

Particularly important to Culyer's position is that

whereas in the welfarist literature utility is interpreted subjectively by each individual and it is these subjective utility numbers that are the arguments in the social welfare function, in extra-welfarism this assumption is not necessarily made and the presumption is that external judgments may be imposed that replace or supplement the subjective utility numbers of principal or agent in the [social welfare function] SWF.

In evaluating health care, in addition to health, Culyer (1990) argues that "[i]t would be natural for extra-welfarists to include other characteristics of individuals as well, especially those related to primary goods". That is certainly in line with Sen. As examples Culyer suggests, "whether they are out of pain, physically mobile, free to choose, enjoying satisfactory relationships with other people". Yet in the remainder of the paper in which he makes the point, and in papers since, he has restricted the focus solely to health. In practical terms therefore, the way that Culyer uses "extra-welfarism" is to shift the contents of the evaluative space from goods to health. Given how Sen attempts to encompass several characteristics within his concept of a person's interests, it is unlikely that he would adopt such a narrow view as Culyer attributes to him.

Extra-welfarism is different from Sen's approach in another key respect. Culyer (1990) excludes the possibility that individuals' diversities with respect to valuing health states should be allowed to count in extra-welfarism. This is the case with QALYs, where variations across individuals in their values of health are not allowed. As Culyer (1990) states: "in extra welfarism ... the presumption is that external judgments may be imposed that replace or supplement the subjective utility numbers of principal or agent in the SWF."

Sen is very much in favour of such variations and indeed he seems to frown upon ignoring or trying to bypass diversities across individuals in their valuations. The exception is when he appears to be in favour of discounting the individual's values in respect of those who are not able to "manage to desire"; see Sen (1992: 149.)

Sen's position is more akin to that adopted by Elizabeth Anderson (1993) in her "expressive theory", which allows a much more nuanced approach to benefit assessment and is quite distant from the monism and consequentialism of extra-welfarism. (This is discussed in detail in Chapter 6.)

In assessing extra-welfarism it remains the case that, as with welfarism, it is founded on individual values. QALYs, for example, do eventually get aggregated across some social grouping or population to provide what might be described as social values of health (see for example Dolan 1998; Nord 1999; and Dolan et al. 2004). They remain, however, based on the individual's values rather than community values; they also often risk being seen in terms of what amounts to individual consumers' values rather than citizens' values.

For QALYs too their derivation is such that being based on the idea that health care systems produce only health—when considerations are made of cost effectiveness in QALY terms (in what are normally referred to as cost–utility studies), the only outputs on the benefit side of the equation are changes in health status as measured by QALYs. The difficulty then is that, to be consistent, the only resources that can legitimately be considered as relevant to the production of QALYs are those where the opportunity cost of their use is QALYs—and, strictly, *only* QALYs. That means (the argument is somewhat circular here) only health care resources qualify. The opportunity cost of QALY production has to be in terms of QALYs, hence only health care resources can be used on the cost side of cost–utility analyses (i.e. those studies which measure technical efficiency in terms of QALYs).

Cost–utility analyses thus cannot legitimately include patient time, educational costs, or other social services costs arising as a result of some health care intervention. These costs might have included, for example, the patients forgoing time to watch television; or, in schools, students missing out on acquiring a greater knowledge of history; or, in social services, having less time to work on reducing domestic violence. Certainly, for many interventions, foregone benefits may well in practice stretch well beyond health, but the opportunity costs of such interventions cannot be included in cost–utility studies of health care interventions.

This issue is equally problematical when we consider "QALY league tables" (see for example Briggs and Gray 2000). These, more accurately, should be known as "marginal cost per QALY league tables". They rank various interventions within some health service budget in terms of what the extra cost per QALY would be if there had been more investment in, say, renal dialysis or chiropody or management of diabetes. The idea is that, if QALYs were to be maximised, then any additional resources in health care ought to be spent on producing extra QALYs as cheaply as possible, thereby maximising any increase in QALYs that might be obtained. Clearly, the marginal costs will be a function of many factors, including, for example, how much renal dialysis, etc. is currently being conducted, the prevalence of renal failure in the population, and the local costs of dialysis, which will be affected by capacity issues, by remoteness, etc. Marginal costs will also change from year to year for various reasons, so that what is top of the QALY league table this year may well not be next year.

It is immediately apparent that, whatever else, QALY league tables need to be based on local information where "local" is to be considered in terms of the scope and spread of the health service budget. Thus we might have an Australian, an Indian, and a Brazilian QALY league table, each of which would be based on information on costs and effectiveness on the margins of programmes in these three countries. Any efforts to "universalise" QALY league tables are misplaced. The idea that the best buy in a Beijing QALY league table would be the best buy in a Brussels QALY league table is clearly illogical. QALY league tables are not transferable across national boundaries. Indeed, where there are yet more localised health care budgets, as in South Africa, within the provinces, or the UK, within the regions, or Australia, within the states, then it is at the level of these jurisdictions that QALY league tables would need to be devised.

This may not be too problematical where some interventions are concerned, such as pharmaceuticals, where the technology is both well designed and very clearly identified. The nature of a nursing home bed or a GP consultation or advice on smoking from a GP are much more complex and less well defined than pharmaceuticals, certainly in their "technological composition" but also in their outcomes. Ideally, what is sought is marginal effectiveness. This will most likely vary depending on both how many interventions there have already been and the incidence of the disease or condition that is being addressed. The same issues arise with marginal costs.

It is thus unfortunate that so many QALY league tables take information, especially on effectiveness, from any area, with scant or no acknowledgment of the problems of doing so. There is seldom any attempt made to establish the marginal effectiveness or the marginal costs of interventions and averages of each or both are used instead. There are thus very real problems in the actual use of QALYs, both in cost–utility analyses and in QALY league tables.

What of the more fundamental conceptual underpinnings of extra-welfarism? The odd thing here is that the whole notion of health maximisation that underlies QALYs appears to be based on an assumption made by Culyer (1988). He argued that it was reasonable to assume that health services are about health and therefore that they seek to maximise health. That is not an outlandish assumption but it is one that is testable empirically. Certainly it seems to fit with what doctors do in their practices and medical researchers do in their randomised controlled trials (RCT).

They assume that all that needs to be tested is how effective the intervention is with respect to *health*. Changes in, say, patient autonomy or respect or information are not measured, only health. Where is the RCT on patient autonomy?

Thus the health economists' traditional extra-welfarist assumption of maximising health and in turn QALYs is in line with much medical thinking and research. I would question whether a medical model is appropriate when we consider health care systems, especially when these are considered as social institutions. Informed citizens seem to demand more than simply health from their health care services. Nonetheless, health economists have built this extra-welfarist paradigm on an untested assumption and they have chosen to ignore the evidence that does exist, albeit in a limited way, that citizens do want more from health services than simply health. So the key assumption underlying extra-welfarism is very much open to question.

Once that assumption is challenged, the basis for extra-welfarism appears to collapse. It is impossible to defend the use of QALYs if, as we must, we let other arguments than health enter the individual's utility function. There are criticisms of QALYs (see for example Gafni et al. 1993; and Gafni and Birch 1997), but for the purposes of this book those outlined are those that represent the case against extra-welfarism. What we need to establish is what the community—the local community—wants from their health services as a social institution. That then provides the thrust for developing a new paradigm.

To argue this is to argue no more than that health services should be designed to reflect the demands of the local population they are to serve and that in so doing these health services should use information about local health problems, local resources, and resource availability to determine how best to use the health services budget. The only truly remarkable thing about such a conclusion is that extra-welfarism is *not* based on these premises!

3.5 Consequentialism

The individualism of both welfarism and extra-welfarism dominates current health economics theoretically. The fact that health services are social institutions and might be valued as such gets lost. The consequentialism that dominates neo-classical economics is adopted in health economics. In excluding the values attached to processes, the humanitarian, caring and compassionate aspects of health care are omitted. The idea of being committed to a community or group is not present. Here the question of consequentialism *per se* is addressed.

In health care there are many paths to better health. These can include going to a GP or to hospital or paying for a prescription. In the main (but not, as it happens, in extra-welfarism, only in welfarism) these would be built into any economic analysis. These all have direct resource consequences. What does get omitted as literally non-consequential are such considerations as whether the encounter with the GP is pleasant or not; whether the GP is caring in the way he or she informs the patient that the patient has, say, Parkinson's disease; whether there is anxiety prior to the operation at the hospital; or whether the chemist gives reassuring advice and information about any possible side effects.

These are not, however, outcomes as such. They are "processes" and they raise the question of whether there can be such a phenomenon as "process utility", as I and others have sought to label this (Mooney 2003). Welfarism and extra-welfarism not only do not include such processes but they deny the relevance of these processes to any assessment of benefits of health care.

Some health economists, such as Jack Dowie, argue not so much that these processes do not exist in welfarism, but that they are better called outcomes. He places health economists on two sides of a debate. One group, he says, wants to "maximise the health or health gain achieved". The other, he argues, wants to maximise "the amount of health care *services* provided" (Dowie 2001: 248; emphasis in original.) He writes:

What [economists such as myself who argue for the inclusion of process utility] are saying is that in allocating the health care budget it is necessary to use a maximand that trades off health gain against other aspects of health care service and provision that people value. For example, people *may* prefer easier access to a local facility which cannot aspire to the standards of care (in terms of health gain outcome) of a centre of excellence, to distant access to the latter. Or, since this example confounds the question of costs to patients with differential effectiveness, patients *may* be willing to trade off health gain against time spent being counselled, provided with information or being "given a sense of autonomy".

What I am suggesting should be maximised is not services but anything that an informed community might seek to maximise. The key difference between Dowie and myself is on the question of whose values are relevant. His answer is the values of health economists who believe that health maximisation is the goal of health care. My answer is the informed community whose health service it is. I am also arguing that the latter may knowingly opt for less health from the available health care resources in return for other benefits.

Thus where a doctor shocks a patient by telling him or her in an uncaring way that he or she has Parkinson's, for example, Dowie might want to argue that this doctor's action will result in a bad outcome for the patient, namely, by then being in a shocked, uncared for state. I prefer to use the language of process to describe this scenario. Alternatively, Dowie might say that to change things so that the patient does feel cared for would mean that the doctor has to spend more time with that patient and thereby the opportunity cost is health foregone for another patient. I agree, but if the community is prepared to make that trade off and have some degree of "caring about" written into the principles of health care then I see no problem with that. I do have a problem with health economists determining the maximand and if that is solely health.

Mile Little (2003) argues for both "caring for" and "caring about" to be part of good health care. He states (p. 211): "We can care for people by following protocols, but to cope flexibly with the needs of the ill, we need to care about them in a more strictly moral sense. Management protocols provide rules that help us to care for. Our consciences and compassion provide guides to caring about." I agree; with Steve Jan, I have argued the need to take account of what we called the "community conscience" (Mooney and Jan 1997: 85). Whether health economist colleagues agree with me in calling this phenomenon "process utility" is a secondary consideration.

Broader process utility arises in terms of the social option good of universal access. This may well have an impact on health *per se* or other outcomes that the society wants from its health care system. Here, however, I want to raise another process effect, which is that knowing that others in a society have access to health care may provide some benefit to those who know this, even if they do not themselves use the health care system. Perhaps additionally but almost certainly overlapping with that might be that this idea of universal access is one sign of a society being decent and might be valued as such.

There are two possible aspects to this. The first is where an individual gets utility from contributing to the creation of the universal access or the decency of society through, for example, paying taxes. This fits with Margolis's ideas on group participation utility (Margolis 1982), where individuals get utility not only in the standard consequentialist way but through participating in the group. Margolis is at pains to argue that such utility is not outcome-based, but is a form of process utility. People like being part of a group or society and as such they want to make a contribution to its overall well being. The more socially cohesive (or "communitarian"—see Chapter 7) the society, the more people will be prepared to contribute. (Margolis's fair share model is discussed in greater detail in Chapter 7.)

This also fits with Sen's agency, but for Sen (1992) this can take two forms. One is where there is utility in contributing to some, say, national goal that an individual sees as being a good thing. This is Margolis's participation utility. Sen also, however, allows for utility being gained when some national goal is achieved even if that individual did not contribute in any way to bringing it about.

Both Margolis and Sen are here very much echoing communitarian sentiments. Neither welfarism nor extra-welfarism is able to handle these sources of utility.

Closely allied to these ideas from Sen and Margolis is the notion of valuing a health care system as a social institution. It does seem that in the UK, for example, people see the NHS as an important and valued institution, and that such value is additional to but not necessarily wholly independent of the benefits it produces by way of health and other outcomes.

It would seem inevitable that process utility does exist despite many health economists seeking to deny it. It is then not surprising that in the health economics literature there is little attempt to examine this issue and in turn little evidence of its proven existence. Brouwer et al. (2005: 86) suggest, however, that "it is increasingly recognised that process does matter". The example they give is as follows:

> consider two patients waiting for a donor heart. When one becomes available, it has to be allocated to one of the two. If the heart is allocated on the basis of probabilities of medical success or need, the patient may not like the outcome but this would have been worse if the same result was reached by allocating on the basis of ability to pay or colour of skin.

In their own study Brouwer et al. (2005 p. 96) find: "Process utility appears to be important in the context of informal care". For other examples of the existence of process utility, see Birch et al. (2003); and Ryan and Wordsworth (2000).

One can see that in a health care system that is tax funded and zero priced at the point of consumption, while interventions that produce health gains efficiently might be funded, there might be more debate about the social value of being cared about or having doctors spend time in reassuring anxious patients when the opportunity cost might instead be measured in lives lost. Some of these non-health processes might be zero weighted or not weighted highly. Alternatively there might be a view that these are issues about which there is less concern for equity and consequently there should be some up front fee for such services.

The point is not strictly whether these process variables are included or not. It is rather that some societies might want the opportunity to include them if they see fit and in ways in which they see fit.

3.6 Conclusion

This chapter has sought to show how health economics to date has failed to devise an alternative paradigm of any substance to replace the market when the market in health care fails. There is an acceptance among most health economists that markets do fail but the most likely contender to replace the market—extra-welfarism—is very limited. This is in two senses First, it is highly restricted by the assumptions it comes with, especially consequentialism and individual values. Second however, the form of its consequentialism is based on an assumption (of health being the only relevant argument in the welfare function) that health economists have seldom bothered to test. In the limited testing that has been done there is no evidence to suggest that it is based in fact.

It has also emerged in this chapter that we need to establish the preferences of local communities on what they want from their health care system before we can begin to evaluate that system as a social institution, its outcomes, and its processes.

The question of what to do when consumer sovereignty fails is critical. Joan Robinson (1972: 274), one of the most eminent economists of the twentieth century, argues in a more general context that "[n]o-one who has lived in the capitalist world is deceived by the pretence that the market system ensures consumer's sovereignty".

Conventional health economics does not defend consumer sovereignty in health care but Robinson's words are quite remarkably pertinent to market failure in health care. She states (Robinson 1972: 274):

The true moral to be drawn from capitalist experience is that production will never be responsive to consumer needs as long as the initiative lies with the producer. Even within capitalism consumers are beginning to organize to defend themselves. In a planned economy the best hope seems to be to develop a class of functionaries, playing the role of wholesale dealers, whose career and self-respect depend upon satisfying the consumer. They could keep in touch with demand through the shops; market research which in the capitalist world is directed to finding out how to bamboozle the housewife could be directed to discovering what she really needs; design and quality could be imposed upon manufacturing enterprises and the product mix settled by placing orders in such a way as to hold a balance between economies of scale and variety of tastes.

The parallels with health care are very real. Consumer's sovereignty very clearly does not exist, and we can go further and argue that consumers do not want it to exist. It is not, as the standard health economics literature implies with agency, that the agent is there to assist the consumer to make decisions that he or she would make in the market if he or she were as well informed as the agent. This role cannot be played by the doctor "agent". We need, as Robinson argues, another type of "functionary... whose career and self-respect depend upon satisfying" not the consumer but the patient. We have *par excellence* in health care the situation where "production will never be responsive to consumer needs as long as the initiative lies with the producer".

As health economists we need to consider this other type of functionary or at least how such a role might be filled. It may be delegated but it is in principle at least a role to be played by the informed community. That idea is central to the paradigm developed in later chapters.

References

Anderson, E. (1993) *Values in Ethics and Economics*. Cambridge, MA: Harvard University Press.

Anand, P. (2003) The integration of claims to health care, *Journal of Health Economics*, 22: 731–45.

Artells-Herrero, J. J. (1981) Effectiveness and decision-making in a health planning context: the case of outpatient ante-natal care. Unpublished M.Litt. thesis, University of Oxford, Oxford.

Birch, S., Melnikow, J. and Kuppermann, M. (2003) Conservative versus aggressive follow up of mildly abnormal Pap smears: testing for process utility, *Health Economics*, 12(10): 879–84.

Briggs, A. and Gray, A. (2000) Using cost effectiveness information. Available at: www.bmj.com/cgi/reprint/320/7229/246.pdf

Brouwer, W. B., van Exel, N. J., van den Berg, B., van den Bos, G. A. and Koopmanschap, M. A. (2005) Process utility from providing informal care: the benefit of caring, *Health Policy*, 74(1): 85–99.

Coast, J. (1999) The appropriate uses of qualitative methods in health economics, *Health Economics*, 8: 345–53.

Culyer, A. J. (1988) Inequality of health services is, in general, desirable, in D. Green (ed.), *Acceptable Inequalities*. London: IEA Health Unit.

—— (1990) Demand-side socialism and health care. Keynote paper presented at the Second World Congress on Health Economics, University of Zurich, Zurich.

Dolan, P. (1998) The measurement of individual utility and social welfare, *Journal of Health Economics*, 17: 39–52.

—— Shaw, R., Tsuchiya, A. and Williams, A. (2004) QALY maximisation and people's preferences: a methodological review of the literature, *Health Economics*, 14(2): 197–208.

Dowie, J. (2001) Analysing health outcomes, *Journal of Medical Ethics*, 27: 245–50.

Fanshel, S. and Bush, J. W. (1970) A health status index and its application to health services outcomes, *Operations Research*, 18: 1021–66.

Gafni, A. and Birch, S. (1993) Guidelines for the adoption of new technologies: a prescription for uncontrolled growth in expenditures and how to avoid the problem, *Canadian Medical Association Journal*, 148(6): 913–17.

—— —— (1997) QALYs and HYEs: spotting the differences, *Journal of Health Economics*, 16(5): 601–8.

—— —— Mehrez, A. (1993) Economics, health and health economics: HYEs versus QALYs, *Journal of Health Economics*, 12(3): 325–39.

Hurley, J. (1998) Welfarism, extra-welfarism and evaluative economic analysis in the health sector, in M. L. Barer, T. E. Getzen and G. L. Stoddart (eds.), *Health, Health Care and Health Economics*. Wiley: Chichester.

Klarman, H. E., Francis, J. O. and Rosenthal, G. D. (1968) Cost-effectiveness analysis applied to the treatment of chronic renal disease, *Medical Care*, 6: 48–54.

Little, M. (2003) Ethonomics: the ethics of the unaffordable, in I. Kerridge. C. Jordens and E.-J. Sayers (eds.) *Restoring Humane Values to Medicine*. Sydney: Desert Pea Press. Originally published in *Archives of Surgery* (1998) 68: 757–9.

Margolis, H. (1982) *Selfishness, Altruism and Rationality*. Cambridge: Cambridge University Press.

Mooney, G. (2003) *Economics Medicine and Health Care*. London: Prentice Hall.

—— Jan, S. (1997) Vertical equity: weighting health outcomes? Or establishing procedures? *Health Policy*, 39(1): 79–88.

—— Ryan, M. (1993) Agency in health care: getting beyond first principles, *Journal of Health Economics*, 12(2): 125–35.

Navarro, V. (2002) *The Political Economy of Social Inequalities*. New York: Baywood.

Nord, E. (1999) *Cost-value Analysis in Health Care*. Cambridge: Cambridge University Press.

Packer, A. (1968) Applying cost-effectiveness concepts to the community health system, *Operations Research*, 16: 227–53.

Reinhardt, U. (1998) Abstracting from distributional effects, this policy is efficient, in M. Barer, T. Getzen and G. Stoddart (eds.), *Health, Health Care and Health Economics*. Chichester: Wiley.

Rice, T. (1998) *The Economics of Health Reconsidered*. Chicago: Health Administration Press.

Richardson, J. (2001) Empirical ethics: or the poverty of ethical analyses in economics and the unwarranted disregard of evidence in ethics. Working Paper No. 120. Melbourne: Centre for Health Program Evaluation, Monash University.

Robinson, J. (1972) Consumers' sovereignty in a planned economy, in A. Nove and D. M. Nuti (eds.) *Socialist Economics..* Harmondsworth: Penguin.

Ryan, M. and Wordsworth, S. (2000) Sensitivity analysis of willingness to pay estimates to the level of attributes in discrete choice experiments, *Scottish Journal of Political Economy*, 47: 504–24.

Sen, A. (1985) *Commodities and Capabilities*. New York: Elsevier.

Torrance, G. (1986) Measurement of health state utilities for economic appraisal: a review, *Journal of Health Economics*, 5: 1–30.

Weisbrod, B. A. (1978) Comment on M. V. Pauly, in W. Greenberg (ed.), *Competition in the Health Care Sector: Proceedings of a Conference Sponsored by the Bureau of Economics, Federal Trade Commission*. Germanstown: Aspen Systems.

4

The Need for a New Paradigm

4.1 Introduction

The need for a new paradigm arises for a number of reasons, but perhaps most fundamentally because of the desire to integrate explicitly three considerations into resource allocation in health care and in public health: institutions, power, and values. Some explanation of these aspects in this context is needed.

The question of institutions and their relevance to health and health care merits a section on its own and is debated in section 4.2. Here attention is drawn to the fact that in conventional health economics, health care systems as organisations are treated as purely instrumental. The value of health care as an organisation is in its outcomes.

Relevant here is that institutional economics treats institutions as representing something wider than simple organisations and includes what amounts to rules in its definition of institutions. As Kasper and Streit (1998: 2) write: "Human interactions, including those in economic life, depend on some sort of trust which is based on an order that is facilitated by rules banning unpredictable and opportunistic behaviour." They add (p. 2): "We call these rules 'institutions'." While recently, especially in the work of Lucy Gilson (2003), health economists are beginning to endorse the value of trust (but primarily within the confines of the doctor–patient agency relationship), the work by health economists on health care systems as institutions is small (although see for example Jan 2000). The idea of public health as a social institution is missing from the health economics literature. Section 4.2 highlights some of the problems that arise for current health economists as a result of these gaps in our approaches.

De Pinho (2005: 7) suggests that there is a need "to create a health system that encourages, supports and sustains increasing inclusion", manifesting itself in terms of "redistribution". She argues that:

In marketized health systems, exclusion of those who cannot pay, is deemed legitimate. Cross subsidisation within these health systems is exposed and driven out, and any redistribution that may occur is regarded as an "unrequited gift from rich to poor" which no matter how desirable in principle, if seen in these terms, will in practice be difficult to gain support for especially from the rich.

To exemplify her point, de Pinho uses the example of the UN Millennium Project Task Force Four which "proposes building a health system around healthcare relationships conceived not as gifts, but as entitlements [which] may move health systems in a more sustainable direction". There is thus, as de Pinho (2005: 7) advocates, a need "to shift the perception and mindset regarding health systems from the prevailing conventional approach that is intrinsically market driven, towards one that is based on two fundamental principles: human rights and equity." A similar shift is needed in the health economics paradigm.

This question of power is one that is missing from most health economics analyses, most importantly from analyses of equity. Ultimately, in the context of equity certainly but in resource allocation in health care more generally, there is a central issue regarding power, with the rich often able to dominate the health care institution, especially if it is private, simply by their purchasing power. They can also influence the structure and workings of public health care systems in their favour, "speaking the same language" as the doctors and administrators in the system and having more voice politically. On either or both counts this can improve their access to better or faster care.

The other main area where a shift is needed in the health economics paradigm is with respect to values. There is a need to examine resource allocation in health care and society more generally with respect to health by considering the health care system and public health as being first and foremost social phenomena (or, better, to describe these as social institutions). An emphasis on social institutions would mean that social values would have to be the basis of both public health and health care systems. There would also be a need to recognise that underlying these social institutions there has to be some set of values or guiding principles (what is referred to in Chapter 9 as "a constitution"). These, it is proposed, might come from the community at large. Conventional health economics thus does not only fail to consider or establish any set of principles on which to base health care as a system; it fails to recognise the need for such principles or constitution to be set.

4.2 Institutional economics, health care, and public health

Neo-classical economics treats institutions as exogenous and not to be valued in themselves. That stance has been extended by health economists to health care systems. Public health would also benefit from being seen in such terms.

To begin, however, it is useful to distinguish two types of institutions: first, what might be called organisations and, second, as rules governing human interactions. The first is the more standard way to think of institutions. That form of institution, especially as a social institution, would include such organisations as the health care sector, the education sector, the justice system, parliament, government, and also private organisations, including private firms and the market itself.

The second, the idea of institutions as rules, is a characteristic of institutional economics. It is not a new idea in economics, however, and Adam Smith, while he did not use the term "institution", clearly endorsed the idea. For example, he wrote (Smith 1759: lll.l.98):

It is thus that the general rules of morality are formed. They are ultimately founded upon experience of what, in particular instances, our moral faculties, our natural sense of merit and propriety, approve, or disapprove of. We do not originally approve or condemn particular actions; because, upon examination, they appear to be agreeable or inconsistent with a certain general rule. The general rule, on the contrary, is formed, by finding from experience, that all actions of a certain kind, or circumstanced in a certain manner, are approved or disapproved of. When these general rules, indeed, have been formed, when they are universally acknowledged and established, by the concurring sentiments of mankind, we frequently appeal to them as to the standards of judgment, in debating concerning the degree of praise or blame that is due to certain actions of a complicated and dubious nature.

One of the founders of institutional economics, North (1992: 3) argues: "Institutions are the rules of the game and organizations are the players". He also suggests (see http://129.3.20.41/eps/eh/papers/9309/9309004.pdf) that institutions "are the humanly devised constraints that structure human interaction. They are composed of formal rules (statute, common law, regulations), informal constraints (convention, norms of behavior and self-imposed rules of behaviour); and the enforcement characteristics of both."

The need for a shift in the paradigm of health economics can be seen as lying in the acknowledgment of the differences that exist between the individualism that traditional health economics retains, and the more social or group context of the models of institutional economists. As Dugger (1984: 314) indicates of Veblen (1924), one of the founders along with Commons (1931), of institutional economics, "an institution is a set of norms and ideals which is imperfectly... reproduced or internalized through habituation in each succeeding generation of individuals. Such an institution serves as stimulus and guide to individual behavior."

Dugger (1984: 314) continues: "The preferences of an individual are not original or fundamental causal factors, *hence they are not the place to start a theory* (emphasis added)." He argues then for the focus being not on individuals or their preferences but "[s]ince, in the institutionalist view, the range of alternatives open to men is determined by the institutional structure or context into which they are born, the place to start is with that institutional structure."

Jan (2000 and 2002) is one of the very few health economists to attempt to bring institutional economics into health. As a result he is quoted here at some length. He identifies certain key differences between institutional and neo-classical economics. Two of these are particularly germane to the arguments in this assessment of the need for a new paradigm in health economics. These are: "Analysis of social rather than individualistic behaviour" and "a 'holistic' approach to the analysis of economic phenomena" (Jan 2002: 27).

Gruchy (1947) argues on the first point that neo-classical economics is founded on a psychological theory that is both static and individualistic where there is no explicit recognition of any base in society. While that is again about neo-classical economics, health economics retains this theoretic underpinning where society *qua* society is absent. What is thus needed is a recognition of what Jan (2002: 27) describes as "social norms and standards which govern conduct".

Jan (2002: 44) draws attention to the failure of representative democracy as portrayed in the analysis of government regulation by Stigler (1971). Jan states: "[Stigler's] theory of regulation is remarkable because of its rejection of the often-held 'public interest' view of representative democracy that assumes that the preferences of the majority of the population prevail in the formulation of policy and regulation."

This is perhaps a little simplistic, but it nonetheless acknowledges the importance of maintaining some very clear public policy role for the "public interest". How to achieve that is critical, yet the issue is one that is missing from health economists' research on health and health care. Bringing the public interest centre stage is what is needed.

Jan (2002: 47) argues that in health economics,

the use of public choice theory could be useful in explaining the behaviour of public sector organisations, particularly in the context of decisions where there are winners and losers. Often such decisions in practice do not reflect the predictions of conventional welfarist perspectives and as such, tend to be explained in an ad hoc manner within the health economics literature.

In the sense used in institutional economics, institutions are what Elster (1989) refers to in the title of his book as *"The Cement of Society"*. They are the links that bring together various organisations. In the context of health care they set the scene for how the different actors interact and influence each other as well as the output of the organisation. In all countries those working in the medical profession are important players in their influence on the decision making processes. In some countries, for example the US, their influence is yet greater; in others, such as Denmark, less so. The pharmaceutical industry is a strong player everywhere, but some governments are better placed to exercise control over them than others. Private health insurance companies in some countries, in Australia for example, have much influence on governments, less so in other countries, such as the UK. The power of GP organisations varies from country to country. Governments can be the handmaiden of the medical association or they can seek to control their power.

How these different organisational components interact, easily or with difficulty, well or badly, equitably or in an unequal power relationship is what institutional health economics would be about. While setting out these interactions and the fact that they can vary from country to country or culture to culture is useful in trying to understand the decision making processes in health care systems; standard health economics ignores these factors. As Jan (2002: 17) states: "the characteristics of a particular institutional setting can have powerful and highly pervasive consequences in health care because they can facilitate, or indeed hamper, economic transactions and other forms of interaction between organisations and individuals".

In conventional health economics, economic evaluation studies, for example, take place in an institutional vacuum. The results are assumed to hold good whatever the nature of the health care organisation and whatever the rules of interaction between the key players. Yet such evaluations in the clinical arena will be more or less effective in practice depending on, for example, the power relationships between the relevant doctors and the administrators or managers. Can the latter encourage, cajole, or force doctors to change their practice so that it becomes more efficient in the ways that the economic evaluation study suggested? Is the organisation of health care, for example the funding procedures and the remuneration systems for doctors, able to facilitate or hamper such changes?

In Australia the organisational institutional arrangements are such that the Pharmaceutical Benefits Advisory Committee, a government body, determines which drugs are listed for tax payer subsidy. This listing is determined on the basis, *inter alia*, of efficiency as judged in economic evaluation studies. This organisational structure is favourable to having such economic evaluation studies played out successfully in policy action. The institutional rules, however, mean that the power vested in doctors through clinical freedom to prescribe leaves the door open to inefficient practices. Thus the tensions that can exist at both these levels can have substantial impacts on the efficiency of health care resource use. Ignoring these institutional arrangements, as current health economics tends to, can create problems in pursuing efficiency of institutions, both as organisations and as sets of rules.

Public health is even more in need of being considered as an institution. At least health care is a recognised organisation while public health is, as it has been labelled here, more of a "movement" or a collection of various "bits and pieces". These might sit in a variety of organisations, including the finance ministry, housing departments, parliament, and private companies, its organisational arrangements much more a loose network of agencies. Trying to attain a more coherent organised entity would almost certainly result in a more efficient and equitable approach to public health, so that the question of a public health institution would have real advantages.

The fact that this is missing is not something that can be laid at the door of health economics. Its absence is, however, problematical for health economics. As identified in Chapter 8, the proposed paradigm in this book addresses that issue.On institutions as rules, a potentially yet stronger case can be made for there being such a focus for public health in conventional health economics.

The lack of an entity of public health makes the consideration of interactions between the players on the public health stage critical to the effectiveness and in turn efficiency and equity of planning and management of interventions in population health. Too often it seems public health is underfunded vis-à-vis other health actions and this is despite the fact that informed citizens have wanted such measures to have high priority (see Chapter 9). A number of explanations can be offered for this underfunding, but most centre on the lack of a coherent strategy, no "ownership" at governmental level of the endeavour as a whole, and a lack of a political base with real power for the public health "movement". National medical associations are not renowned for their support but rather for their rhetoric on public health. It is seldom that those in power weigh in politically to promote greater funding for public health, especially if the opportunity cost is to be borne in treatment services. Public health lacks Stigler's "cement".

4.3 Individualism (with dignity as an example)

There is a need for a major shift in the thinking of the disciplines of medicine and health economics. Both of these draw heavily on the values of individuals *qua* individuals, with, for example, medical ethics being very much focused on the individual doctor to individual patient relationship, economics drawing on the concept of consumer sovereignty in the market place, and health economics retaining the importance of individual values.

Medicine as a discipline is concerned very much with individual ethics—duty and virtue. In medical eyes, the health care system is seen primarily as the vehicle through which individual patients are treated by individual doctors. In turn the social good that health care systems produce is then interpreted simply as the sum of what individual doctors do to individual patients, often restricting the social good to the aggregation of individual health gains.

There are various problems with this view, which are primarily centred around the question of restricting the good of health care to health. Here the question of respect for dignity is used as an example. While in principle the medical ethics literature does acknowledge the importance of the dignity of the patient, in practice this is all too often ignored. More importantly in the context of this book, it is ignored by health economists.

The issue of respect for dignity, however, should not be restricted to patients but rather it should be expanded to include all citizens. There are areas of health care about which citizens might legitimately argue they should be able to express their values. To ignore or fail to elicit these values shows a lack of respect for the citizen and, *inter alia*, may contribute to undermining their self-esteem. That can in turn have a negative impact on population health both directly and indirectly in that citizens are more likely to be compliant with services that are underpinned by their values and so, as patients, they are then more likely to use these services, which in turn are more likely to be effective.

Abortion and euthanasia are interventions which immediately come to mind in considering the potential relevance of both community values and the consulting of citizens. But there are many others, such as screening services, which might ideally be "community-preference"-based. For example it can be asked whether screening for Down's syndrome is about minimising the risk of disability (adopting that position does little for the dignity of disabled people or of the broader society) or about creating greater choice for women and their partners (which enhances their dignity and potentially the dignity of citizens in general). Again the question of informing patients about patient care and the citizenry about health care system choices more generally involves respecting both these groups' autonomy and their values. To fail to do so is disrespectful, treating them as no more than instruments. In the case of the care of people in their own homes who are chronically sick, such as those suffering from multiple sclerosis, the value of respite care for the informal (family) carers can be seen not only in terms of helping them to cope, but also it reflects a desire to acknowledge them and to respect their dignity as carers. Knowing that such recognition is forthcoming is of potential benefit to society at large.

Williamson (1986: 177), the institutional economist, identifies this issue in labour markets, suggesting that dignity "has special relevance for the economics of process . . . since the means as well as the ends have a bearing on dignity." He argues (Williamson 1986: 177) that one of the problems that arises from ignoring considerations of dignity is that this "encourages the view that individuals can be considered strictly as instruments", and this is a trap into which conventional health economists do seem to have fallen. He maintains (Williamson 1986: 177) that "sensitivity of human needs for self- and social-esteem become important when the organization of work . . . comes under scrutiny." Williamson does not consider health or health care. Were he to do so, the arguments he uses in considering dignity in labour markets would be yet stronger. The patient in health economics currently is seen almost entirely as an instrument, a vessel that can be filled with more or less health—in essence a passive "bearer" of health or ill health.

Williamson (1986: 178) also draws out the importance of dignity at a social level.

Society is the loser if the political and social competencies of the parties are degraded. Such effects are all the more serious if a private utilitarian approach to dignity in economic transactions impairs not only the political and social competencies of the immediate parties but has adverse spillover on others as well. Such results are avoided only by a recognition that society has a stake in dignity and that otherwise neglected systems-effects may need to be recognized and economic incentives corrected appropriately.

The idea is thus born that the set of principles underlying the health care system might embrace respect for both patients' dignity and citizens' dignity.

Other characteristics that might be built into a set of principles on which the health care system as a social institution might be based include autonomy, participation, preference elicitation, etc. These will be addressed in Chapter 9. The key points here are two: first, acknowledging the desirability of establishing such principles; and, second, recognising that conventional health economics ignores or side-steps these issues.

4.4 Varying perspectives

Concentrating solely on health as an outcome may be a justified view of health care from a medical perspective (see Coast 2004). There are, however, other perspectives such as the patient's, the health care system's, the donor's, the society's, and the global perspective, as exemplified by WHO. It might be argued that a change in perspective does not alter the value base of health care, but that it is challenged by the proposed new paradigm as set out later (see Part II). The most relevant change is from the social perspective.

It is acknowledged, even if rather inadequately, that the health economics paradigm does consider a form of patient perspective. In (rightly) abandoning the market, most health economics literature casts doubt on the willingness to pay by "consumers" as a measure of value, largely because of the problems of lack of information held by the consumer as compared to the information they hold on other goods in the market place.

The patient, at least in extra-welfarism, is assumed either to have values of health common with all other patients or to be the only patient but clearly with multiple and several health problems. Once the notion of a constitution or set of principles is established as necessary or desirable, then such issues as these would need to be addressed explicitly.

Another way to consider the patient's perspective in health is through the idea of a right to health. The relevant literature here is complex. The Universal Declaration of Human Rights, Article 25 (see: www1.umn.edu/

humanrts/edumat/studyguides/righttohealth.html) states: "Everyone has the right to a standard of living adequate for the health and well being of himself and of his family, including food, clothing, housing and medical care." This is very broad and would be difficult to implement at a policy level. One elaboration on this idea, however, is that

to improve the standard of living in developing nations immediate attention should be directed towards the following challenges:

- Increasing the distribution of clean water
- Establishing sanitary living conditions
- Maintaining sufficient food supplies
- Administering widespread vaccinations and medications
- Providing prenatal and maternal care
- Educating people about disease prevention and malnutrition.

This idea of a "standard of living" for health is at some distance from the health economics extra-welfarist paradigm with its goal of health maximisation. That goal is challengeable on three fronts. First, people can want more than simply health from their health care system. Second, with respect to distributional concerns, they may want to value increments in some people's health more highly than increments in others, for example, the poor (Mooney 1998, 2000). This means that they do not want health *per se* maximised but rather some form of *weighted* health. Third, there is a problem in arguing that health is a common construct across all groupings in society, most clearly across different cultural groupings but perhaps also across different classes (see for example Adams 2004; and Houston 2004). There is evidence, for example, that the poor have higher discount rates for health. Whether this is due to a different construct or different values is not clear. As Chapter 11 reveals, different cultural groupings have different constructs of health.

The health care system's perspective also needs to be noted. While there is every reason to think that this might be different, what is striking is that this is very often synonymous with the medical perspective. The values of health care systems are very much those dominated by the medical profession. That tells us a lot about the distribution of property rights in health care and the "medicalisation" of this social institution. It also helps to explain why the standard health care system's objective function is very often couched in terms of health maximisation, which is largely an aggregation of the sort of thinking that pervades clinical trials. This medical thinking has infiltrated health economics.

This medical perspective is also reflected in the approach that donors often adopt in their giving of aid to developing countries. This is most frequently set along disease programme lines—malaria, heart disease, etc. What this means is that the emphasis is on investing in improving health outcomes directly. Too little attention is then given to building up the governance structure and the institution that is to deliver good health care. In other words the narrow consequentialism of medicine is adopted by the donors. The principles they adopt in their aid-giving then fail to reflect the wider perspective of the health care system as a social institution or simply to reflect local values in deciding on investment strategies for health.

Again, too often the principles on which WHO and the World Bank operate are based on the adoption of a medical perspective, most notably with the WHO's burden of disease programme for priority setting (see for example Murray and Lopez 1996), which sought to argue, *inter alia*, that the setting of priorities ought to be along the lines of disease. This is particularly odd as the question of priority setting arises because of the scarcity of resources. It logically follows that priorities ought to be about resource allocation and hence about the question of what are the best buys for intervention. It is therefore interventions that need to be prioritised not diseases. Yet the medical model prevails here as well.

Turning to the social perspective, there are at least three reasons for challenging the standard health economics paradigm. First, as indicated previously, while the health care system might be valued for itself, the consequentialism of most health economics prevents this.

Second, the value base of the existing paradigm is individualistic, yet again reflecting the medical model and encouraging the idea that a health care system is primarily a medical entity rather than a social institution. It also means that health economists thereby endorse the power of the medical establishment in their property rights over resource distribution in health care.

Third, the medical profession exercises very great power over resource allocation in health care. Once it is conceded that health care is a medical entity, it is more or less inevitable that this will happen. This results in the medicalisation of the values underpinning health care systems and creates problems for the involvement of not just patients but also citizens in determining the value base of health care. The basis of medical ethics is individualistic, drawing in essence on the Hippocratic Oath and its emphasis on virtue (the individual doctor doing good to individual patients) and on duty (to the individual doctor's individual patient). This is not just different from the ethics needed for health care systems, it is inimical to such ethics.

The ethics of social institutions must be social ethics, where considerations of the common good come into play, but with due cognisance of the fact that society's resources are scarce and that whatever it is that society seeks from its resources it will be more than any health service can provide. The notion of social opportunity cost must be central. Yet it seldom occurs that medical values drive health care resource allocation.

Why health economists have adopted the health maximisation objective is based on a degree of pragmatism. First, it means that at a technical level they have been able to concentrate their efforts on measuring health and not other outputs or valued processes. Second, and perhaps only subconsciously, they have in this way sought to make their analyses have an impact on health care resource allocation.

It is worth noting that where health economics has had its greatest impact is through the use of economic evaluation, especially, but not solely, in pharmaceuticals. This is where the medical profession can make most use of economics and not feel that their status or power is threatened. Where health economists, however, have had very little impact has been in addressing priority setting at the level of, for example, investments in community services rather than in the hospital sector or in different client groups (such as the elderly versus the mentally ill versus maternity care) or in different disease groups. As discussed in Chapter 1, this seems odd, as such priority setting is exactly where economics ought to be able to make the greatest contribution. It is also where economic analysis would have a direct impact on the power base of individual clinicians. Currently in most health care systems the way in which decisions are made about priorities and resource deployment is often less than transparent. It is in the interests of powerful clinicians that it remains so, as they are then better placed to influence where resources are invested. Explicitness in such decision making, through economic analyses such as programme budgeting and marginal analysis (PBMA), bringing out as it would the opportunity costs involved and so opening up debate about different options, is not welcomed. There has thus been far less investment of health economists' time and effort in analysing these priority setting issues. What investment there has been has had little impact. Given this appraisal of the power structure within health care this is not surprising. Unless the distribution of property rights on resource allocation in health care is challenged by health economists, little will change in how priorities are currently established. The paradigm developed in this book acknowledges and seeks to change the existing distribution of property rights in health care.

Setting health care systems central stage as social institutions shifts the value base away from what has traditionally been the health economics value set. Most crucially certain key values shift from the individual to the community, and from the individual consumer to the citizen. There is also a shift of power from the doctors to the community. The previous chapter showed how health economics has not gone far enough in breaking out from the market. The emphasis has still been on health care as a commodity rather than on health care as a social and community good, or social service, produced in a social institution, which may have value in itself.

4.5 Public health

The economics of health outside of health care is essentially that of public health. The fact that the paradigm built in Part II of this book emphasises the social and community means that it is well placed to handle this issue. Public health is very clearly a social entity and can be seen as a social institution in its own right. In the context of the social determinants of health, which embrace a number of social institutions, public health can be seen as the summation of the workings of these different social institutions.

While the work by many disciplines and policy makers on the social determinants of health and public health more generally has blossomed, oddly, although with some notable exceptions such as Bob Evans (see for example Evans et al 1994) and Vicente Navarro (2002), health economists have been rather thin on the ground. This situation is, however, improving. There are a number of possible explanations for the relative paucity of health economics research in public health. The most obvious is that public health would be difficult to interpret as a commodity. Health care can be and is; public health as an entity is not marketable (although some individual aspects, such as jogging shoes or healthy food, might be).

In analysing public health, it also seems critical (again!) that the value base of the current health economics paradigm is individualistic. Somewhat like the economist's social welfare function, for health economists population health represents an aggregation problem with no workable solution, either conceptually or empirically, in sight. Add to the individualism the consequentialism of health economics and it is not surprising that traditionally health economists have struggled to analyse both public health and population health.

There is the related problem that population health is a big, broad entity in which issues other than "health gains" or QALYs figure even larger than in individual health. These are not adequately taken care of by conventional externalities (such as caring externalities). Population health measures can fall under the heading of social option values, which in the public health literature are known as "preparedness", and which has been defined as follows (RAND Corporation 2007):

The capability of the public health and health care systems, communities and individuals to prevent, protect against, quickly respond to and recover from health emergencies, particularly those whose scale, timing or unpredictability threatens to overwhelm routine capabilities. Preparedness involves a coordinated and continuous process of planning and implementation that relies on measuring performance and taking corrective action

Public health is also about addressing population risk and its reduction, which in turn raises questions around population anxiety and reassurance—intangibles that individual health measures such as QALYs struggle to encompass. Fear of bird flu, SARS, and AIDS are all population-based fears as well as individual-based. Preparedness can be seen as being more about reducing population anxiety than about health gains *per se*.

Traditional health economics is able to deal with some of this, but only inadequately. The beauty of a public health construct that starts at the social level is that the aggregation problems are largely avoided and issues of measurement start at the aggregate level and do not need then to be worked up to that level.

A good example of some of these issues is the question of evidence-based policy, which has become so prevalent in clinical medicine. While one might argue that the question of being evidence-based is one of which the virtue cannot be disputed, it is at the same time worrying that it has become something of a religion in clinical medicine (Kristiansen and Mooney 2004). One can see that evidence-based RCTs in evaluation of pharmaceuticals are both valuable and valid. Within clinical medicine, however, such evaluation in home care versus hospital care for MS sufferers becomes more problematical. Extend the focus to evaluation of atmospheric pollutants or income inequality or indigenous land rights and evidence is not just harder to come by but it is of a very different type. It follows that the individualistic consequentialism of clinical evaluations is not only more difficult to apply in public health, but it risks being described as an attempt to "weigh heat". In the competition for resources for health, instead of the public health trying to compete with clinical medicine on the individualistic consequentialist paradigm of clinical medicine, it needs a separate paradigm. Otherwise it will continue to fail at that level. What is needed, as the paradigm developed in Part II explains, is for all judgements about resource allocation for health, whether individual health or population health, to be based on the notion of health as a social and cultural construct. Thus population health is a function of different sub-populations' health, where each sub-population (which might be some cultural grouping, for example) can have a different construct of health.

It is also likely that what different societies and different cultures want from public health will vary. Some will place more weight on reducing anxiety, others on being involved in decision making around public health.

Beyond the question of interpreting both health care systems and public health as social institutions, there is what is perhaps best described as "ownership" of the institution, but with "responsibility" perhaps being a better term. The question of who "owns" the health service can readily be answered as "the people", especially if it is a public health care system. The same question—who owns public health?—is less readily answered but there are elements, if not of ownership, then at least of responsibility and obligation, such as there being responsibility of the strong for the weak (Juul Jensen 1987); the well for the sick; and those more secure (in many senses) for those more at risk.

The above considerations raise questions not only about the optimal allocation of scarce public health and health care resources, which, as currently conceived are set in terms of outcomes and especially of individuals' health outcomes, but also how such optimal resource allocation might be better based and according to whose values. What is needed is a process that allows an informed community to have its values driving resource allocation in principle—setting a constitution for health—and in a way that allows them to have a form of ownership of the process, where health care and public health are valued not just for their outcomes but also as social institutions that are a part of the overall common good of society, being both pillars supporting that society but also being an integral part of the good provided.

4.6 Compassion

It can also be hypothesised that moving away from individualism to more of a community focus will lead to creation of a more compassionate society. A society where people see themselves as members of a community, they are more likely to behave reciprocally with other members and be concerned about issues of mutuality and trust than if they were to see themselves as individuals with few social ties. While these traits in a society cannot guarantee that it or its citizens will be more compassionate, where there is a commitment to one's community, the soil is likely to be more fertile for this compassion to grow, and so compassion for others in that community may become more prevalent. The question of social compassion is yet more likely to occur in some sectors of the social fabric than others, with health care and public health looking to be better candidates for the presence of caring and compassion than say energy policy or transport. There are in many societies a greater concern for the health of others and/or the access to health care for others than for, say, the education of others. It is then possible to hypothesise that societies that are more communitarian in nature, such as the Scandinavian countries, will tend to be more concerned to protect the weak, such as the sick, and to see a social role for this protection (Juul Jensen 1987). That would in turn suggest the presence of a larger public sector, higher taxes, and possibly a more progressive taxation systems. It is difficult to measure compassion and even more so to measure differences in levels of compassion between different societies, but a case can be made for these characteristics listed above as providing proxy measures of compassion. (In the specific context of addiction policy, I have tried previously to argue that more compassionate societies have different attitudes to both prevention and treatment of addicts; see Mooney 2005.)

Compassion on its own without power, however, may not result in any significant differences in a society's overall policies relating to vulnerable or disadvantaged people. It can be difficult for ordinary citizens to convey to those in power a desire to see a more compassionate society or a more compassionate work place or a more caring school environment. The ruling ideology may be lacking in altruism or compassion and often it is this ideology that then shapes social attitudes rather than the compassionate community persuading those in power to act compassionately.

The work of Nussbaum (2001) on compassion, especially public compassion, is germane to the issues here and builds on these comments from Dugger (1984). Nussbaum (2001: 403) asks

what would a compassionate society look like? Given that there is reason to think that compassion gives public morality essential elements of ethical vision without which any public culture is dangerously rootless and hollow, how can we make this compassion do the best work it can in connection with liberal and democratic institutions? ... The insights of an appropriate compassion may be embodied in the structure of just institutions, so that we will not need to rely on perfectly compassionate citizens. This idea is used both by Smith (with his idea of the compassion of the "judicious spectator") and by Rawls, who creates an artificial model of an appropriately constrained benevolence via the Original Position. This ideal of moral benevolence is the lens through which we see how institutions and basic political principles should be designed.

Nussbaum (2001) argues that there are many different ways in which compassion might be built into our institutions. She does not, however, go so far as to argue that we can leave all of this to our institutions, instead she suggests (p. 404) that we must "rely on compassionate individuals to keep essential political insights alive and before our eyes".

Nussbaum (2001: 405) thus sees the relationship between compassion and social institutions as "a two-way street: compassionate individuals construct institutions that embody what they imagine; and institutions, in turn, influence the development of compassion in individuals".

Building the social institutions of a health care system and of public health on public or social compassion is attractive. (This idea is a part of Anderson's expressive theory on which the paradigm developed in Part II is based.) Current health economics, being both consequentialist and based on individual values, would struggle to incorporate compassion, either at a social level or at the level of the individual patient. The idea of more value being attached to a health care system that is compassionate as compared with one that is not is also alien to traditional health economics. Further, the construct of public health, being based as it so often is on social justice, can benefit from being seen as an institution that, in Nussbaum's terms above, can "influence the development of compassion in individuals".

4.7 Conclusion

What this new paradigm shift requires is thus the following.

- A move from individuals' values to citizens' and community values.
- The acceptance of both health care systems and public health as social institutions.
- A shift away from the property rights currently in the hands of medical associations and individual doctors to investing power in the

community whose health is at stake, whose health service it is and who are members of the population whose public health it is.

- An acknowledgment that while there is often a recognition within health economics that the market fails, health economists have done too little to come up with some other paradigm.
- An acceptance that compassion matters in the delivery of health care; it also matters in designing our social institutions including health care systems and public health.

References

Adams, V. (2004) Equity of the ineffable: cultural and political constraints on ethnomedicine as a health problem in contemporary Tibet, in S. A. Anand, F. Peter and A. Sen (eds.), *Public Health, Ethics and Equity*. Oxford: Oxford University Press.

Avineri, S. (1974) *Hegel's Theory of the Modern State*. Cambridge: Cambridge University Press.

Coast, J. (2004) Is economic evaluation in touch with society's health values? *British Medical Journal*, 329: 1233–6.

Commons, J. (1931) Institutional economics, *American Economic Review*, 21: 648–57.

de Pinho, H. (2005) *Transforming health systems to strengthen implementation of the Beijing Platform for Action and the Millennium Development Goals*. Baku: United Nations Division for the Advancement of Women.

Dugger, W. (1984) Methodological differences between institutional and neoclassical economics, in D. M. Hausman (ed.), *The Philosophy of Economics: An Anthology*. Cambridge: Cambridge University Press.

Elster, J. (1989) *The Cement of Society*. Cambridge: Cambridge University Press.

Evans, R., Barer, M. and Marmor, T. (1994) *Why are Some People Healthy and Others Not?* New York: de Gruyter.

Gilson, L. (2003) Trust and health care as a social institution, *Social Science and Medicine*, 6(67): 1452–68.

Gruchy, A. G. (1947) *Modern Economic Thought: An American Contribution*. New York: Prentice Hall.

Hegel, G. (1820) *The Philosophy of Right*. Available at: www.marxists.org/reference/archive/hegel/works/pr/prfamily.htm (accessed 20 Nov. 2007).

Houston, S. (2004) The past the present the future of Aboriginal health policy. PhD thesis, Curtin University, Perth.

Jan, S. (2000) Institutional considerations in priority setting: transaction cost perspective on PBMA, *Health Economics*, 9: 631–41.

——(2002) Institutionalist perspectives in the economics of health and health care. PhD thesis, University of Sydney, Sydney.

Jensen, U. J. (1987) *Practice and Progress: A Theory for the Modern Healthcare System*. London: Blackwell Scientific Publications.

Kasper, W. and Streit, M. (1998) *Institutional Economics*. Cheltenham: Edward Elgar.

Kristiansen, I. S. and Mooney, G. (2004) *Evidence Based Medicine: In its Place*. London: Routledge.

Mooney, G. (1998) Beyond health outcomes: the benefits of health care, *Health Care Analysis*, 6: 99–105.

—— (2000) Vertical equity and health care resource allocation, *Health Care Analysis*, 8(3): 203–15.

—— (2005) Addiction and social compassion, *Drug and Alcohol Review*, 24(2): 1347–141.

Murray, C. and Lopez, A. (1996) *Global Burden of Disease*. Cambridge, MA: Harvard University Press.

Navarro, V. (ed.) (2002) *The Political Economy of Social Inequalities*. New York: Baywood.

North, D. (1992) Institutions and economic theory, *American Economist*, 36(1): 3–6.

—— (1993) Institutions and credible commitment, *Journal of Institutional and Theoretical Economics*, 149(1): 11–23.

Nussbaum, M. (2001) *Upheavals of Thought: The Intelligence of Emotions*. Cambridge: Cambridge University Press.

Rand Corporation (2007) Conceptualizing and defining public health emergency preparedness. Available at: www.news-medical.net/?id=23254 (accessed 12 Dec.2007).

Smith, A. (1759) *Theory of Moral Sentiments*. London: A Millar.

Stigler, G. (1971) The theory of economic regulation, *Bell Journal of Economics and Management Science*, 2(1): 3–21.

Veblen, T. (1924) *The Theory of the Leisure Class*. London: George Allen and Unwin.

Williamson, O. (1986) The economics of governance: framework and implications, in R. N. Langlois (ed.) *Economics as a Process: Essays in the New Institutional Economics*. Cambridge: Cambridge University Press.

5

Neo-liberalism and its Impact on Health

5.1 Introduction

There is a shift of focus in this chapter to issues of a more ideological nature and how these underpin health economics. The chapter sets public health and health care in more of a political economy context. Without this context, which is largely missing in current health economics, the efforts of health economists are greatly reduced in their effectiveness.

The chapter will argue that neo-liberalism, the form of free market economic philosophy and ideology that has increasingly pervaded the globe in the last 30 years, is bad for the health of the people of those nations that embrace it. It will also argue that global institutions, such as the World Bank and the International Monetary Fund (IMF), further the hegemony of neo-liberalism, and that, with few exceptions, these issues too have been mostly ignored by health economists.

As previous chapters have shown, health economists traditionally have mainly concentrated their skills on the analysis of health care rather than on public health. Additionally, the emphasis on health care has meant that the political economy of health has also become largely the political economy of health *care*. The power of the medical profession that tends to dominate health care politics has thereby extended into the politics of public health. Whatever the legitimacy of the former situation, the legitimacy of the latter is questionable. Doctors, perhaps inevitably, are most interested in medicine and the health of their individual patients and much less so in population health.

As it happens, a very sizeable proportion of the social determinants of health can be collapsed into just two categories: poverty and inequality. There is, and has been for a long time, excellent evidence that poverty is bad for our health. Recently, suspicions have been confirmed (see for example Wilkinson 2005) that, additionally, inequality is bad for our health, although the interpretation of this evidence remains disputed in some quarters. Being poor is bad for population health; but the evidence is growing that inequality makes it yet worse. Importantly in the context of this book, this is especially true if such inequality is set in terms of what Wilkinson and Pickett (2006) call "social stratification or how hierarchical a society is" or what Navarro (2007) calls a "class analysis".

There are various explanations for the impact of inequality on health but most relate to loss of autonomy, power, and powerlessness. Being powerless and lacking autonomy are bad for health, as is being overpowered. The greater the inequality in a society, the less cohesive the society becomes, and the less solidarity it has. Where societies lack compassion for the disadvantaged, inequalities are likely to be greater and the impact of inequality of health will also be greater. A class analysis (such as Navarro 2007 advocates) is needed to allow a fuller understanding of the impact of inequality on health. This is thus to be seen not just in terms of inequality of income but also in inequality of power.

I have earlier attempted to set the issue of addiction in this context of compassion. In writing on that issue I quoted Cohen (1997: 160) who said that "the dominant opinion in the US seems to hold that the individuals who suffer such conditions [of addiction] are the cause of them". He suggests (p. 161) that "American politicians have neither the tools to fight the presence of growing masses of underclass poor nor the political support for creating such tools". Drawing on that I wrote (Mooney 2005: 140):

Public compassion matters . . . We need to care not simply because people who are poor in income or have had their culture destroyed by colonization or are addicted to gambling or drugs, or have fled from some vile regime, but simply because they are badly off . . . The need is to embrace rather than push away "the other" . . . To embrace must be for the sake of building a decent society, a caring community, for the sake of a common humanity, for community autonomy. The individualism of the market belongs to the market; it is not the basis for building a community or society.

The chapter discusses the individualism that neo-liberalism is based upon and in turn further engenders, and its impact on population health. Where neo-liberalism has been abandoned or denied, population health tends to be better. Where it has been imposed, population health has declined.

In the next section neo-liberalism is defined and some of the ramifications for relations between rich and poor nations are discussed and set in a health context. Some of the problems for health globally are created by global institutions, such as the World Bank, and these issues are set out in section 5.3. Section 5.4 then indicates the impact of neo-liberal globalisation on health. It is concluded in section 5.5 that health economists need to pay more attention to neo-liberalism and its effects on health, both in individual countries and more especially globally.

5.2 Neo-liberalism, compassion, and institutions

Neo-liberalism can be described in many different ways. I want to *define* it, primarily in economic terms, but to go on and suggest that, with respect to its impact on population health, the concerns about the effects of neo-liberal globalisation extend beyond the impact on incomes and income distribution into questions of power and class, and that these in turn have major implications for cultural diversity and the diversity of economic systems (which are inevitably related). I also draw attention to the fact that the selfish individualism that neo-liberalism engenders spills over into global power relations between rich and poor countries, but also it increases inequality within countries. These issues, despite their very real influence on both world health and the health of individual societies, especially its distribution, are not issues that health economists have spent much of their research efforts in exploring. See, however, the various contributions from a political economy stance in *Neoliberalism, Globalization and Inequalities* (edited by Vicente Navarro 2007).

As highlighted in Chapter 1, evidence from the leading health economics journals, our key world conference, and important review articles by non-health economists on inequalities in income and health confirms the neglect by health economists of considerations of poverty and inequality. It is then not surprising that we might have failed to look behind this to see what role neo-liberalism might have played in these two leading social determinants of health.

The Canadian philosopher Charles Taylor (1991) argues that individualism is a major source of "the malaise of modernity". In this book he describes what he calls "the dark side of individualism" with its "centring on the self, which both flattens and narrows our lives, makes them poorer in meaning, and less concerned with others or society" (Taylor 1991: 4). While Taylor does not write as specifically about society, culture, or global concerns, this flattening and narrowing must also threaten the cohesion and solidarity of some societies and, in its hegemonic influence, reduce the diversity of culture across the globe. Individualism encourages us to look inwardly, introspectively, at ourselves, which then affects our capacities to see ourselves as part of a wider society or community or to recognise the importance of the culture in which we live.

Such individualism leaves little room for the building of compassionate societies and in turn equitable social institutions. This is confirmed in the smugness of Francis Fukuyama (1992) in *The End of History*, where he argued that neo-liberalism and the market represent the summit of social and political endeavour.

Harvey defines neo-liberalism as (Harvey 2005: 2):

a theory of political economic practices that proposes that human well-being can best be advanced by liberating individual entrepreneurial freedoms and skills within an institutional framework characterized by strong private property rights, free markets and free trade...State interventions in markets...must be kept to a bare minimum.

That definition is adequate for the deliberations in this book.

Globalisation, today, is primarily motivated by and has its driving force in neo-liberalism. Watkins (1997) suggests that "globalisation encapsulates both a description of changing patterns of world trade and finance, and an overwhelming conviction that deregulated markets will achieve optimal outcomes for growth and human welfare". He adds: "Seldom since the heyday of free trade in the nineteenth century has economic theory inspired such certainty—and never has it been so far removed from reality."

However, the writer who historically forecasted the difficulties that would arise from what is now called neo-liberalism is the philosopher Hegel (Muller 2003). While rather neglected by economists, his words on economics are very insightful. In the use of the health economics paradigm developed in this book and considerations around neo-liberalism and in turn globalisation, what is crucial is the role that Hegel saw for the state.

Muller (2003: 157) writes of how Hegel argued that

[t]he pressures of competition...gave market societies an outward thrust. The search for markets in which to sell these products for which supply now exceeded demand led entrepreneurs to push on into areas that were relatively backward economically, both internally and beyond the nation's borders...Hegel recognised (as Smith had not) that entrepreneurs were a major force in the expansion of the

imagined wants of consumers...the market did not just satisfy wants it created them.

Hegel saw the importance of the state in terms of social institutions. Today's neo-liberal freedom would have been dismissed by Hegel as an assault, first, on the state and, second, on freedom. He would have viewed neo-liberals as being slaves to their passions. What provides the framework for freedom for Hegel and hence a framework for a good life and society is the establishment of social institutions that, based in culture, can provide a way of socialising people into good habits. He saw duties not as limiting freedom, but enhancing it. The free person in liberal terms inevitably leads a turbulent life with no real sense of direction. Hegel saw virtue in terms of living up to one's institutionally imposed duties. "In an ethical community, it is easy to say what someone must do and what the duties are which he has to fulfil in order to be virtuous. He must simply do what is prescribed, expressly stated, and known to him within his situation" (Hegel 1820: 150). In his conceptualisation of freedom, Hegel emphasised the crucial role of institutions "so that self-conscious individuals could become more aware of the meaning of the institutions in which they participated—a step towards feeling at home in these institutions" (Muller 2003: 150).

This notion of "institutionally imposed duties" is alien to neo-liberal values. It is much easier, however, to see it as being part of community life and in turn community freedom. This is apparent at the level of both duties *to* the community and duties *by* the community, a form of reciprocal agreement that, for example, is present in many Indigenous communities.

The need for the poor to be organised was recognised by Hegel, lest they be left as isolated powerless individuals. He writes (in Avineri 1974: 166):

it is of the utmost importance that the masses should be organized, because only [by] so do[ing do] they become mighty and powerful. Otherwise they are nothing but a heap, an aggregate of atomic units. Only when the particular associations are organized members of the state are they possessed of legitimate power.

If the poor are not organised into some communal grouping, thereby giving themselves power, as individuals they will lose their autonomy. Community autonomy for the poor, but also for societies in general, matters. It is best achieved through institutionalising it.

It is of note that the literature on improvement in institutions for the poor does so largely on the basis of empirical evidence on how existing institutions are failing the poor (see for example Acemoglu et al. 2004).

The process here is likely to prove much easier if questions of distribution (for example between rich and poor) are assessed using some *social* construct of fairness. It will be easier still if there is a wholly explicit constitution worked out by the citizenry whose social institution this is. If the citizens are in a position to determine the criteria for allocating resources to different disadvantaged groups—those with ill health, risk, capacity to benefit, etc.—and to exercise their strengths of preferences for one group over another according to their degrees of compassion for different vulnerabilities or disadvantages, then the prospects for analysing equity as a genuinely social phenomenon are greatly enhanced. This is what is allowed by the approach based on communitarian claims. The question of equity under the new paradigm is, however, left for discussion to Chapter 11.

Hegel thus confirms that social institutions matter. It is important that we as citizens of our own countries but also citizens of the world "feel at home" in our institutions, and that participation in social institutions, as integral parts of the state, is encouraged. There is a further need to defend our social institutions and, most fundamentally to recognise the importance of, and in turn celebrate, the institution of community autonomy.

In health economics the social institutions that are health care, public health, and health policy need to be recognised more often as valuable in their own right. Societies do value them for the health and other outcomes they produce, as conventional health economics implies, but they can also be valued as contributing to a better, more decent society. They also need to be valued in more direct Hegelian terms as providing protection (along with other social institutions) to the state not least from being overrun by the forces of the neo-liberal market place.

Today the state is increasingly threatened by both globalisation and neo-liberalism. Hegel argued against the market's conception of the good society. The market seemingly allows each individual the right to define his or her own good by promoting the right to be free to choose whatever maximises that person's own good. This is the classic liberal freedom. Yet, importantly, and too often played down by neo-liberals, there are three prerequisites lying behind this construct of the good. First, individuals must have the means to choose in terms of money or income; second, there must be a coincidence of values and desires; and, third, the social good can be interpreted purely in terms of individuals' values and their aggregation.

Social justice, which is essential for building public health, does not require close definition in the context of globalisation. There is clear evidence that the gap between rich and poor both across the globe and within countries has been increasing. As a minimum, this has been exacerbated by neo-liberal globalisation.

In the United Nations Development Programme's (UNDP) *Human Development Report* of 1999, it is stated (UNDP 1999: 3):

Inequality has been rising in many countries since the early 1980s. In China disparities are widening between the export-oriented regions of the coast and the interior: the human poverty index is just under 20% in coastal provinces, but more than 50% in inland Guizhou. The countries of Eastern Europe and the CIS [the former Soviet Union] have registered some of the largest increases ever in the Gini coefficient, a measure of income inequality. OECD countries also registered big increases in inequality after the 1980s—especially Sweden, the United Kingdom and the United States.

Across countries the report (UNDP 1999: 3) also exposes growing inequality: "The income gap between the fifth of the world's people living in the richest countries and the fifth in the poorest was 74 to 1 in 1997, up from 60 to 1 in 1990 and 30 to 1 in 1960." The maldistribution is summed up as follows:

By the late 1990s the fifth of the world's people living in the highest-income countries had 86% of world GDP—the bottom fifth just 1%; 82% of world export markets—the bottom fifth just 1%; 68% of foreign direct investment—the bottom fifth just 1%; and 74% of world telephone lines, today's basic means of communication—the bottom fifth just 1.5%.

While it is clear that poverty leads to loss of self-esteem, the impact of that loss is furthered by a lack of caring by the rich for the poor. This is then fed by neo-liberalism's individualism, which in turn leads to ill health and the prospect of yet greater poverty. There are various analyses of these phenomena (see for example Coburn 2000; Navarro 2002; and Wilkinson 2005), but few by health economists.

Added evidence that the rich nations appear not to care about the poor is provided by the fact that the UN target of 0.7% of GNP for donor countries to give in aid to the developing world is met by few. The average is considerably below this (0.2%–0.4%) with only five OECD countries above 0.7% (three of which are Scandinavian), and Greece and the US at the bottom of the ladder with 0.16% and 0.17% respectively.

In addition to this lack of caring, there are cases of exploitation of the poor by the rich. For example, Rosenberg (2002: 28) identifies the problems for poor countries of the laws that surround patenting, which give rise to "intellectual property rules that require poor nations to honour drug patents [which] will result in a transfer of $40 billion a year from poor countries to corporations in the developed world".

Another form of exploitation that arises through neo-liberal globalisation and the freeing up of trade is the movement of labour, especially doctors and nurses, from developing to developed countries. Maureen Mackintosh (2007: 159) writes:

Migration from Africa to high-income countries ... worsens an already intolerable gulf. Its distributive effects may be measured by the perverse subsidy generated ... Migrant African health care professionals were trained in sub-Saharan Africa at public and private expense; the benefits of that training are then experienced in the UK [and other rich countries] and lost to those dependent on African health services. The subsidy arises because UK health care users benefit from the skills the UK did not create through investment; it is perverse because it worsens global health inequity ... Training costs in the UK are estimated at £220,000 for a doctor and £37,500 for a nurse. This implies a one-off saving in training costs ... of about £64.5 million from hiring 293 Ghanaian trained doctors in the UK in 2004, and about £38 million for an estimated 1021 nurses trained in Ghana

Poor countries are subsidising industrialised countries by about US$500 million a year through the migration of health care workers. In South Africa the outflow of doctors between 1989 and 1997 amounted to over 82,000. That represents a loss of training investments of US$5 billion (Padarath et al. 2004).

In considering third world health and third world poverty, the neo-liberal West lacks compassion. We fail to hear the voices of the world's poor. We do not want to feel their humiliation. The lack of solidarity across the globe hinders such solidarity, and governments who have embraced neo-liberal ideology do too little to foster a sense of community and social cohesion. The situation is not only supported by our international organisations—our global institutions—it is also encouraged by them, as the next section shows.

5.3 International organisations

In considering the impact of neo-liberalism on health care as an institution, two points are worth making. First, despite the pressures from neo-liberalism, industrialised countries have continued to prefer health care policies, which are heavily funded publicly (with some exceptions such as in the US). Second, at the same time and hypocritically, they, WHO and the World Bank, have encouraged the commercialisation and privatisation of health care in poor countries. This is evidenced by the data that show that the lower the income of a country, the higher the proportion of the health care spending that is private (Padarath et al. 2004). Thus, in general, the richer a country (but the US is again clearly an exception), the less likely it is to privatise health care.

Global institutions have tended to see the world though a Western perspective and assume that Western values, and often neo-liberal values, are or can be universal. An example is WHO. While that body *does* do good works, too often the good is defined by WHO rather than by those whose health they seek to improve.

In 2000, for example, WHO (2000) issued a report on world health based on what they considered were the key criteria for judging the quality of a health care system. Using these criteria they also worked out a world league table: who had the best health care system; who the second best; and so on. The criteria included such considerations as overall population health, responsiveness, access, and equity.

With respect to equity, in health care delivery the goal can be defined in various ways, such as equal health, equal access, or equal use. The same is true of equity in health care financing. Whatever the definition chosen, there is a need to make the case for defining it other than as a cultural-social phenomenon where equity in one country may be conceived and valued differently from equity in another country. WHO did not make this case, neither did it recognise the need to do so, but instead it adopted a universalist position, with equity and its relative value as compared with other health care objectives being assumed to be the same in all countries.

WHO used *their* criteria and *their* weights to judge what constitutes a good health care system. They defined the nature of the objective function and then used this for all countries. This might not have mattered except that policy makers do use these league tables. It is also symptomatic of a wider phenomenon where the imposition of universalism dominates global institutions.

Again, in its Commission on Macroeconomics of Health (CMH), WHO did too little to seek to disturb the existing political economy of world development. The Commission (WHO 2001: 23) commented on the

many reasons for the increased burden of disease on the poor. First, the poor are much more susceptible to disease because of lack of access to clean water and sanitation, safe housing, medical care, information about preventative behaviors, and adequate nutrition. Second, the poor are much less likely to seek medical care even when it is urgently needed ... Third ... out of pocket outlays for serious illness can push them into a poverty trap from which they do not recover.

All of this is true, but it is a description of the problems, not an analysis. It does not address the global political economy that creates the situations listed. It is a seemingly ideologically neutral stance. In practice, in not offering a critique of the status quo, it becomes a part of that status quo. The key recommendation of the report of the Commission (WHO 2001: 4) was that "the world's low- and middle-income countries, in partnership with high-income countries, should scale up the access of the world's poor to essential services". More health care is seemingly the answer and appealing to the governments of the high-income countries to fund it is the vehicle to bring health to the world's poor. Such appeals have fallen on deaf ears before. Unless they are backed by some good analytical evidence and address the power and class structures arising through neo-liberalism in individual countries and promoted internationally by global institutions nothing will change.

The CMH, as Katz (2007) confirms, was "deeply conservative and unoriginal". She argues (p. 381):

The report encourages medico-technical solutions to public health problems; it ignores macroeconomic determinants and other root causes of both poor health and poverty; it reverses public health logic and history; it is based on a set of flawed assumptions; and it reflects one particular economic perspective to the exclusion of all others ... It faithfully reproduces conventional "free" market, "free" trade prescriptions that have been so resoundingly successful in accelerating poverty and social inequality—and in turn poor health status of populations—over the last 20 years

What is particularly worrying in Katz' criticisms is her point that the report "reflects one particular economic perspective to the exclusion of all others". The point is echoed by Banerji (2007): "A striking aspect of the report is that it has almost systematically 'blacked out' alternative viewpoints on health economics."

The CMH provided much evidence of the nature of the problems for low- and middle-income countries to develop and some very useful analyses of the links between macroeconomics and health. It then failed to analyse what needs to be done to make the necessary changes. In particular, it ignored the impact of neo-liberalism on both global development and the policies of the global institutions that oversee such development. Some have placed much of the explanation for the failings of the CMH at the door of its chair Jeffrey Sachs who is known for having been an advocate of neo-liberalism, especially in Chile and Russia (Klein 2007). To place the blame there, however, misses the point that there was no secret about Sachs' ideological position when he was appointed and, without seeking to diminish the role of others on the commission, it must have been known when he was appointed what sort of ideological stance he would bring to his work.

There is clearly a problem here, not just with the neo-liberalism of globalisation *per se*, but with the neo-liberalism of current global institutions. WHO, for example, is made up of representatives of its member states; it does not represent world citizenry. The same criticism but on an even greater scale can be directed at the WTO. In doing so I want to highlight the fact that the nature of today's world and the nature of today's world institutions are dictated by the forces of the market, often powerful corporate interests, and they are not democratic.

The WTO is concerned with three issues (Ranson et al. 2002: 19):

1. to assist in the free flow of trade by facilitating the removal of trade tariffs or other border restrictions on the import and export of goods and services.
2. to serve as a forum for trade negotiations; and
3. to settle trade disputes based upon an agreed legal foundation.

An example of the workings of the WTO serves to illustrate the neo-liberal focus of its power base. In 2002, in the wake of a well publicised campaign, the South African government sought cheaper drugs from the pharmaceutical companies for their AIDS patients. The companies were forced by Amnesty International and public opinion to back down and agree. At the WTO meeting in November 2002, it was announced that the WTO would allow cheaper drugs for developing countries (Mason 2003).

Then, a month later, the WTO changed its mind. They did so because the US pharmaceutical companies objected to the impact that cheaper drugs for South African AIDS victims would have had on their profits. As Mason (2003) writes, explaining the backing down:

the pharmaceutical companies . . . are determined to maintain their profits. The largest US drug company made $37 billion in profits [in 2001], a rate of return to shareholders of 39 percent. Although less than 20 percent of these profits are made from the 80 percent of the world's population in the developing world, they are not prepared to allow cheap drug production to continue.

This is an example of neo-liberalism at work at the WTO—in this instance through the power of the pharmaceutical companies.

One facet of the workings of the WTO which is particularly relevant to health economics is the TRIPS Agreement—the Agreement on Trade-Related Aspects of Intellectual Property Rights. The aims of the TRIPS are "promotion of technological innovation; transfer and dissemination of technology; and contribution to the mutual advantage of producers and users of technological knowledge in a manner conducive to social and economic welfare" (Ranson et al. 2002: 22).

Such stated intents, however, have not in practice delivered economic or social benefits to the poor, especially not to those in the developing world. TRIPS, if it were acting "in a manner conducive to social and economic welfare", ought to have positive impacts on population health, especially through pharmaceuticals and vaccines. The South African example above clearly indicates that there is a need for reform. The UNDP (1999) show for example that while three-quarters of the world's population live in the third world (and bear a yet higher percentage of the world's burden of disease), they consume only 14 percent of global pharmaceuticals. Pécoul et al. (1999) show that of the 1,223 new chemical products marketed between 1975 and 1997 only 13 were applicable to tropical diseases. Ranson et al. (2002: 29) report: "Developed countries currently hold 97 per cent of all patents world wide; more than 80 per cent of the patents that have been granted in developing countries also belong to residents of developed countries."

There can be no surprise at such figures or any expectation that TRIPS, or the WTO more generally, will have much if any positive impact on them. It is market forces that determine these figures. The poverty and inability to pay of the developing world mean that the developing world stays underdeveloped. This will remain the case as long as the world's governing body on trade is driven by neo-liberal principles.

In his criticisms of the neo-liberal West, and on TRIPS, Stiglitz (2003a: 105), a former senior vice-president and chief economist of the World Bank and co-winner of the 2001 Nobel Prize in economic science, goes yet further: "TRIPS reflected the triumph of corporate interests in the United States and Europe over the broader interests of billions of people in the developing world. It was another instance in which more weight was given to profits than to other basic values—like the environment, or life itself."

Underlying these issues is a problem identified by Ranson et al. (2002: 30): "At present only 0.2 per cent of the annual global health expenditure related to R&D is for pneumonia, diarrhoeal diseases and tuberculosis, despite their accounting for 18 per cent of the global disease burden."

One much publicised attempt to reduce world poverty (and, it is implied, to improve world health) is contained in the WTO's Doha agreement on world trade. Adopted originally in November 2001, that agreement has undergone various transformations since, mainly to weaken its initial intent.

In its original form it was stated, *inter alia* (see: www.wto.org/English/thewto_e/minist_e/min01_e/mindecl_e.htm):

International trade can play a major role in the promotion of economic development and the alleviation of poverty. We recognize the need for all our peoples to benefit from the increased opportunities and welfare gains that the multilateral trading system generates. The majority of WTO members are developing countries. We seek to place their needs and interests at the heart of the Work Programme adopted in this Declaration... We recognize the particular vulnerability of the least-developed countries and the special structural difficulties they face in the global economy. We are committed to addressing the marginalization of least-developed countries in international trade and to improving their effective participation in the multilateral trading system.'

What is the likely impact of the Doha agreement as it now stands some seven years later? In a book edited by Hertel and Winters (2006), the various contributors present their assessments of the likely impact of implementing the Doha agreement in full in a range of countries. Some examples are presented here. Emini et al. (2006: 371) suggest for Cameroon that the Doha agreement is "likely to relieve poverty mildly... with falls in both overall poverty and income inequality, allowing 22,000 people to escape from poverty in net terms". In the Philippines (Cororaton et al. 2006: 401), however, it is likely to "slightly increase poverty... especially in rural areas and among the unemployed, self-employed, and rural low-educated". Annabi et al. (2006: 463) suggest for Bangladesh:

The Doha agreement is found to have minor negative implications for the overall macro economy, household welfare and poverty in Bangladesh, because the [terms of trade] deteriorate and consumer prices rise more than nominal incomes... The net effect is greater welfare losses and poverty increases among the poorest households. The greatest beneficiaries of the Doha agreement appear to be rural large farmers who capitalize on rising returns to agricultural capital (primarily land).

Rutherford et al. (2006: 468) see more gains for Russia: "Russian WTO accession in the medium term will result in gains averaged over all Russian households equal to 7.3 per cent of Russian consumption ... with virtually all households gaining." It is also likely to be more or less neutral across rich and poor in Russia. The policy will do little to help the poor of Mexico

(Nicita 2006: 126) "unless it is complemented by domestic reforms aimed at facilitating the response of households to these new market opportunities".

Finally, for Mozambique, Arndt (2006: 150) states: "To rise out of poverty, Mozambique must achieve rapid growth over a long period...Seen from this perspective, the static results presented...are disappointing because they do not contribute to the growth required for such sustained poverty reduction."

The overall picture as to whether the Doha agreement, if implemented in full, would have a positive or negative effect on poverty remains uncertain. Whatever the direction of the effect, even if positive, it would be small. That already small effect is yet further reduced, as the Doha agreement is not being implemented in full. Only if the Doha targets were to be "ambitious", as Hertel and Winters (2006: 28) put it, (and, as they currently stand, they are not) would they have a "measurable impact...on poverty" (Hertel and Winters 2006: 28). The reason for this, as summarised by these authors, is that the Doha agreement, even as originally conceived, was not sufficiently far reaching. Hertel and Winters (2006: 4) write:

Sustained long-term poverty reductions depend on stimulating economic growth. Here, the impact of the [Doha agreement] on productivity is critical. To fully realize their growth potential, trade reforms need to be far reaching, addressing barriers to services trade and investment in addition to merchandise tariffs.

The Doha proposals never were far reaching; they are much less so now.

Such "far reaching" reform does not happen, however, because the Western neo-liberal societies do not want it. Anderson et al. (2006: 521), taking the central Doha scenario of three (which is almost certainly optimistic in terms of poverty reduction), estimate that "the overall gains from a WTO accord could amount to US$96 billion, of which US$80 billion would be reaped by rich countries".

There is an appearance of reluctance on the part of the rich nations to do more. But is "reluctance" the best way to describe this? Stiglitz (2003a: 131) argues: "Trade negotiators have little incentive to think about the environment, health matters or even the overall progress of science... Trade ministers tend to negotiate in secret. Trade agreements are long and complex." The implication is that it is the process that matters rather than the outcome and that the question of bettering the lot of poor countries is simply not on the agenda when governments are negotiating trade deals.

It is of note in the context of the communitarian emphasis in the later parts of this book that, on establishing the preferences of the community,

Stigltiz (2003b) writes: "If the issue of access to AIDS drugs were put to a vote, in either developed or developing countries, the overwhelming majority would never support the position of the pharmaceutical companies or of the Bush administration." The vote of world citizenry is not called so such health issues are not addressed. They are left to our global institutions. Stiglitz' comments here come close to endorsing the idea of a global communitarianism (of which more in Chapter 9).

These observations lead to the question of global governance and how the effects of corporate interests that Stigliz identifies can be countered. That issue (see Chapter 9) might entail global communitarian claims as a way of handling global health. Certainly these issues are highly pertinent to the economics of health and health care.

There is a need to examine how global financial decisions are currently made as these are important to the considerations in this book. In turn, such decision making needs to be seen in terms of the history of global financial management since the Bretton Woods Agreement of 1944.

The Bretton Woods Agreement was primarily about setting up a new international monetary system. It established the International Monetary Fund (IMF) and the International Bank for Reconstruction and Development, later called the World Bank. The role of the IMF is to provide loans or guarantee credits to its member countries. It also provides money for various projects including roads, schools, etc. Further, it gives loans to help to restructure economies that are in difficulty through what are called "structural adjustment programmes" (SAPs). The IMF is also involved in lending money to countries, but usually only where there are short-term balance of payments problems. Such loans are, again, dependent on countries agreeing to certain reforms of their economies, which in practice means SAPs.

What has emerged over time is a split in the power of the global institutions. In essence (Raffer and Singer 2001: 7),

the UN was not to be trusted with the "hard" instruments of development such as finance and macroeconomic policy making; that was to be the preserve of the Bretton Woods institutions [the IMF and the World Bank] with their system of weighted voting and firm control by the Western industrial countries.

This meant that the UN was left with what Raffer and Singer (2001) describe as "the 'soft' instruments" which include "food aid, technical assistance, children, women, social policy and, more recently, the environment".

This power split is important. The UN is based on one nation, one vote; the World Bank and the IMF are based on one dollar, one vote. That has meant that the rich nations control the IMF and the World Bank, and as a result put most of their efforts into these institutions, seeking to deny as best they can power to the UN, where the poorer nations have equal rights of voting. In turn, what the UN might have controlled has been shifted to the G7 and the G8, i.e. again to the rich and powerful nations (the former Canada, France, Germany, Italy, Japan, the UK and the US; the latter these same countries plus Russia). As Raffer and Singer (2001: 10) state, these organisations are "clearly undemocratic . . . representing less than 20 per cent of the world's population."

Thus power within the World Bank and the IMF rests on quotas where these are based on economic size. For the World Bank: "Inequity among member countries is reinforced further . . . with the five largest quota holders appointing their own representatives to the Executive Board, while the remaining 179 countries are grouped into constituencies and represented by 19 Directors, each having just one vote." (World Bank/IBRD at: www.oneworldtrust.org?display=wb).

The Global Exchange provides more detailed data on the voting structure of the IMF and the World Bank. "Currently, in the IMF, the United States has 17.81 percent of the vote, Germany and Japan 5.55 percent each, France and the United Kingdom 4.99 percent each, the G-7 countries a combined total of 44.9 percent, and the G-10 plus Switzerland account for 51.2 percent of the total voting power." They suggest that the World Bank is similar, with the "voting power . . . currently distributed as follows: the United States 17.14 percent of the vote, Japan 6.47 percent, Germany 5.0 percent, France and the United Kingdom 4.79 percent each, the G-7 countries a combined total of 44.4 percent, and the G-10 plus Switzerland 50.8 percent."

This situation is exacerbated, however, because the IMF and the World Bank also have an impact on voting at the UN. Dreher and Strum (2006), in their study of 188 countries over a 30-year period at the end of the last century, show that the IMF and the World Bank use their power over other nations to "influence voting in the UN General Assembly" (p. 25). They also argue, following Stiglitz (2003a: 26), that "the influence of governments could also be reduced by transferring the control of international organizations to the member countries' citizens".

Against that background of the power structure of the World Bank and the IMF, it is perhaps not surprising that there is little evidence that the structural adjustment programmes work in favour of reducing poverty in the poor- and middle-income countries. As the Global Exchange (see: www.globalexchange.org/campaigns/wbimf/faq.html) states: "Structural adjustment has exacerbated poverty in most countries where it has been applied... since the 1980s, adjustment has helped create a net outflow of wealth from the developing world, which has paid out five times as much capital to the industrialised countries of the North as it has received."

A second issue with respect to global governance that has become a central feature of international financial arrangements in recent years is what is called "conditionality". This phenomenon grew out of a recognition on the part of the IMF that the approach to monetary policy that might suit developed countries was less appropriate in the developing world, since the latter lacked the institutional arrangements to make such policy viable. (See Chakravarti 2005: 75.) So the IMF adopted the idea of "conditionalities" which are conditions aimed at providing a country with the necessary ability to achieve short-term stability which might then be the basis on which to build economic growth. By the late 1980s the IMF and the World Bank had agreed that "structural adjustment or economic reform packages were necessary to reduce distortions introduced by inappropriate government policies, eliminate structural rigidities, and permit the development of liberalized and more competitive markets". To bring this about (Chakravarti 2005: 76) "the programmes would bind the borrower to a set of conditionalities intended to bring about sustainable budget deficits, monetary discipline, competitive exchange rates, and a general liberalization of the economy". These conditions represent the imposition of neo-liberal economic reforms.

The use of these conditionalities is very different from what many originally sought in the 1944 Bretton Woods Agreement. As Raffer and Singer (2001: 3) report, in Keynes' early thinking about these institutions, he opposed the idea of conditions associated with "a 'grandmotherly' fund" but "[w]hen he had to accept the idea of conditionality, he did so on the basis of a very large Fund... equal to half of annual world imports... It was as late as 1969 that conditionality became explicitly enshrined in the Articles of Agreement [of the IMF]."

What we have today is a fund that is not 50 percent but 2 percent of the world's annual imports. This greatly diminished fund is, as Raffer and Singer (2001: 3) state, "a measure of the degree to which our vision of international economic management has shrunk". The prize of a visionary global governance, along what were Keynesian lines, has been replaced by a yet greater reliance on the neo-liberal forces of the market place.

This embracing of neo-liberalism by global institutions has also meant, as Mishra (1999: 129) suggests, that "social policy [including heallth] has remained essentially a national concern". He argues:

The main reasons for limited progress in developing effective transnational social protection are two fold; first the absence of global institutions of governance with the authority to formulate binding standards and to ensure their implementation. The second and a related point is that although the important difference between civil and political rights on the one hand and economic and social rights on the other has been recognized, the implications of the difference have not been worked out.

What is critical here is to reform the structures of global governance. That issue is addressed in more detail in Chapter 9.

The global institutions of the World Bank and the IMF have considerable potential to influence world poverty and inequality and in turn to improve health and health inequalities across the globe. They choose not to do so. But where are the health economics assessments of the policies of these organisations that look at the gap between what they might achieve for world health and what they do achieve? Health economists cannot by themselves hope to change world governance. We can at least better identify the health problems that current governance creates, and assess what reforms might do for global health. As explained in Chapters 8 and 9, yet more could be done if health economics were to adopt a communitarian stance.

5.4 Impact of neo-liberal globalisation

This section gives a brief outline of the impact of neo-liberalism on health through considerations of economic growth, inequalities in income and health, and culture. First, the idea that neo-liberalism has resulted in faster rates of economic growth is challenged. Second, the issues around neo-liberalism and inequalities in income (and power) is set in a class analysis to identify better what lies at the heart of the explanation of the relationship between neo-liberal-induced inequalities and health. And, last, the way in which neo-liberalism imposes alien cultures on existing local cultures is examined and the impact this has on population health.

5.4.1 *Impact on growth*

There is a belief that neo-liberalism is an important contributor to economic growth. Thus as Li (2004) writes: "The advocates of neo-liberalism promised that the neo liberal 'reforms' or 'structural adjustments' would usher in an era of unprecedented economic growth, technological progress, rising living standards, and material prosperity."

Again Navarro (2002: 35) argues: "One claim made by neo liberal authors in support of the superiority of neo liberal policies is the increased rate of economic growth experienced in the 1980s, which is assumed to have resulted from the implementation of important elements of neo liberal policies in the OECD countries."

Li (2004) suggests, however, that:

the world economy has slowed towards stagnation in the neo liberal era. The average annual growth rate of world GDP declined from 4.9 percent between 1950 and 1973, to 3.0 percent between 1973 and 1992, and to 2.7 percent between 1990 and 2001. Between 1980 and 1998, half of all the "developing countries" (including the so-called "transition economies") suffered from falling real per capita GDP.

Navarro (2002) compares various economic indicators for a series of countries from the 1960s through to the 1990s. He takes the starting point of neo-liberalism as being 1979–80 with the election of Margaret Thatcher in the UK in 1979 and Ronald Regan in the US in 1980. He then compares growth rates in a number of countries over the 1960s through to the 1990s.

He presents figures which indicate (Navarro 2002: 36) "that the rate of economic growth was higher in the 1980s than in the 1970s". He points out beyond that two issues (p. 36) "that question the superiority of such policies". These are: "First, the rate of economic growth in the 1980s was lower than in the 1960s, when state intervention policies were in full swing. Second, in the 1990s, when neo liberal policies were still in operation, the rate of economic growth declined quite substantially, to even lower levels than in the 1970s."

He continues (Navarro 2002: 36):

If, rather than looking at the annual growth of GDP, we look at the GDP per capita and for longer periods in the 1990s...we find that, for most of the developed OECD countries, the rate of growth was lower in the 1990s than in the 1980s and lower in the 1980s than in the 1970s. Only in Germany, Denmark, Ireland, and Norway were rates of economic growth per capita greater in the period 1989–1997 than in the period 1979–1989. All these countries—all with highly regulated labor markets and extensive social protection [one might say "more communitarian"]—had greater economic growth than the United States.

He summarises: "one cannot conclude that neo liberal policies were more successful in stimulating economic growth than the state interventionist policies they replaced. Quite to the contrary: they were less successful."

These analyses give the lie to the idea that neo-liberalism is necessarily good for economic growth. In the time frames in a before and after analysis of neo-liberalism that are relevant to the comparison, Navarro shows, as reported above, that just four countries stand out as bucking this trend—and these four were "protected" by "highly regulated labor markets" and "extensive social protection", i.e they were the subject of *non-neo-liberal* policies.

Navarro looks at other macro indicators to try to assess the impact of neo-liberalism over this same time period. His assessment is that these policies have controlled inflation and led to higher profit shares and rates; increased social inequalities; and that "the welfare state, rather than being a drag on the economy, contributes to the creation of employment". A key finding by Navarro (2002: 71) is that there is "a political relation rather than economic determinism (which is behind the globalization position) that underlies the level of inequalities in any country".

5.4.2 Impact on inequalities in income and health

With respect to the impact of neo-liberalism on income inequality, there is good evidence (see for example Coburn 2000) that neo-liberal societies tend to be less equal. Evidence also exists that inequality is bad for a society's health (Wilkinson 2005).

There has been some considerable debate about the interpretation of the literature on inequalities in income and in health. What is important here is whether inequality at an aggregate social or, more accurately, at a societal level (e.g. the nation state) and population health are related. Such inequalities may or may not be related at other more micro levels, but the social stratification issue or class issue is what is of interest here. The only study that I have been able to identify that looks at this question specifically is that of Wilkinson and Pickett (2006). They conclude (p. 1778) as follows:

Our interpretation of 168 analyses of the relationship between inequality and health is that *income distribution is related to health where it serves as a measure of the scale of social class differences in a society*... In small areas, where income inequality is unlikely to reflect the degree of social stratification in the wider society, it is [as the authors show] less likely to be related to health. The overwhelmingly positive evidence for studies of larger areas suggests that this interpretation is correct. The fact that social stratification is such a fundamental feature of social organisation explains why there are so many socioeconomic factors correlated with inequality (emphasis added)

Navarro (2002: 71) shows that the growth of inequalities in most OECD countries in the last few decades is due to tax policies that favour the rich; the attack on trade unions; the erosion of the welfare state; and "economic policies that gave priority to the reduction of inflation via monetarist policies that reduced the rate of economic growth and increased unemployment".

The influence of neo-liberalism and of globalisation can be exemplified by the situation in South Africa. Fourteen years on from the democratic elections, nearly 60 percent of the health care spend in South Africa remains private for 16 percent (nearly all white) of the population. Of the remaining spending of just over 40 percent in the public sector, the formula adopted for allocating these public resources was such that there was a bigger weight per capita for those provinces that were rich and growing fast economically (i.e. whiter provinces) than there is for the "'catch up" and, under Apartheid, neglected, homelands provinces. The result was that the province that got more—far more—*public* sector health care, rand per capita, was Gauteng, the richest, whitest, and most privately insured province in the country.

The reason appears to be that in essence the democratically elected South African government is caught in the web of neo-liberal international politics and regulations as put in place by the IMF and the World Bank. They have a concern that if they go too fast in reforming their society, in this case in health care, this will have financial repercussions on their ability to obtain loans from the IMF and the World Bank.

Across the globe it is apparent that current policies on social justice in the health sector have failed. This is at least in part because the values of Western societies are so dominated by the atomistic liberalism of the neo-classical market place, by the move to globalisation, and by the loss of country sovereignty that has then ensued. The threat of being penalised by the World Bank and/or the IMF is very real for many countries.

The impact of neo-liberal policies in the form of a "trickle up" effect on inequalities is exemplified by Navarro (2002) in Brazil. In the period 1968–81 the Brazilian economy grew very rapidly and was held up as a model neo-liberal performer by the World Bank as that country had rigorously pursued the edicts of the World Bank. Yet, oddly, infant mortality rates increased over this same time. Navarro (2002) investigated this issue more closely and showed that for the top 5 percent of the Brazilian population their share of national consumption increased from 20 percent to 48 percent; for the bottom 50 percent, their share fell from 20 percent to 12 percent.

So much of health care policy is influenced, even dictated, by the World Bank, IMF, WHO, and WTO. As Homedes and Ugalde (2005: 94) write on the basis of their assessment of neo-liberal reforms in Latin America:

The formidable concentration of power in the hands of a few IMF and [World Bank] policy makers and bureaucrats weakens [both] national policy making and [attempts to find] correct answers to each country's health problems based on local political, cultural, and historical realities more than on [some] generic formulation based on ideology.

5.4.3 *Impact on culture*

Vandana Shiva (2000) outlines how the neo-liberalism of globalisation can have social and cultural impacts beyond the economic. She states:

Globalisation is the rule of commerce and it has elevated Wall Street to be the only source of value. As a result things that should have high worth—nature, culture, the future are being devalued and destroyed. The rules of [neo-liberal] globalisation are undermining the rules of justice and sustainability, of compassion and sharing.

It can readily be argued from the literature on the social determinants of health that these are all factors that are can be used to building social cohesion. As such, Shiva's comments suggest that neo-liberalism can be seen as undermining population health. On health issues more specifically she goes on to argue that a "global monoculture is being forced on people by defining everything that is fresh, local and hand made as a health hazard". And she points out that: "When patents are granted for seeds and plants, as in the case of basmati rice, theft is defined as creation, and saving and sharing seed is defined as theft of intellectual property."

Shiva's notion of a monoculture is potentially a major problem for the health of populations, since it threatens cultural diversity. Where people are comfortable in their own cultures, where their cultures breed self-respect and are respected by others, then population health is more likely to flourish. In many Indigenous cultures, in the wake of colonialism and neo-colonialism, self-respect culturally has been lost. Neo-liberal globalisation is destroying the diversity of cultures. This is not to argue that all cultures are healthy or health promoting, but rather that before any attempts are made to reform various cultural practices, the net effects of doing so need to be determined. More generally, however, neo-liberal economic reformers need to recognise that too often their economic reforms result in the imposition of Western cultural values, usually neo-liberal values, which have negative effects on population health and especially the health of the poor.

The more insidious impact of Western neo-liberal ideology in destroying local cultures is apparent in the account from Mander (1996) of the introduction of TV in the societies of the Dene Indians and the Inuit in the Arctic (p. 58): "children lost interest in the native language, they wanted to learn Canadian English; they refused to learn how to fish on the ice or go hunting... Young people did not want to be Indians, in fact they hate being Indians—they want to be Canadians and Americans." As a result (p. 352) "the effect has been to glamorise behaviours and values that are poisonous to life up here [in the Arctic]. Our traditions have a lot to do with survival. Community co-operation, sharing, and non materialism are the only ways that people can live here."

Bagchi (2005: 40) emphasises an apparent paradox in neo-liberalism. "Concurrent with stereotyping whole peoples as superior or inferior, capitalist ideology also propagates the fallacy that the behaviour of societies can be portrayed as that of a simple aggregate of atomized individuals." He recognises, however, that "human beings, men, women and children, almost from the time they are born, become socialized individuals. Capitalism socializes individuals in particular ways." He continues:

Even as it endows a small group with control over means of production and, through the "culture industry" over the means of acculturation, it converts large numbers of people into propertyless workers who can survive only by selling their labor power and who become objects of manipulation by the culture industry.

Thus it is not just neo-liberalism *per se* through its individualism and attacks on social cohesion that is problematical for health. Worse still is the hegemony of neo-liberalism.

Individualism and disengagement are bad for individual and population health, as are any policies that divide societies. There is a need to defend and protect diversity of cultures. As UNESCO (2005) on cultural diversity states: "Globalization, in its powerful extension of market principles, by highlighting the culture of economically powerful nations, has created new forms of inequality, thereby fostering cultural conflict rather than cultural pluralism."

The links between health and culture can be strong. As UNESCO (2005) claims, in "our increasingly diverse societies... [p]olicies for the inclusion and participation of all citizens are guarantees of social cohesion".

5.5 Global public goods for health

One of the themes explored in this book is that conventional health economics inadequately acknowledges that many of today's health problems extend beyond national boundaries and raise questions about their management internationally. One of the most obvious examples is the emergence of new infectious diseases (Plant and Watson 2008) that can affect people across the globe. While such diseases and their effects may be difficult to contain, a question arises for health economics on how best to design and finance relevant health intervention programmes to deal with them. That rather open question is narrowed down in this section to ask whether Global Public Goods for Health (GPGH), as promulgated by health economists and others at the WHO, are the way forward.*

The poor bear the greatest burden of disease. Equity, then, demands that health care and public health more generally be supported by a desire for social justice by governments, donors, etc. Donors, for example, could finance inputs targeted at the health of the indigent and they themselves, i.e. the donors, might then derive some satisfaction from doing so. Although the benefits of such programmes are private to the recipients, insofar as the donors also obtain benefits there is a positive externality. Again, if the consumption of the service (by the recipient) were also to prevent the spread of an infectious disease to the community, then the reduction in the level of carriers for that disease would also constitute a form of external benefit. In most cases of government intervention, the motivation is to achieve levels of consumption in keeping with what is deemed socially desirable. While the goal relates to consumption, this can be achieved, either by governments altering in some way the level of production and thereby altering the level of consumption that would otherwise have prevailed, or by more direct intervention on consumption. Goods of this ilk mostly fall into those categorised as public goods. This section briefly examines the concept of GPGH as presented by the WHO (Smith et al. 2003).

The concept of global public goods, according to Kaul et al. (1999a), is based on the assertion that public goods (bads) which traditionally are national in character are becoming global. From this perspective they define a global public good as

---

* This is based in part on Mooney, G. and Dzator, J. (2003) Global public goods for health: a flawed paradigm?, in R. Smith, R. Beaglehole, D. Woodward and N. Drager (eds.), *Global Public Goods for Health*, pp. 233–40. By kind permission of Oxford University Press.

a public good with benefits that are strongly universal in terms of countries (covering more than one group of countries), people (accruing to several, preferably all, population groups) and generations (extending to both current and future generations, or at least meeting the needs of current generations without foreclosing development options for future generations) (Kaul et al. 1999a).

The proposed objectives of the WHO's GPGH project are to identify potential GPGH of particular importance to poor people in developing countries that might also provide more general benefits at a global level; to outline how they could be provided and financed; and to gauge their economic merits and political feasibility.

The concept of GPGH, while it may be appealing to the WHO, is worrying. For example, the consumption of the benefits from the three key types of public goods that might be identified as influencing health (i.e. infrastructure systems for the provision of health services, clean water and sanitation; policy and regulatory regimes; and knowledge and technologies that help to (i) understand health risks, (ii) provide preventive, curative and palliative interventions, and delivery systems) is mostly determined in many developing countries by market forces. Thus, even if national governments are coerced into providing these intermediate goods, many consumers would be excluded from benefiting because of, for example, fee-for-service policies. Ironically, the WHO's GPGH concept rules out the important and significant cross-border activities that can have strong externalities on health.

Global governance in the case of producing global public goods appears to be one of the difficult issues. Such governance must involve the interaction of states, international organizations, and non-state actors to shape values, policies, and rules, and is perceived to be different from international governance, defined as intergovernmental cooperation (Fidler 2001).

GPGH remain essentially welfarist in nature. It is then relevant to think through some of the implications that may be ascribed to welfarism. For example, in discussing distributive justice in the context of welfarism, Sumner (1996: 221) poses the question: "What is the good of which citizens are to be assured equal shares?"

Sumner (1996: 221) goes on:

Does welfarism suggest an answer to this question?...On a subjective account, some aspects of our wellbeing (our aversion to pain, for instance) are relatively unaffected by our idiosyncrasies of taste or our freely chosen projects. But others are not: what counts as the best life for you will be strongly influenced by your particular constellation of personal values or aspirations. Suppose that, having convinced yourself that you are the sort of person who deserves the best, you are unable to be satisfied with less than the fastest cars, the flashiest clothes, and the best cosmetic surgery, while your more modest neighbours are able to achieve the same level of wellbeing with much more limited resources. A theory of justice which requires that resources be distributed so as to ensure equality of welfare will, in effect, enable you to tax your neighbours for the maintenance of your expensive life style. And that seems unfair, not least because . . . you too could have chosen to cultivate more humble tastes.

Sumner (1996: 222) then argues that

most theories will . . . counsel the adoption of a strategy consisting of whatever set of rules or dispositions is calculated, given realistic assumptions about the nature of human agents and their circumstances, to increase the likelihood of success in making the right decisions.

The GPGH literature inadequately addresses the problems, particularly the equity problems but also the valuation problems, that bedevil welfarism. Since GPGH rest on welfarism, these problems need to be addressed.

As identified earlier in this chapter, a major problem with globalisation and now in turn with GPGH is that the terms of trade, whether it be in goods or in benefits (health and other) from GPGH, are set in a world where the distribution of property rights is very firmly skewed in favour of rich countries. This is the key argument against free trade where free trade only equals fair trade if it is between more or less equally powerful nations or if there is altruism present in the negotiations. What happens in practice is that the more powerful (i.e. the richer) nations can often ensure that the terms of trade work much more in their favour than can the poor—unless the rich are altruistic.

It is worthy of note in the work of Kaul et al. (1999b) how they grapple with very similar issues in assessing how to finance GPGH, which is a parallel situation to the terms of trade argument. A fair outcome would be for the rich to take the greatest majority of the burden of financing. In practice, however, as Kaul et al. (1999b) identify, they will not do this without some sort of incentive. They suggest that a global participation fund be established. They argue that participation is a useful starting point for equity and suggest that "equity in participation should be embedded in the structures of international governance". If one were drawing up a manual on how to make free trade fair, one might well have a central clause which would read: "equity in participation should be embedded in the structures of international governance". As explained and for the reasons stated above, given the distribution of property rights between rich and poor in the terms of trade, free trade does not end up as fair trade. No global participation fund for free trade has been set up. Why would we expect more success with GPGH?

An alternative approach to these issues that avoids the problems of GPGH and that builds on the paradigm developed in later chapters is outlined in Chapter 9.

5.6 Conclusion

In his assessment of the impact of neo-liberal globalisation, Mishra (1999) emphasises the importance of social institutions, echoing a theme already picked up in this book. He argues that the push to globalise along neo-liberal lines results in pressures to deregulate, to privatise, and to reduce social programmes. This follows as a result of the weakening of the welfare state, which protected workers' incomes both through seeking full employment and by providing well paying jobs. Additionally, the welfare state provided social protection in unemployment or sickness. In response to this threat (Mishra 1999: 115) states: "The neo liberal thrust of globalization . . . is to strengthen market forces and the economic realm at the cost of the institutions of social protection."

He points to the clash between globalisation and communities:

human communities are defined above all by language and culture and are thus rooted in a place . . . Economies have gone global but societies and communities remain national. The result is a growing hiatus between the needs of the economic realm . . . and those of the social realm for stability, security and a sense of belongingness and cohesion.

Mishra also, importantly, distinguishes between social rights and social standards, noting that welfare states have by and large been based on the former. He states (p. 117):

Since the late 1970s, social rights have taken a beating, both ideologically and in practice . . . The basic weakness of social rights as a concept is that it is not [on] a par with the other two rights, i.e. civil and political. Whereas these two are essentially *procedural* and can be institutionalized as universal human rights, social rights are substantive in nature . . . They raise issues of mobilizing and redistributing material resources. The bottom line is that the granting of social rights comes into conflict with economic or property rights, one of the basic rights in liberal capitalist societies.

We return to Mishra's ideas in Chapter 9.

Our global institutions do not reflect the voices of people globally. They do not in any sense represent world authority. They are dominated by the US and other large Western countries and in turn by their neo-liberal ideology. These countries see social policy, including health policy, in residual terms. The global institution of the WHO remains wedded to welfarism and seems unprepared to challenge neo-liberalism.

The neo-liberal West see global institutions in the image of their own national institutions and are prepared to impose where necessary (in their opinion) institutions that are foreign to the local cultures. The allowance that there is, in conditionalities and in structural adjustment programmes for cultural relativities, is minimal. Those institutions, in both senses of the word—the organisations and "the cement" (Stigler 1971)—that have been deemed to work in country X and country Y are deemed to be suitable for country Z.

The question of respecting and often of maintaining local institutions—not inflexibly but relying on local values and listening to local values—is critical. As Narayan et al. (2000) argue:

What emerges is that, despite the global efforts to create institutions that serve the poor, many of these institutions created by outsiders—whether from the state, civil society, the private sector, or international organizations—often do not have the character poor people value. Only when all these institutions embody the characteristics laid out by poor people will they make a sustained difference, a difference that matters in poor people's lives. Poor people want institutions they can participate in and that they can trust to be relevant, to care and to listen.

That is a key issue and we return to it in Chapter 9.

References

Acemoglu, D., Johnson, S. and Robinson, J. (2004) Institutions as the fundamental cause of long run growth. Available at: http://elsa.berkeley.edu/~chad/handbook9sj.pdf (accessed 20 Nov. 2007).

Anderson, K., Martin, W. and van der Mensgrugghe, D. (2006) Global impacts of the Doha scenarios on poverty, in T. W. Hertel and L. A. Winters (eds.), *Poverty and the WTO*. Washington, DC: The World Bank.

Annabi, N., Khondker, B., Raihan, S., Cockburn, J. and Decaluwe (2006) Agreements and unilateral trade policy reforms for poverty in Bangladesh: short- versus long-run impacts, in T. W. Hertel and L. A. Winters (eds.), *Poverty and the WTO*. Washington, DC: The World Bank.

Arndt, C. (2006) The Doha trade round and Mozambique, in T. W. Hertel and L. A. Winters (eds.) *Poverty and the WTO*. Washington, DC: The World Bank.

Bagchi, A. K. (2005) *Perilous Passage. Mankind and the Global Ascendancy of Capital*. Oxford: Rowman and Littlefield.

Banerji, D. (2007) Report of the WHO Commission on macroeconomics and health: a critique, in V. Navarro (ed.), *Neoliberalism, Globalization and Inequalities*. New York: Baywood.

Bretton Woods Agreement (1944) Available at: www.ibiblio.org/pha/policy/1944/440722a.html (accessed 21 Dec. 2007).

Buchanan, J. and Vanberg, V. (1994) Constitutional choice, rational ignorance and limits of reason, in V. Vanberg (ed.), *Rules and Choice in Economics*. London: Routledge.

Chakravarti, A. (2005) *Aid, Institutions and Development*. Cheltenham: Edward Elgar.

Coburn, D. (2000) Income inequality, social cohesion and the health status of populations, *Social Science and Medicine*, 51: 135–46.

Cohen, P. (1997) Crack in the Netherlands: effective social policy is effective drug policy, in C. Reinarman and H. G. Levine (eds.), *Crack in America*. Berkeley: University of California Press.

Cororaton, C., Cockburn, J. and Corong, E. (2006) Doha scenarios, trade reforms and poverty in the Phillippines: a GCE analysis, in T. W. Hertel and L. A. Winters (eds.), *Poverty and the WTO*. Washington, DC: The World Bank.

Dreher, A. and Strum, J.-E. (2006) Do IMF and World Bank influence voting in the UN General Assembly? Available at: www.yale.edu/polisci/info/Workshops/IR/11–14–06-Sturm.pdf (accessed 12 Oct. 2007).

Emini, C., Cockburn, A. and Decaluwe, B. (2006) The poverty impacts of the Doha round in Cameroon: the role of tax policy, in T. W. Hertel and L. A. Winters (eds.), *Poverty and the WTO*. Washington, DC: The World Bank.

Fidler, D. P. (2001) The globalization of public health: the first 100 years of international health diplomacy, *Bulletin of the World Health Organization*, 79(9): 842–9.

Fukuyama, F. (1992) *The End of History and the Last Man*. London: Penguin.

Harvey, D. (2005) *A Brief History of Neo Liberalism*. Oxford: Oxford University Press.

Hertel, T. W. and Winters L. A. (eds.) (2006) *Poverty and the WTO*. Washington, DC: The World Bank.

Homedes, N. and Ugalde, A. O (2005) Why neo liberal health reforms have failed in Latin America, *Health Policy*, 71(1): 83–96.

Katz, A. (2007) The Sachs Report: Investing in health for economic development: or increasing the size of the crumbs from the rich man's table?, in V. Navarro (ed.), *Neoliberalism, Globalization and Inequalities*. New York: Baywood.

Kaul, I., Grunberg, I. and Stern, M. A. (1999a) Defining global public goods, in I. Kaul, I. Grunberg and M. A. Stern (eds.), *Global Public Goods: International Cooperation in the 21st Century*. New York: Oxford University Press.

———— —— —— (1999b) Global public goods: concepts, policies and strategies, in I. Kaul, I. Grunberg and M. A. Stern (eds.), *Global Public Goods: International Cooperation in the 21st Century*. New York: Oxford University Press.

Klein, N. (2007) *The Shock Doctrine: The Rise of Disaster Capitalism*. London: Allen Lane.

Li, M. (2004) After neo-liberalism: empire, social democracy, or socialism? *Monthly Review*. Available at: www.monthlyreview.org/0104li.htm (accessed 12 Nov. 2007).

Mackintosh, M. (2007) International migration and extreme health inequality: robust arguments and institutions for international redistribution in health care, in D. McIntyre and G. Mooney (eds.), *The Economics of Health Equity*. Cambridge: Cambridge University Press.

Mander, J. (1996) Technologies of globalisation, in J. Mander and E. Goldsmith (eds.), *The Case Against the Global Economy: And for a Turn Toward the Local*. San Francisco: Sierra Books.

Mason, B. (2003) US blocks cheap drugs for undeveloped world January 2003. Available at: www.wsws.org/articles/2003/jan2003/drug-j17_prn.shtml (accessed 1 Nov. 2007).

Mishra, R. (1999) *Globalization and the Welfare State*. Cheltenham: Edward Elgar.

Mooney, G. and Dzator, J. (2003) Global public goods for health: a flawed paradigm, in R. Smith, R. Beaglehole, D. Woodward and N. Drager (eds.), *Global Public Goods for Health*. Oxford: Oxford University Press.

Muller, J. Z. (2003) *The Mind and the Market: Capitalism in Western Thought*. New York: Anchor Books.

Narayan, D., Chambers, R., Shah, M. K. and Petesch, P. (2000) *Voices of the Poor: Crying Out for Change*. New York: Oxford University Press for the World Bank. Available at: www1.worldbank.org/prem/poverty/voices/reports/crying/cry9.pdf (accessed 14 Dec. 2007).

Navarro, V. (2002) Development and quality of life: a critique of Amartya Sen's *Development as Freedom*, in V. Navarro (ed.), *The Political Economy of Social Inequalities*. New York: Baywood.

—— (ed.) (2007) *Neoliberalism, Globalization and Inequalities*. New York: Baywood.

Nicita, A. (2006) Multilateral trade liberalization and Mexican households: the effects of the Doha development agenda, in T. W. Hertel and L. A. Winters (eds.), *Poverty and the WTO*. Washington, DC: The World Bank.

Padarath, A., Chamberlain, C., McCoy, D., Ntuli, A. and Rowson, M. (2004) Health personnel in Southern Africa: confronting maldistribution and brain drain. Equinet Discussion Paper No. 3. Available at: www.equinetafrica.org (accessed 20 Dec. 2007).

Pécoul, B., Chirac, P., Trouiller, P. and Pinel, J. (1999). Access to essential drugs in poor countries: a lost battle? *Journal of the American Medical Association*, 281(4): 361–7.

Plant, A. and Watson, C. (2008) *Communicable Disease Control: An Introduction.* Melbourne: IP Communications.

Raffer, K. and Singer, H. W. (2001) *The Economic North South Divide. Six Decades of Unequal Development.* Cheltenham: Edward Elgar.

Ranson, K., Beaglehole, R., Correa et al. (2002) The public health implications of multilateral trade agreements, in K. Lee, K. Buse and S. Fustukian (eds.), *Health Policy in a Globalising World.* Cambridge: Cambridge University Press.

Rosenberg, T. (2002) Globalization: the free trade fix, *New York Times,* Aug. 18: 28.

Rutherford, T., Tarr, D. and Shepotylo, O. (2006) The impact on Russia of WTO accession and the DDA, in T. W. Hertel and L. A. Winters (eds.), *Poverty and the WTO.* Washington, DC: The World Bank.

Sen, A. (1992) *Inequality Re-examined.* Oxford: Clarendon Press.

—— (1999) *Development as Freedom.* Oxford: Oxford University Press.

Shiva, V. (2000) *The Reith Lectures.* Available at: www.bbc.co.uk/radio4/reith2000/lecture5.shtml (accessed 18 Dec. 2007).

Smith, R., Beaglehole, R., Woodward, D. and Drager, N. (eds.) (2003) *Global Public Goods for Health.* Oxford: Oxford University Press.

Stigler, G. J. (1971). The theory of economic regulation, *Bell Journal of Economics and Management Science,* 2(1): 3–21.

Stiglitz, J. (2003a) *Globalization and Its Discontents.* London: Norton.

—— (2003b) The global benefits of equality. Available at: www.guardian.co.uk/wto/article/0,,1036367,00.html (accessed 20 Dec. 2007).

Sumner, L. W. (1996) *Welfare, Happiness and Ethics.* Oxford: Oxford University Press.

Taylor, C. (1991) *The Malaise of Modernity.* Toronto: Anansi.

UNDP (United Nations Development Programme) (1999) *UN Development Report.* Available at: http://hdr.undp.org/en/media/hdr_1999_front.pdf (accessed 11 Nov. 2007).

UNESCO (United Nations Educational, Scientific and Cultural Organization) (2005) Cultural Diversity in the Era of Globalization. Available at: http://portal.unesco.org/culture/en/ev.php-URL_ID=11605&URL_DO=DO_TOPIC&URL_SECTION=201.html (accessed 16 Dec. 2007).

Watkins, K. (1997) Globalisation and liberalisation: implications for poverty, distribution and inequality. Occasional Paper No. 32. Available at: http://hdr.undp.org/en/reports/global/hdr1997/papers/kevin_watkins.pdf (accessed 12 Dec. 2007).

WHO (World Health Organization) (2000) *The World Health Report 2000.* Geneva: WHO.

—— (2001) *Investing in Health for Economic Development.* Report of the Commission on Macroeconomics and Health (chaired by Jeffrey D. Sachs). Geneva: WHO.

Wilkinson, R. (2005) *The Impact of Inequality.* London: Routledge.

——Pickett, K. (2006) Income inequality and population health: a review and explanation of the evidence, *Social Science and Medicine,* 62: 1768–84.

Part II

A New Paradigm

6

Building the Base for the
New Paradigm

6.1 Introduction, values, and a constitution

Values, the choosing of values, and the eliciting of values underlie much of the emphasis of this book. In these respects there are echoes of some of the sentiments expressed by Victor Fuchs (1996) in an address to the American Economic Association Conference when he reviewed the state of the art of health economics. He suggested (p. 20) that as health economists "we must pay more attention to values than we have in the past. Through skilful analysis of the interactions between values and the conclusions of positive research, we will be able to contribute more effectively to public policy debates." Fuchs' point is endorsed by Uwe Reinhardt (1992) when he wrote (p. 315) that "to begin an exploration of alternative proposals for the reform of our [US] health system without first setting forth explicitly, and very clearly, the social values to which the reformed system is likely to adhere strikes at least this author as patently inefficient; it is a waste of time." Reinhardt (1992: 315) continues: "Would it not be more efficient to explore the relative efficiency of alternative proposals that do conform to widely shared social values?"

Economists also need to consider the questions of the origin and the formulation of preferences. We normally take preferences as givens and not the subject of inquiry, for example, as to whether they are rational or not. Notably, preferences over beliefs are typically not investigated by economists. These omissions may help to explain the relative lack of interest in moral and ethical matters by most economists. As Hausman and McPherson (1993: 29) point out: "utility theory places no constraints on what individuals may want." They argue that utility theory cannot be viewed as a positive theory "without further assumptions concerning the extent to which people are rational, and it is not merely a model or definition, because rationality is itself a normative notion". The need to accept the importance of ethics in economics is also the focus of work by Hurley (1998: 391) when he writes: "economists...who conduct evaluative economic analyses must appreciate more deeply that such analyses are inherently exercises in social ethics...The development of methods for such...analyses needs to occur in conversation with the broader literature on social ethics and moral philosophy."

It thus emerges that there is a need for some set of social rules—a constitution—when conducting our analyses. With Virginia Wiseman (Mooney and Wiseman 2000), I have previously set out the idea of a constitution for health services. Such a constitution is a set of principles on which policy and actions might be based: such as equity, how important it is, and how it might be defined. Is there to be concern only with horizontal equity, the equal treatment of equals, or also with vertical equity and the unequal but equitable treatment of unequals? A constitution might cover issues of respect for individual autonomy, of ensuring the freedom of individuals to refuse treatment, of the extent to which only outcomes matter or whether processes (such as decision making *per se*) are also to be valued. It might even state in which contexts in public health the community's preferences should count and when valuation issues might be left to the experts. (There is more discussion of this notion of a constitution in health in Chapter 9.)

Drawing on this idea of a constitution, this chapter begins to build the new paradigm. First, it sets the stage by introducing the "expressive theory" of Elizabeth Anderson (1993). This revolves around a rejection of consequentialism and especially the context-free monistic value systems of both welfarism and extra-welfarism. It seeks to incorporate a type of democracy that embodies some form of collective decision making in which all citizens are equal, arguing that "[a]utonomy can be realized on a collective scale through democratic institutions" and where such "collective autonomy" involves "collective self-governance by principles and valuations that everyone, or the majority, reflectively endorse" (p. 142). Anderson argues that some goods—she uses education as an example—need to be labelled "political goods". These "are provided by the community as a whole to its members". They are not public goods in the technical sense, but are distributed "in accordance with a conception of members' needs". Given these facets of Anderson's expressive theory, even if she does not argue specifically for communitarianism, nonetheless I perceive her theory as a useful base on which to build a communitarian approach to health and health care (see Chapter 7) and a communitarian paradigm (as in Chapter 8).

This chapter also addresses two issues that are important to any communitarian-based approach to values. The first looks at preferences, the elicitation of preferences, and the impact of reflection on such preferences. The second considers the extent to which preferences elicited in a group may be different from the aggregation of the preferences of the individual members of the group.

Communitarianism is discussed in detail in the next chapter. Here it is important to identify that there are at least four pillars to communitarianism, which will apply to both health care and public health. First, in determining the nature of the values that are to underpin health care, these will be based on the community's preferences. The emphasis is on the fact that health care as a system is a social institution. Similarly for public health, this will be approached through community preferences and where population health is much more than simply the sum of individuals' health. For example, what is acceptable to a society by way of advertising and health promotion will be determined by the society rather than, as is currently often the case, by health promotion experts.

Second, community preferences may not equate with the summation of individuals' preferences. There are contexts in which individual votes cast in secret can be the way to reach decisions, but having people debating and reflecting on issues as a community can result in different answers that, in some instances, may be preferred.

Third, establishing what may be best described as the social good of health care, perhaps but not necessarily, through the capabilities of Sen (1992) or Nussbaum (2001), is important.

Fourth, since different groupings within society (poor people, ethnic minority people) may have different abilities to manage to desire adequately, even if we wanted to place all of these preferences on a single measuring rod (such as utility), we cannot legitimately do so. The idea of a single and thereby common measuring rod is even more problematical if health and/or health need are different constructs in different social groupings, as they may well be, for example, across different cultural groups. This is discussed at greater length in Chapter 11.

6.2 Building a constitution

In respect of building a constitution, the research by James Buchanan on what he calls "constitutional" choices is highly pertinent. For example, Brennan and Buchanan (1985: 2) argue: "if rules influence outcomes and if some outcomes are 'better' than others, it follows that to the extent that rules can be chosen, the study and analysis of comparative rules and institutions become proper objects of our attention." The notion of a "constitution"—which (even if the language has changed) dates back to Adam Smith's "laws and institutions"—then becomes important, and in turn the idea of what Vanberg (1994: 135) describes as a "constitutional paradigm". He argues (p. 135) that instead of concentrating on the "goals that organizational action is supposedly directed at, [the constitutional paradigm] draws attention to the procedural foundations that organizational action is based upon". (This constitutional paradigm and Vanberg's ideas more generally are discussed again in Chapter 9.)

Bob Evans (1998: 478) appears to be writing about something akin to a constitution when he states: "we can set up an analytical framework postulating that consumer behaviour can be represented as the outcome of maximizing some objective function, but the framework tells us nothing at all about the arguments of the objective function."

With respect to the choices that arise regarding such a constitution, Buchanan and Vanberg (1994: 184, et seq.) argue that there are two problems. The first they refer to as differences in theories (which is perhaps better interpreted as differences in preferences) and, the other, differences in interests. The example they give is that two individuals may disagree about a law prohibiting smoking in public places. They may differ in whether it will succeed and they may differ in terms of their own different interests, e.g. if one is a smoker and the other a non-smoker.

It is the costs and complexities of involving the community in such choices that are most commonly put forward as reasons for not going down the road of community values for a constitution. On the informational requirements of doing this, Buchanan and Vanberg (1994: 186) state:

As one moves from collective choice among alternative constitutions, to collective choice among constitutional experts to, finally, individual choice among alternative constitutional arrangements, not only are the informational requirements for an intelligent choice dramatically reduced, the individual's incentives for making an informed choice significantly increase. While it may be very difficult to predict reliably the working properties of alternative constitutional rules, and also difficult to assess the true competence of constitutional experts, individuals will have fewer difficulties in assessing the relevant working properties of actually operating constitutional systems. And as they individually and separately choose their own "constitutional environment" they also have much more reason to make an informed choice, compared to their participation in a collective choice among constitutional rules or among constitutional experts.

This points to a need to consider different levels of choice or preferences, for example one at a community level and another at an individual level. That separation is not made in conventional health economics. The new paradigm set out in Chapter 8 makes this distinction.

The question of who is to get what and how collective decision making is to be carried out—two issues that Vanberg (1994) emphasises—are clearly important in any organisation. Vanberg (1994) outlines different paradigms for analysing the behaviour of organisations: these are the goal paradigm; the exchange paradigm; the nexus of contracts paradigm; and the constitutional paradigm. His starting point in doing so is to acknowledge that often collective entities (such as business firms or governments) are assumed to be decision making bodies, just like individual people. In the context of this book often health services or departments of health or hospitals are assumed to take on this role of being a decision maker. This is what Vanberg (1994: 125) calls "the principle of methodological individualism".

Vanberg's reflections are important in considering the application of the new paradigm because health care is normally seen as being composed of doctors, nurses, syringes, and hospitals, and these "actors" then deliver health care to patients. This is a part of the goal paradigm, since the delivery of health care is clearly not an end in itself. Patients are not a part of the health care institution. Citizens in this model are not present except perhaps as passive funders. In the private health care sector, citizens become consumers of health care or health care insurance and, again, they have little say in the nature of the organisation that delivers their health care.

Vanberg describes his constitutional paradigm as follows (p. 135):

The constitutional paradigm ... reverses ... the logic of the goal paradigm. Instead of concentrating on the "goals" that organizational action is supposedly *directed at*, it draws attention to the procedural foundations that organizational action is *based upon*. It concentrates on the social mechanisms that bring about the intraorganizational co-ordination of individual choices and actions that make us think of organizations as corporate actors.

Vanberg (1994: 136) draws on the work of Coleman (1990) to argue that

procedural rules that underlie organized or corporate action can justly be viewed as a constitution because they constitute organizations as corporate actors. When a group of persons establishes an organization by pooling resources for joint or combined use, they establish—explicitly or implicitly—a constitution.

This constitution is not only about decision making but also about the modus operandi, the culture, and the governance of the organisation.

"This means... that it must contain provisions for the kinds of problems that tend to arise whenever persons unite for organized or cooperative action, problems that are essentially of two kinds: collective decision problems and distributional problems."

Constitutions are needed for both health care and public health. There is much doubt about what the social goals of health care are, even if health economists have assumed they are about health maximisation. Without a constitution, there is no explicit value base, no set of principles to determine the modus operandi of the health care institution. There is a need for Vanberg's "procedural foundations that organizational action is based upon".

The situation in public heath is yet more perilous, as there is no organisational entity that is public health and no clear institutional governance in the sense of sets of rules. The new paradigm overcomes this problem.

As an alternative to setting a constitution, Jo Coast (2004) suggests a way out of the problems surrounding the current application of economics in health care, in the form of economic evaluation. She writes of the "increasing emphasis on cost–utility analysis [which] results in a conflation of 'health' with QALYs gained by the patient" (Coast 2004: 1235). She argues (p. 1235): "This 'funnelling' of various health outcomes into one, simplistic, single measure, is a further camouflaged assumption receiving less attention than it should." Coast proposes a move back from economic evaluations to what she calls "the approach of cost-consequences" (p. 1235) where " '[d]ifferent options are contrasted clearly and explicitly in tabular form for all the relevant costs (resource use) and consequences" (p. 1235). She suggests that using this approach "allows decision makers (on behalf of society) to impute their own values to these costs and consequences, which could differ according to local context" (p. 1235).

There is clearly merit in this approach, in its desire to allow the decision makers to include more than QALYs in what amounts to a constitution. The questions then are what elements they will include and what weights they will attach to the different elements. The prospects for manipulation here are very real. I would argue, as I did in Chapter 3 in promoting Joan Robinson's ideas of "functionaries", that the danger of manipulation can be overcome by separating the people given the responsibility to make decisions from those charged with setting the constitution. That separation is a major component of the new paradigm set out later in this book.

The extent to which health economists have concentrated on economic evaluation is itself a product of the social environment in which we work and will therefore vary from one society or culture to another. Indeed the US-based Edwards (2005: 311) argues that the UK-based Coast (2004) "fails to convey that the development of methods of economic evaluation by UK health economists does in fact reflect deep seated UK societal values and commitment to socialised medicine" (p. 311). While Edwards may overstate the point, nonetheless the social environment in which any discipline works must influence its objectives and its role. There is little doubt that more generally the focus and locus of health economists in the US are different from their counterparts in the UK—the former dealing much more with the market and hence financing and insurance issues, and the latter more with equitable resource allocation matters and economic evaluation.

6.3 Anderson's expressive theory

Anderson (1993: 18) describes her expressive theory as one which

reflects not a conventionalist but an anti-individualist theory of rationality. It claims that individuals are not self-sufficient bearers of practical reason: they require a context of social norms to express their attitudes adequately and intelligibly in action, to express them in ways others can grasp.

Her theory "defines rational action as action that adequately expresses our rational attitudes toward people and other intrinsically valuable things".

Anderson's expressive theory also takes us beyond consequentialism, since "expressive theories ... are intentional, backward looking, distributive, and non-instrumental" (Anderson 1993: 33). By intentional she means that they "tell people to intend or aim at certain things" (p. 33). Thus this theory is about doing things that express some sort of attitude towards a person or thing: there is a form of recognition on people's parts that their actions do express their attitudes. An example is deliberately tripping someone rather than doing so accidentally. Consequentialism does not distinguish between these two. An example closer to health is allowing someone to die as opposed to killing that person; or treating two people successfully, but only in one case with the person's informed consent. At the health care systems level, Anderson's expressive theory would allow us to distinguish between two systems that are identical except that one is designed on the basis of the local community's values and the other makes no effort to elicit community values.

With respect to being "backward looking", "what it makes sense to do now essentially depends on what one has done in the past" (Anderson

1993: 34). The past is contextual in that it can give special meaning to current acts that might well have a different meaning if the past had been different. A public health example would be distinguishing between two groups with an equally low life expectancy, say smokers and Indigenous people. An example at the level of individual patient care would be taking account of the emotional impact on a couple of whether this is their first IVF cycle or their sixth. A health care systems level example would be respecting the traditions of a community with respect to the use of land that might have spiritual significance to the local people and that was scheduled for development for the siting of a health care facility.

A third feature of Anderson's expressive theory relates to what she calls the "distributive structure" of the norms involved (Anderson 1993: 35). Expressive norms are about the particular—there is a person or thing that is the target or aim or end of the act. Thus "the distributive structure of expressive norms typically imposes constraints on a person's maximising behaviour, since not every way of maximising something expresses the appropriate respect, benevolence, or other attitudes we owe to each person affected by our actions" (p. 35). This is different from consequentialism where emotions *per se* are not evaluated except in terms of what they result in, i.e. their outcomes and where the way of expressing such emotions across different "persons affected" might influence them differentially. Expressive norms allow mixed emotions—satisfaction and guilt, happiness and regret, fulfilment and shame. In health care the trade-off between efficiency and equity might be a case in point—in, say, choosing to weight efficiency more highly than equity and thus gaining more benefit overall, but at the expense of foregoing some lesser benefit to a more deserving group. Having one's dignity respected, one's autonomy protected, or one's shame acknowledged can matter to patients, but not necessarily equally across all patients or across all situations for any particular patient. Expressive norms allow these.

Screening programmes raise questions of the "distributive structure" of expressive norms. Compare an individual who refuses to be screened and subsequently regrets not having been screened to an individual who lives in a country where no such screening is available. The "outcome" is the same whether or not the screening programme existed, but the negative benefit is greater where there is the opportunity for regret. In screening (or indeed other programmes) there may also be what I have previously called "deprivation disutility" (Mooney and Lange 1993). If a screening programme is implemented in region A but not in region B, people in region B are in one sense no better or worse off than before, as they still do not have a screening programme; but if they now know that region A has a screening programme they may feel deprived. Anderson's expressive theory would allow deprivation disutility to be included; consequentialism would not.

Using the private health care sector to queue jump can affect benefits by more than simply achieving outcomes faster for the queue jumper. The queue jumper may feel guilty, and those who do not or cannot queue jump may feel envious or deprived. In the context of health care systems as social institutions, the very existence of the private sector can create similar emotions: it can be divisive and undermine social solidarity.

A final feature of expressive norms is that they are "non-instrumental" (Anderson 1993: 37) in the sense that they "are justified not by reference to any independent value that the consequences they recommend are thought to have, but by reference to the rational attitudes they express" (p. 38). Thus "expressivists recognise different frames for different actions". This is in contrast to consequentialists who recognise only one. While expressivists "disagree over the relevant terms of description... pleasures... satisfactions... intrinsic values... they all agree that there is some noncontextual value inherent in states of affairs which is given independent of interpretations of expressive meanings" (p. 38).

Anderson uses the example of the captain of a sinking ship who might get relief from his tasks of coordinating rescue efforts by slipping off for a quiet drink. Consequentialism has no choice but to treat such action as valuable. In her expressive theory "[t]he relevant decision frame bearing upon the captain's actions accords it no value at all".

She (Anderson 1993: 38) states: "Because states of affairs have only a context-dependent extrinsic value, it doesn't make sense to globally maximise the value of states of affairs. This is as incoherent as trying to globally maximize the instrumental value of tools, apart from the contexts which give them any usefulness."

Most fundamentally for health economics this "non-instrumentality" suggests that the consequentialist idea of QALY maximisation is flawed in the sense that health is context dependent so that the idea that "a QALY is a QALY is a QALY" is unsustainable. Its value will vary from one context to another, for example between leisure and work; between surviving to see one's child graduating from university or simply surviving; between performing one's normal daily duties and being present at the concert of a lifetime.

The "non-instrumental" feature of health is also present at the population end of the spectrum especially when comparisons are being made, say, between the rich and poor. The value of the health of each is affected by the fact that it is being compared with the other. Indigenous health in Australia, with a life expectancy 17 years less than that of other Australians, cannot be valued independently of this sort of comparison with the non-Indigenous population. In a mixed public–private heath care system, the value of the outcomes of the private sector is affected by the existence of public sector health care and its outcomes—and vice versa.

Anderson (1993: 211) further argues that democratic institutions "provide the social conditions of autonomy people need to articulate, change and promote their own values in ways they can reflectively endorse". She is derisive of the idea of commodity fetishism: that all that is valued by people is available in the market place. She calls for "institutions of voice" (Anderson 1993: 211) that can "allow people to articulate their concerns directly and thereby empower them to put new items on the agenda without depending on 'experts' to speak for them". She argues too that "the preference for an education of a particular sort is not, like the preference for chocolate over vanilla ice cream, merely a matter of given, primitive tastes for which no reason can be offered. Such a preference is formulated in the light of particular ideals" (p. 162).

The same argument can be used for health care consumption and for health in general. Anderson's "institutions of voice" are particularly important in a health care system seen as a social institution. There is very clearly a need for agency—the expert doctor assisting the ill informed patient—at the level of the doctor–patient relationship. There is a tendency, however, for such agency to have a spill-over effect, with doctors seeking to become embroiled in discussions about the health care system as a system; whether it is adequately funded; what the priorities ought to be in terms of diseases or types of beds; lengths of waiting lists; etc. Such involvement is not necessarily problematical in itself, but it is too often conducted in terms which suggest that doctors are experts at these levels. They are not.

Anderson (2000: 170) is also interested to determine or explain "why people comply with social norms" where such a norm "is a standard of behaviour shared by a social group, commonly understood by its members as authoritative or obligatory for them".

In addressing this question she dismisses the rational choice theory of economics suggesting that it falls down on various counts: people's inability to calculate probabilities; people not ordering preferences in the consistent way they are asked to by expected utility theory; etc. She opts instead for models of *"Homo sociologicus"* and what she calls "social" or "cultural" rationality (Anderson 2000: 171). This "explains conformity to social norms in terms of the normativity of norms, and grounds that normativity in the ways individuals see norms as meaningfully expressing their social identities, their relationships to other people, or shared intentions and values" (p. 171). She adds (p. 175): "Trust appears to be a key factor behind the willingness to cooperate. The norm of trust tells people to act as if they believe others will reciprocate their own cooperation."

Anderson's ideas on different value "perspectives" allow a very specific bridge to be built to communitarianism (Anderson 2003). She suggests that certain types of judgements are much the same seen from any perspective. The example she gives is $2 + 2 = 4$: what might be described as a technical judgement. Anderson (2003: 242), however, states that

value judgments essentially lay a normative claim on people's mental states, directing them to feel, desire or deliberate in certain ways with respect to the valued object. Value claims, then, are perspectival in that they essentially assert a relation between the valued object and an agent's will or emotion.

This question of different perspectives based on the relation between the subject and the object, so to speak, she then presents according to four motives. These are very much tied to the nature of the society, or community, or group in which the individual exists.

The first of these (p. 242) is what she calls "*ascriptive identification*". This is where people see others "as extensions of oneself—as tied by relations of birth, such as of kinship, ethnicity, race, and caste, or related in some other socially ascribed way, as sharing a common language, culture or religion". This form of identification may (p. 243) "motivate loyalty, solidarity, and attachments to the in-group members which take the form of feeling group members' joy, pain, pride, and indignation as one's own".

Her second motive is "*sympathy*" which is (p. 243) "distinct from and of wider scope than identification . . . It can lead people to evaluate the world through the eyes of others whom we do not identify as extensions of ourselves."

Practical identification occurs when people see themselves as . . . participants in a common cooperative enterprise . . . or as committed to living and hence reasoning together about what to do, as in a democracy . . . The key point is that to engage in effective cooperation . . . people must construct a shared point of view from which reasons are assessed (p. 243).

Her final motive is (Anderson 2003: 243)

respect [which] involves recognizing and valuing others by acting only for reasons that they can reasonably accept as a permissible basis for anyone similarly situated to act. It is to commit oneself to act only on principles that can be reasonably shared by those one respects . . . When one acts out of sympathy for another, the aim of one's action is the other's good. When one acts out of respect, the other's good places a constraint on what one may do in pursuit of one's own aims, but one's own ultimate aims need not be devoted to the other's good.

These four motives from Anderson can be seen as being context driven in two senses. First, the extent to which any particular motive is present will be a function of the degree to which a society is individualistic or communitarian; and, second, the extent to which the issue at stake is one that leads to its being a concern or interest to the collective or the community will influence what motive is present or dominates.

The former will clearly vary from society to society with the individualistic United States at one end of the spectrum and Indigenous communities or, say, Cuba at the other, and Scandinavia lying somewhere in between. The claim is made in establishing a new paradigm for health economics in this book that health care systems and public health are concerns that are collective in nature in that they are social institutions where motives of citizens extend beyond ascriptive identification and embrace potentially one or more of the others. What fits best with the communitarianism of this book is clearly "practical identification" where "people must construct a shared point of view from which reasons are assessed". That practical identification of "people see[ing] themselves as . . . participants in a common cooperative enterprise" allows public health and the health care system as social institutions to be viewed from a communitarian stance.

Anderson stresses that these features are very different from the economist's concept of utility, which is individual focused and where in essence there is an isolated preference set. They are just as different from extra-welfarism. She (Anderson 2003: 245) states:

Utility measures are deeply positional, immediately tied to the individual agent's parochial and idiosyncratic view of the world. They are so positional that they do not permit interpersonal utility comparisons. This makes them ill-suited to inform practical projects grounded in sympathy for others, because sympathy directs our helping efforts to more urgent cases—those more disadvantaged, or more in need, within a given domain of concern.

Anderson (2003: 245) also identifies that utility measures have difficulty in dealing with "the ways people adapt their preferences to circumstances of deprivation and oppression". Tellingly, for the building of the new paradigm in this book and therefore for interpreting her ideas in the context of QALYs, she adds: "In fact all welfare measures that rely on the subjective valuing of individuals fall prey to the problem of adaptation to deprivation" (p. 245).

Anderson (2003: 250) is an advocate for deliberative democracy (see Chapter 9 for more detail), as she believes this

stresses the universal accessibility of a state's permanent residents to equal citizenship, freedom of speech, assembly, and the press, and mechanisms for holding public officials accountable for their actions... as the core institutions of democracy. These institutions enable collective deliberation, feedback mechanisms informing democratic bodies about the performance of their policies as judged by the public, and opportunities for changing these policies in light of that feedback.

She maintains that this form of democracy "is the institutional embodiment of practical reason for a collective agency composed of equal citizens".

These ideas from Anderson are very much in line with those of Sen (2000: 29).

In sympathizing with others, there are two quite different uses of identity: an "epistemic" use, in trying to know what others feel and what they see by placing oneself in the position of others, and an "ethical" use, in counting them as if they were the same as oneself. The epistemic use of identity is inescapably important, since our knowledge of other people's minds has to be derivative, in one way or another, on our placing ourselves in the position of others. But the ethical use of identity may be far from obligatory. To respond to the interests of others, we can see ourselves as "impartial spectators", as [Adam] Smith describes the role; but this demand of impartial concern is not the same thing as promoting the interests of others on the ground that they are, in some sense, extensions of oneself. As people capable of abstraction and reasoning, we should be able to respond humanely to the predicaments of others who are different and are seen to be different.

Anderson (1988: 63) concludes:

what is needed is an institutional framework within which people can better express their values and choose among alternatives... The idea of letting people make decisions about life and health for themselves would be better realized through institutions of democratic participation. The people who are placed at risk should have the opportunity to participate directly in the decisions which affect them. They should have the power to propose, debate, and vote on alternative health and safety projects, and to participate in the implementation of these projects.

For building a new paradigm for health economics, Anderson's expressive theory is most useful even if it does not in itself necessarily point to the adoption of a communitarian paradigm. The social liberalism of Habermas (see for example White 1995) would be another vehicle for Anderson's expressive theory but in my view a less helpful one. If we were dealing with some other social institution, such as education, then the balance between the individual and the community might shift and Habermasian social liberalism might be preferred. Health care systems and public health are such socially orientated goods or, to borrow Anderson's expression, so clearly "political goods" and with, for most societies, such an emphasis on equity, that the dominance of the community over the individual is justified. In choosing between communitarianism and Habermas (as well as other models), the social solidarity, mutuality, and reciprocity that communitarianism can embrace, certainly more so than Habermas's discursive deliberative model, are not neutral with respect to their possible impact on the health of a population. It is important to recognise that social solidarity, mutuality, and reciprocity, being important social determinants of health, can have positive impacts on health.

Habermas (1984) accepts that there is unlikely to be a single uniquely best form of political and social institution, and his discursive, deliberative model seeks to strike a balance between liberal models and communitarian models. As White (1995: 13) contends: "For Habermas, the former [liberal models] neglect the need for a social solidarity obtainable only by a radicalization of public communication processes, while the latter [communitarian models] seek to constitute such solidarity around notions of community that are too thick." In turn what is "best" for the social institutions of health care and public health will not necessarily be best for other social institutions.

6.4 Reflective and group preferences

Anderson thus argues, *inter alia*, for "democratic participation" in institutions. This is a major part of the ideas in this book. Some form of deliberative democracy is advocated (for the detail of this see the Appendix to Chapter 9), getting people generally, but crucially people who are suitably informed citizens, to participate in some sort of reflective way, in groups or communities. Such deliberative democracy will make a difference to decision making or as a minimum to the values used in decision making. The question then arises whether such preferences will be different from individual non-reflective preferences.

The amount of research on the issue of reflective preferences for health and health care and on the question of whether group preferences may be different from the aggregation of individual preferences is surprisingly little. Erik Nord (2006), writing about valuations of health status, states: "One of the reasons for [philosophers'] scepticism [of such valuations] is that many investigators seem to do too little to ensure a satisfactory level of reflection in subjects from whom preferences are elicited."

Abelson et al. (2003) suggest that "[h]ow to involve the public in setting health and health care priorities is a constant challenge for health system decisions" (p. 95). They continue: "Policy maker interest in involving the public in increasingly complex and value-laden priority setting processes has led to the use of deliberative public involvement methods designed to promote discussion and debate among participants with the objective of obtaining more informed and consensual views" (p. 95).

The research that has been done has had mixed results. It has been at two levels: priority setting and health status. On the former, Dolan et al. (1999: 918) claim that:

The public's views about setting priorities in health care are systematically different when they have been given an opportunity to discuss the issues . . . if the considered opinions of the general public are required, surveys that do not allow respondents time or opportunity for reflection may be of doubtful value.

Murphy (2005) suggests, again with respect to priorities in health care, that there is another dimension to this question of reflecting in a group.

In reasoning about embedded values, citizens may gain insight into the kind of community they aspire to be, and, in that process, examine their intentions, including whether to serve self or other(s). Citizens who articulate and share values such as respect, generosity or equity may justify health-care priorities that create opportunities for all community members to gain mastery over their lives.

Abelson et al. (2003: 104) argue that "it does appear that deliberative processes can and do make a difference to participant views". They also claim that on the basis of their exploratory study "on average, deliberation is less likely to change more dominant views (e.g. top rankings, highest priorities, etc.) but that with increased deliberation comes the opportunity for these views to become more rather than less entrenched". They conclude (Abelson et al. 2003: 95): "we are still at an early stage in understanding the process through which these differences come about and what difference deliberation makes to broader outcomes such as civic competence, civic engagement and health policy decisions."

In looking at the second level, namely the valuation of health states, Stein et al. (2006)

found that a brief period of discussion of the scenarios and initial preference values resulted in few changes to values, although a substantial proportion of the group (40%) made at least one change during the course of the study. Importantly, the impact of changes made at the group level, even in this small group, was negligible.

Their study is interesting at another level. They state that, despite this negligible change, "members of the group rated the discussion period as very important, for four main reasons: providing reassurance about initial preferences, checking procedural performance, increasing group cohesion and satisfying curiosity".

In a test-retest study of health outcomes, Alan Shiell et al. (2000) indicate that one-third of their sample said that they had reflected on their answers after the first survey and many had changed their responses one week later.

The issue of reflection and involvement in a group become intertwined since reflection can often be more easily achieved when this occurs in a group setting. Stein et al. (2006) claim:

We are not aware of any studies which have examined the effect of discussion on preferences elicited in a group setting. Dolan *et al* studied the impact of discussion in a focus group setting but this examined theoretical health care purchasing decisions and not preferences on health states. An effect of discussion was shown but the choices made by participants were subject to a wide range of considerations which do not enter into preference elicitation in the context examined here.

The fact that people were given the opportunity by Stein and colleagues to sit together and think through certain issues was of value to them: "the group were unanimous in finding discussion helpful." This was despite the group's acknowledging that their values had changed little. The act of deliberating together was valued in itself.

The very limited literature on this question has concentrated on whether strengths of preferences or values for certain given states (e.g. priorities or health states) change in the wake of reflection or as a result of group deliberation. One issue that is not clarified by the literature is whether the values are different between reflective individuals and groups. This needs to be investigated.

To summarise, group valuations of health states may or may not be different from individual valuations. The evidence currently is patchy. Given the focus in health economics on the values of individuals *qua* individuals and the acceptance largely of unreflective values, the fact that health economists have not done more to investigate these issues is not surprising. What the studies to date do not clarify is whether groups, on reflection, value different characteristics of health care. Might they define the good of health care as an institution differently in the wake of reflection? Does the group want something different from health care than what the sum of the individuals want? We do not know from the literature because these issues have not been addressed. What the literature does suggest is that allowing Anderson's expressive theory to come to bear and in particular the "intentional characteristic" is likely to prove useful. People may well value having the opportunity to reflect on their health care system and on public health, even if they do not subsequently change their preferences.

6.5 Conclusion

The links between Anderson's expressive theory and communitarianism are potentially strong, even if Anderson herself does not argue specifically for a communitarian approach. The "intentional, backward looking, distributive, and non-instrumental" (Anderson 1993: 33) facets of her theory provide an alternative base on which to build a new health economics. It will not lead to the neat quantifiable, measured outcomes of current health economics, but then the idea that either health or health care systems can be made quantifiable to the extent that health economics currently seeks to make them is only tenable in the consequentialism of welfarism or extra-welfarism. Anderson's "political goods" represent much better the complexities of the health care system and public health. As she indicates, these are not public goods, they are distributed "in accordance with a conception of members' needs" (Anderson 1993: 142). She leaves open, however, what this "conception of members' needs" might be. Neither does she address how these "members' needs" might be assessed. Communitarian claims, as outlined in Chapter 7, suggest how this might be done.

The extent to which research has tried to assess what differences arise in measured preferences where reflection is allowed is limited. Even more limited is the research on whether group preferences are different from the summation of individual preferences. There is no research that I can identify on whether groups' preferences are such that what they want from the health care system and public health is something different after they have had time to reflect as a group as compared to what they might want as an aggregate of unreflective individuals. Clearly more research is needed on these matters.

Taking Anderson's theory, linking it to the philosophy of communitarianism, and accepting the need for more research on community reflective preferences, we can build a new paradigm for health economics. The next chapter provides the communitarian base. Chapter 8 outlines a new paradigm for health economics.

References

Abelson, J., Eyles, J., McLeod, C., Collins, P., McMullan, C. and Forest, P.-G. (2003) Does deliberation make a difference? Results from a citizens panel study of health goals priority setting, *Health Policy*, 66(1): 95–106.

Anderson, E. (1993) *Values in Ethics and Economics*. Cambridge, MA: Harvard University Press.

—— (1988) Values risks and market norms, *Philosophy and Public Affairs*, 17: 54–65.

—— (2000) Beyond *homo economicus*: new developments in theories of social norms, *Philosophy and Public Affairs*, 29(2): 170–200.

—— (2003) Sen, ethics and democracy, *Feminist Economics*, 9: 239–61.

Brennan, G. and Buchanan, J. (1985) *The Reason of Rules: Constitutional Political Economy*. Cambridge: Cambridge University Press.

Buchanan, J. and Vanberg, V. (1989) A theory of leadership and deference in constitutional construction, *Public Choice*, 61: 15–28.

Coast, J. (2004) Is economic evaluation in touch with society's health values? *British Medical Journal*, 329: 1233–6.

Coleman, J. S. (1990) *Foundations of Social Theory*. Cambridge, MA: Harvard University Press.

Dolan, P., Cookson, R. and Ferguson, B. (1999) Effect of discussion and deliberation on the public's views of priority setting in health care: focus group study, *British Medical Journal*, 318: 916–19.

Edwards, R. (2005) Economic evaluation and society's values: view from the other side of the pond, *British Medical Journal*, 330: 311.

Evans, R. G. (1998) Towards a healthier economics, in M. L. Barer, T. E. Getzen and G. L. Stoddart (eds.), *Health, Health Care and Health Economics*. Chichester: Wiley.

Fuchs, V. (1996) Economics, values and health care reform, *American Economic Review*, 86(1): 1–24.

Habermas, J. (1984) *The Theory of Communicative Action. Vol. 1. Reason and the Rationalization of Society*, (trans. T. McCarthy). Boston: Beacon Press.

Hausman, D. and McPherson, M. (1993) Taking ethics seriously: economics and contemporary moral philosophy, *Journal of Economic Literature*, 31(2): 671–731.

Hurley, J. (1998) Welfarism, extra-welfarism and evaluative economic analysis in the health sector, in M. L. Barer, T. E. Getzen and G. L. Stoddart (eds.), *Health, Health Care and Health Economics*. Chichester: Wiley.

Mooney, G. and Lange, M. (1993) Ante-natal screening: what constitutes benefit? *Social Science and Medicine*, 37: 873–8.

—— Wiseman, V. (2000) A constitution for health services, *Journal of Health Services Research and Policy*, 4: 1–2.

Murphy, N. J. (2005) Citizen deliberation in setting health-care priorities, *Health Expectations*, 8(2): 172–81.

Nord, E. (2006) Severity of illness and priority setting: worrisome lack of discussion of surprising finding, *Journal of Health Economics*, 25(1): 170–2.

Nussbaum, M. (2001) *Upheavals of Thought*. Cambridge: Cambridge University Press.

Reinhardt, U. (1992) Reflections on the meaning of *efficiency*: can efficiency be separated from equity? *Yale Law and Policy Review*, 10(2): 302–15.

Sen, A. (2000) Other people, *The New Republic*, Dec., p. 18.

Shiell, A., Seymour, J., Hawe, P. and Cameron, S. (2000) Are preferences over health states complete? *Health Economics*, 9: 47–55.

Stein, K., Ratcliffe, J., Round, A., Milne, R. and Brazier, J. (2006) Impact of discussion on preferences elicited in a group setting, *Health Quality of Life Outcomes*, 4: 22. Available at: www.pubmedcentral.nih.gov/articlerender.fcgi?artid=1440847 (accessed 20 Dec. 2007).

Vanberg, V. J. (1994) *Rules and Choice in Economics*. London: Routledge.

White, S. K. (1995) Reason, modernity and democracy, in S. K. White (ed.), *Habermas*. Cambridge: Cambridge University Press.

7

Communitarianism

7.1 Introduction

This chapter examines the philosophy of communitarianism, arguing that this can be used as a basis for the values on which to build the proposed new paradigm for health economics. It points to the emphasis that communitarians place on public life and community in general, and the fact that people are not free floating atoms but members of communities, citizens with identities that are in part formed by their social setting.

It is identified that communitarianism means more than the inclusion of interpersonal effects (externalities) in the individual's utility function. The intrinsic and not just the instrumental value of social relationships is important. Community is valued in and of itself as are commitment, reciprocity, and public participation.

As signalled in the previous chapter, adopting Anderson's (1993) expressive theory, philosophical bases (such as Habermas's 1984 discursive, deliberative model) other than communitarianism could be adopted to build a new paradigm for health economics. The advantages of the communitarian approach as laid out in this chapter are, first, in its recognition of the value that community and community institutions can contribute to population health and, second, in allowing the development of communitarian claims, as outlined in the next chapter.

Beyond this introduction, the notions of community and citizenship are set out. In section 7.3 the essence of communitarianism is outlined. There is then an excursion into the work of Margolis (1982) and his idea of dual utility functions, the second of which is based on the utility of participation in the group, which can be seen as the basis of a communitarian approach (even if Margolis does not label it as such). In section 7.5 the relationship between communitarianism and liberalism is discussed.

The link between communitarianism and economics is made more explicitly in section 7.6. There is a conclusion in section 7.7, which points forward to the new paradigm as set out in the following chapter.

7.2 Community and citizenship

The term "community" is an ancient one and "goes back to Greek philosophy, to Aristotle's works, through Cicero and the Roman community of law and common interest...and the works of Rousseau in France and Hegel in Germany" (Avineri and de-Shalit 1992: 1). A sense of Community can involve such values as mutuality, reciprocity, sharing, and caring among a group of people. A community will be more communitarian the more these attributes are prevalent. It may be defined geographically, but it need not be, for example health economists can be looked upon as a community. Communities can be small, local, they can be formed by minority groups, or they can encompass whole nations, such as Australian society. There is, finally, also a global community.

In the context of this book, since we are dealing with issues of resource allocation in health care and in public health, and since budgets and expenditures for these activities and their scope tend to be geographically based, so community tends to take on a geographical identity. There are county health services, provincial population health policies, and national health systems. There are global health issues and policies, for example as set out by WHO. It may also be that there are ethnic groupings that have their "own" health services, such as Aboriginal Medical Services in Australia. While in communitarian philosophy more generally, community can be seen in many different dimensions; for the purpose of this book the emphasis is on geographical communities.

The question of what it means to be a citizen is central to communitarianism. The definition of a citizen is not uncontroversial. What is critical in this text is the distinction between a consumer (the utility maximising individual of the market place), and a citizen (someone who belongs to and is a member of a community). The distinction between consumers and citizens is made well by McPherson (1977: 99–100).

One can acquire and consume oneself, for one's own satisfaction or to show one's superiority to others...whereas the enjoyment and development of one's capacities is to be done for the most part in conjunction with others, in some relation of community. And it will not be doubted that the operation of participatory democracy would require a stronger sense of community than now prevails.

Boswell (1990: 31) makes another distinction between citizens and consumers.

The participatory democracy model has been sharply contrasted with the view which sees democracy primarily as an output mechanism, a begetter of wealth and economic growth. It has been said that this latter concept essentially views human beings as "infinite consumers and accumulators"...whereas under the participatory model we are to regard ourselves primarily as "exerters and enjoyers of our capacities".

As Boswell indicates, from this there is a clear "communitarian moral" to be drawn. The role of participatory democracy in communitarian society is discussed in greater detail in Chapter 9.

On citizenship Wiseman (2003: 72) states: "Citizenship has at least two meanings. One is narrow and fairly technical and legal, the other broad and social." It is the latter that is the focus of communitarianism.

The concept of citizenship that has gained most acknowledgement in the literature is that of Marshall (1950: 10). He suggested that citizenship might be considered in

three parts...civil, political and social. The civil element is composed of the rights necessary for individual freedom...the political element...[involves] the right to participate in the exercise of political power...the social element [is] the whole range from the right to a modicum of economic welfare and security to the right to share to the full in the social heritage and to live the life of a civilised being according to the standards prevailing in the society.

Going yet closer to what is meant by citizenship in this book the Australian Senate Legal and Constitutional References Committee (1995) states: "Without individuals and organisations prepared to participate and take responsibility; without a concept of the public interest, without the values of tolerance and compassion, and some sense of solidarity and belonging, citizenship would be impossible."

7.3 The essence of communitarianism

There are two related but separate ways of viewing communitarianism—the one is methodological or descriptive, the other is normative. On the former, Avineri and de-Shalit (1992: 2) state: "the premises of individualism such as the rational individual who chooses freely are wrong or false and...the only way to understand human behaviour is to refer to individuals in their social, cultural and historical contexts." The latter, the normative view, results in communitarians asserting (Avineri and de-Shalit 1992: 2)

that the premises of individualism give rise to morally unsatisfactory consequences. Among them are the impossibility of achieving a genuine community, the neglect of some ideas of the good life that should be sustained by the state, or others that should be dismissed, or—as some communitarians argue—an unjust distribution of goods.

Avineri and de-Shalit (1992: 3) suggest that from a communitarian perspective: "the community is a good that people should seek for several reasons and should not be dismissed." They argue that "communitarians conclude that, in order to justify the special obligations that we hold to members of our communities—families, nations, and so forth—one must attach some intrinsic (i.e. non-instrumental) value to the community" and that, as compared with any individualistic theory, communitarian theory "better justifies obligations that are not universal but rather specific and particular, because these obligations are part of what constitutes the self".

It is this latter normative stance that drives the communitarianism of this book. Public health and health care systems are important social institutions that are valued as parts of the good of society. The upkeep of the health of the population is a community obligation. Acceptance of that obligation by the community in its fostering of solidarity in the community with respect to health is itself good for population health. Such social solidarity is an important social determinant of health.

Thus communitarians believe that the self and social relations are very much influenced by the community and indeed that the question of identity itself is formed, in part, by the community. The construct of individual identity is thereby only to some limited extent individual; we are all more or less shaped by the society and the social relations within which we live. The self can only be understood in relation to others (Avineri and de-Shalit 1992).

Communitarians emphasise the importance of mutuality, reciprocity, and sharing of not just identities, but also values, moral commitments, and obligations. As Sandel (1992: 23) states:

Allegiances are more than values I happen to have and to hold at a certain distance. They allow that to some I owe more than justice requires or even permits, not by reason of agreements I have made, but instead in virtue of those more or less enduring attachments and commitments that, taken together, partly define the person that I am.

Identity is thus wrapped up in social reciprocity and mutuality, which are often cultural and historical in origin. Issues of social change, for example, are not driven simply by some aggregation of individuals with common values. They are more often about some sense of mutuality or reciprocity in attaining shared ends. They are fuelled by sentiments that stretch beyond some commonality of self-interest. There clearly are and also have been various social institutional reform structures with respect to liberation movements, civil rights actions, and pro-environment and anti-war protests. The various facets of these stretch well beyond the individual identity of those who believe in, endorse, or fight for social justice or any more specific cause.

These ideas can be related to the agency of Sen (1992). To form an overall assessment of an individual's interests, Sen suggests we need to consider the individual's own well being (which is derived, first, from what he or she achieves, but also, second, from her freedom to achieve) and her agency achievement and agency freedom (both of which relate to the person's goals that stretch beyond her personal well being). In explaining agency Sen (1992: 56) writes:

A person as an agent need not be guided only by her own well-being, and agency achievement refers to the person's success in the pursuit of the totality of her considered goals and objectives. If a person aims at, say, the independence of her country, or the prosperity of her community, or some such general goal, her agency achievement would involve evaluation of states of affairs in the light of these objects, and not merely in the light of the extent to which those achievements would contribute to her own well-being.

On reciprocity and mutuality Sullivan (1986: 10) states: "A public life develops only when a society realizes that reciprocity and mutual aid are worthy of cultivation both as good in themselves and as providing the basis of the individual self." Tawney goes further (in Terrill 1974: 216–19): "The mutual relationships of all citizens should be the yardstick for all social and economic decisions."

Another communitarian attribute is fraternity. On this Boswell (1990: 42) writes:

the principle of fraternity has little sympathy for notions of community which are monopolizing, focused exclusively on grass roots, or opposed in principle to large-scale organization and to the nation state. Such ideas cannot be reconciled with the diversity of social groupings which is needed if fraternity is to unfold fully, in complementary ways, for each and every person. Only a pluralistic pattern within a substantially sized society can allow the diverse groupings room to develop. Only such a pattern, too, is consistent with considerations of diffused power, personal choice, social inclusiveness and openness to change—considerations on which democratic communitarianism equally insists.

Boswell (1990: 39) also argues that "although fraternity is a fundamental impulse, all too many forces indirectly obstruct it. The first test of a democratic communitarian society is that it constantly attacks the needless obstacles to fraternity."

Trust is also a feature of communitarianism. A more closely knit community is more likely to be a trusting one. Where people are in a divided community that lacks cohesion and where individuals do not associate themselves to any extent with the community and do not participate in community activities, they are likely to be more distrustful of others.

Boswell (1990: 39) also provides a picture of a communitarian society.

Such a society would try...to enable people to live reasonably close to their workplace. It would provide for social spaces between buildings, and public places so that people could mix more freely. Jobs and work processes would be restructured; socially balanced neighbourhoods would be encouraged; opportunities would be built for different classes and social groups to mingle across barriers, at least at certain critical points in everyone's life.

Communitarianism as a school of philosophy is both old and new and not one about which there is a neat or tight agreement as to its precise content. It can be argued that Aristotle endorsed a form of communitarianism in his consideration of social relations and relationships (Macintyre 1985). The philosophy is applicable in many sectors of the economy and society, but it is particularly well placed to provide a conceptual basis for analysis of the health care sector and health, especially public health, more generally.

Partly the reason for the lack of a precisely agreed definition of communitarianism is that different communitarian writers start from different angles, either from the concept of autonomy or from the nature of the self. Some forms are "looser" than others with regard to the strengths or bonds of the community involved. Etzioni (1993) has also labelled communitarians as being either liberal or social. Others (Ross 2002 for example) argue for socialist communitarianism. What is common to all conceptualisations is that there is a key recognition that the community and social relations are valued and not just instrumentally, but for themselves. There is also a notion of a good society where that society is recognised as communal, but with different degrees of acceptability between different communitarians of the "trade-off" between individual rights and the value of community.

As indicated in the next section, this has echoes in the Margolis (1982) model of "fair shares" with his notion of dual utility functions where individuals gain utility in two ways—the standard "selfish" individual outcome utility and a "group" utility which is obtained not as an outcome but as a process through some sort of participation in some group or community.

7.4 An economist's approach to communitarianism

Normally, the expression "fair shares for all" is thought of in terms of the distribution of some set of goods or services that is declared to be just in terms of society at large or of some sub-group.* It is thus about giving out good things fairly. In an, at the time, ground breaking way of thinking about social policy, Margolis (1982) turned around this standard way of viewing fair shares for all. Margolis considers fair-sharing as being not about what one gets but about what one does; that is, he sees it as *doing* one's fair share rather than *getting* one's fair share. He too argues that we are all social and political animals, and that we view ourselves as more than just individuals with the ability to enjoy the good things of this life. Additionally, we want to do our "fair share" for society, the community, the group, or the family—at least some set of individuals wider than but including our individual selves. Margolis does not explicitly label this a communitarian approach, but it clearly is.

The motivation for this willingness to "do our bit" is not based on the output from our actions in helping or assisting the group; it is not consequentialist. It is much more at home in Anderson's expressive theory. It is the action *per se* that generates the utility, which serves as the motivation. It is the knowledge that we are participating in the group or the community that counts.

It might be argued that this is based on altruism, but it is not altruism in a pure form, since Margolis (1982) stresses that in participating in the group and devoting resources to the group, we as individuals are equal members of the group. Also, the motivation is not strictly or directly to help others. It is not so much feeling useful as feeling good through group participation. It is thus communitarian in form. His "fair shares model" is developed in the context of social policy generally. Here I want to describe

---

* Some of this section draws on Mooney, G. (2004) *Economics, Medicine and Health Care*, 3rd edn. Reprinted with kind permission of Pearson Education.

his approach briefly and then in the next chapter show how it can apply to health care and public health.

The basic postulate on which Margolis builds his approach is that individuals obtain utility in two ways: first, in the normal sense of goods utility, and, second, through *participation* in group orientated activities. The utility derived from this group related activity is not directly a function of either the utility of the output that the individual receives as an equal member of the group or the utility of the output that the group receives. However, the willingness of individuals to participate is in part a function of the degree of efficiency with which the group orientated activities are organised, as perceived by the individual. In other words, individuals are more willing to take part in efficient groups or efficient group activities than in inefficient ones. Thus, the utility in this second form is process rather than output utility: it is the doing itself rather than what is given or received that counts.

The individual divides his or her resources between activities through which he or she obtains utility selfishly and those through which he or she obtains utility as a result of participating in the group. The individual continues to seek to maximise his or her expected utility, which means ensuring that the sum of the selfish utility and group participation utility is the greatest possible. Thus, if the individual can get even greater utility from using some of his or her resources to participate in group orientated activities than from spending them on him- or herself, he or she will do so. Such switches of resources will continue until the individual cannot increase his or her total utility any more. At this point he or she will have the optimum balance between allocations to the self and those to the group.

7.5 Communitarianism and liberalism

In more recent times part of the explanation for the difficulty in pinning down any precise content of communitarianism philosophy lies in the fact that its more modern raison d'être takes its shape from being opposed to or, as a minimum, disagreeing with liberalism. This liberalism can take many forms all of which, however, are based on individualism. For example Kymlicka (1992: 165) argues that one of the "most persistent criticisms of Rawls's theory [of justice] is that it is excessively individualistic, neglecting the way that individual values are formed in social contexts and pursued through communal attachments". He and others also argue how a "distinctive feature of contemporary liberal theory is its emphasis on 'neutrality'—the view that the state should not reward or penalize particular conceptions of the good life but, rather, should provide a neutral framework within which different and potentially conflicting conceptions of the good can be pursued" (p. 165). Individualism lies behind this sentiment. Taylor (1992: 29) suggests that liberals "try to defend...the priority of the individual and his rights over society". His attack on "atomism" is an attack on theories based on "the primacy of rights" (Taylor 1992: 30). These theories "are those which take as the fundamental...principle of their political theory their ascription of certain rights to individuals and which deny the same status to a principle of belonging or obligation". Sugden (1981: 10–11) suggests there are four key tenets of liberalism: individualism, the pluralism of values, the importance of rights, and equality. Dworkin (1977: 180) places emphasis on the state treating citizens not just with "concern and respect but with equal concern and respect".

The varied positions of liberal thinkers on their philosophy and individualism more generally are summed up by Avineri and de-Shalit (1992: 11):

Individualists define liberalism in different ways, rather far-removed from one another. The concept of neutrality serves to advocate the variety in interpretations of liberalism...Some argue that liberalism is a theory of the minimal government, others argue that it is a theory of basic individual rights, and yet others, especially Dworkin and Rawls define liberalism as an egalitarian philosophy, Dworkin arguing that the main idea of liberalism is equality rather than liberty.

Liberalism is thus a very broad church. It then follows that communitarianism is almost bound to be as broad in its definition. It can even seem at times to overlap with liberalism, as some liberal philosophers protest that liberalism already embraces much of communitarianism, and in some instances they challenge its very existence.

There is, nonetheless, a series of common threads to communitarianism. Liberalism of the form developed by Rawls (1971) in his theory of justice seems to suggest that liberalism is universally applicable. Communitarians see both justice and social values more generally as being embedded in a society and thus their conceptualisation is particular to each society. Communitarianism thus can allow for, indeed it endorses the idea that, justice together with other social values are culture- and community-specific. The institutions that underpin or uphold any society or culture vary. These variations need to be taken into account when assessing such social factors as health, especially population health but also individual health, and such social institutions as health care and public health systems. For example Aboriginal Australians have a different construct of health from that of non Aboriginal Australians. To the former, health is holistic, involves certain culturally determined obligations (in some instances a son-in-law has a responsibility for his mother-in-law's health should she fall sick), and can embrace spiritual health, the physical environment, and economic well being in ways that Western biomedical constructs of health do not (Houston 2004). There is also evidence that self-rated individual health is to some extent a function of the health of the community in which the individual is living (Wiseman 1997). It is also not happenstance that the social institution that is the US health care system is much more individualistically based than is, for example, the Danish health care system.

Much of the debate in the last 30 years or so around liberalism and in turn communitarianism centres on the work of John Rawls and his theory of justice (1971). Rawls famously argued that to arrive at key principles regarding a just society individuals would be placed behind a veil of ignorance where they would be equal in terms of their decision making power, but in this "ignorant" position they would have no knowledge of their own position in society and no knowledge either of the nature or shape of the society in which they were placed.

From this Rawls derives two principles on the basis of how people might be expected to reason, given the veil of ignorance. First, "each person is to have an equal right to the most extensive basic liberty compatible with a similar liberty for others" (Rawls 1971: 136) and, second, that those to be most advantaged should be those who are least advantaged.

Sandel (1992: 23) argues: "What the [Rawlsian] difference principle requires, but cannot provide, is some way of identifying those *among* whom the assets I bear are properly regarded as common, some way of seeing ourselves as mutually indebted and morally engaged to begin with." He suggests (1992: 22):

The difference principle, like utilitarianism, is a principle of sharing. As such, it must presuppose some prior moral tie among those whose assets it would deploy and whose efforts it would enlist in a common endeavour. Otherwise, it is simply a formula for using some as means to others' ends, a formula this liberalism is committed to reject.

This implies that Rawls' efforts to allow individuals the freedom to be free floating atoms fails. This is for two related reasons. First, behind Rawls' veil of ignorance there is no society, community, or group *per se* where reason alone can allow us to say with whom we are competing in terms of advantage or disadvantage. And, second, there is no moral force present that will then allow any right in this process to take from one in order to give to another. The sharing thus risks becoming arbitrary. As Sandel (1992: 24) argues, the "liberal ethic puts the self beyond the reach of its experience, beyond deliberation and reflection. Denied the expansive self-understandings that could shape a common life, the liberal self is left to lurch between detachment on the one hand, and entanglement on the other."

The "new" public health (Baum 2008) and some of the literature on the social determinants of health can sometimes recognise this. For example Wilkinson (2005: 296) writes, and with echoes of the four pillars of Anderson's expressive theory (see section 6.2):

it is important to recognize that our emotional ability to identify with each other is broadening, if not deepening. Where once people apparently felt quite unaffected by the suffering of any but their nearest and dearest, it looks as if the boundaries of our moral universe have been expanding: our tendency to identify with each other is slowly spreading from family to class, from class to nation, and now, for some at least, to most of the human race.

It is also significant that Wilkinson (2005: 318) finishes his most recent book on inequality and health in reminding us of "what people recognized long ago, namely, that the important dimensions of the social environment for human well-being are liberty, equality, and fraternity".

Liberalism is, however, not just a broad church, but is often seen as universalist. As Barry (1995: 3) argues: "I continue to believe in the possibility of putting forward a universally valid case in favor of liberal egalitarian principles." What does come through from most liberal thinkers is that their ideas are based very much on Western liberal traditions and experiences. That may be acceptable as far as it goes, but it does suggest the presence of, if not universalism *per se*, then some sort of desire or claim for universalism, but based on the current particularism of Western liberalism. As Sugden (1981: 10) states: "Liberalism is one of the main strands in the history of political and economic thought *in Western Europe and the English speaking world*" (emphasis added). It is also significant that in making his case against liberalism one major part of Taylor's argument (1992: 45) is that (emphasis added):

the free individual *of the West* is only what he is by virtue of the whole society and civilization which brought him to be and which nourishes him; that our families can only form us up to this capacity and these aspirations because they are set in this civilization and that a family alone outside of this context—the real old patriarchal family—was a quite different animal which never tended these horizons.

A concern regarding universalism in the context of health is raised by Adams (2004). She writes (p. 3) about "the idea of an equity of epistemology—about the way we theorize health and its causes—in international arenas". She goes on: "these concerns, cumulatively, point to ineffable areas of ethics in health and health equity"—in essence that we simply cannot find words to explain these phenomena. She draws on an example from Tibet: "because of their religious character, Tibetan medical theories and practices both resist description and quantifiability in a manner acceptable to secularist discourse but may nevertheless remain essential to health." Here the particularism of Western thinking and language moves to the stage of becoming hegemonic. In this case Tibetan medical theories and practice cannot compete with Western medical theories and practice because of this "inequity of epistemology". (More discussion of this issue follows in Chapter 11.)

Larmore (1987: 92) opposes the idea of individuals having the capacity to be fully autonomous in the liberal sense. He favours what might be interpreted as a Hegelian form of freedom supported by the state and its institutions. He states:

Because no one can determine with full autonomy how he shall see the world and what goals he shall pursue, but instead can come to understand himself only through participating in shared traditions and social forms—because in some areas he should not even strive for autonomy, the primary role of the state must not be to sustain a kind of neutrality, but rather to embody and foster some particular conception of the good life.

Rothstein (1998: 39) similarly argues against the idea of a "neutral state" on the basis that people are social beings, not through choice but that they cannot be otherwise. The notion of identity is a social construct. Autonomy is also a social construct (Friedman 2003). This means that both autonomy and identity are carved out of social interaction and social institutions. Rothstein (1998: 39) states:

In the communitarian view...the principles of a neutral state rest on altogether mistaken assumptions about human nature, about what it is that forms our values and character as persons. The principle of political liberalism and individual autonomy is founded, that is, on a series of unrealistic and metaphysical postulates about "the true nature of man". Most critically, it is well-nigh impossible for proponents of political liberalism to handle the empirical fact that citizens achieve their identity through participating in various collectivities. There cannot ultimately be such a creature as an autonomous individual. For human beings are social animals, and their notions of the nature of the good life are governed by their social affiliations.

The possibilities for extending liberalism beyond the Western environment are real, but it is difficult to see that that is possible without some major revisions. For example the process of transplanting liberalism to "new" societies such as the old soviet countries has been a difficult one, with serious and far reaching social and political consequences. As Bell (2004: 2) states, these consequences have included "brutal ethnic warfare, crippling poverty, environmental degradation, and pervasive corruption". The assessment by Chua (2003) of the attempts to bring liberal democracy to Africa, such as in Rwanda, makes clear that where there are major ethnic divides within a country, then liberal democracy may not get beyond the thin version of "one person, one vote", with a less than adequate acceptance of the need to protect minority rights.

Communitarianism has the advantage, *inter alia*, of not being a universalist philosophy and thereby it is possible for it to be more country- and culture-specific. Liberalism, despite its claims to be universal, is particular to the West and, even more narrowly, its primary homes are the US and the UK. Lee Kuan Yew, the ex-prime minister of Singapore, has argued that in Asia there is "little doubt that a society with communitarian values where the interests of society take precedence over that of the individual suits [Asians] better than the individualism of America" (Bell 2004: 3). The values of Australian Aboriginal society are likewise communitarian and threatened by not just post-colonialism as such, but the individualism of Western (Australian) liberal culture. Many urban living Aboriginal people struggle not only with maintaining their own cultural identity, but also with straddling Western individualism and Aboriginal communitarianism. Some younger Aboriginal people can easily succumb to the former and give up on the latter.

In examining the potential for liberalism outside of the West, Bell (2004) takes the example of East Asia and lists three factors that argue for cultural particularism in that region of the world. These are

1. Cultural factors can affect the prioritizing of rights.
2. Cultural factors can affect the justification of rights.
3. Cultural factors can provide moral foundations for distinctive political practices and institutions.

Bell (2004: 5) concludes on this front that the "distinctive communitarian contribution has been to cast doubt on universal theories grounded exclusively in the liberal moralities of the Western world".

While juxtaposed against liberalism, communitarianism sits somewhere on the spectrum between that philosophy and authoritarianism. Communitarianism is particularly useful when analysing social phenomena, such as poverty, but also in assessing what might appear to be primarily individualistic characteristics and placing them or even explaining them in a social context. Suicide, marriage, and divorce would fall into these categories (Baum 2008). More relevant to the analysis in this book come institutions, such as health services, which communitarians see primarily as social rather than, in this case, medical, somewhat akin (as is discussed later) to a Hegelian construct of a social institution. Health, especially population health but also individual health, is also seen in social terms when viewed through communitarian eyes. Individual health is culturally determined (of which more later), and also socially and culturally valued. Our abilities to manage to desire good health and in turn our ability to judge what constitutes good health are functions of community expectations with respect to both individual health and community health.

One of the criticisms that is aimed at communitarianism is that communities can be wicked, such as the community that was Nazi Germany. There can be no guarantee that a community deemed to be communitarian would be universally recognised as good. However, just as Sagoff (1986) argues that the satisfaction of individual preferences is good only insofar as such preferences are for good things, so I would argue that communitarianism is only good if the community it is applied in is good (as judged on the basis of some universalist principle). The prospects for goodness, however, do seem greater in a community where individuals are more rather than less embedded. The concern here is primarily that a community may be wicked in the sense of being unjust. Yet Dworkin (1989) suggests that the greater the embeddedness (or "integration" as he calls it) in a community, the more the community will provide a source of stability and legitimacy with respect to justice. In an integrated community "everyone, of every conviction and economic level, has a personal stake . . . in justice not only for himself but for everyone else as well". There is no guarantee here of avoiding wickedness, but the probability of it occurring is reduced. Further, given the attitudes of many individuals to the health problems of others, the prospects for a community being "integrated" and just, and therefore less likely to be wicked are perhaps greater with respect to health and health care than in other facets or sectors of a society.

There is a prospect here for a different paradigm for both public health and health care in which each is considered as contributing to the welfare of individuals in a society or community, but is also valued in its own right. Thus public health may be valued in itself and not just for the functioning of individuals but for the functioning of a society or community; and health service systems may be valued as social institutions and not just for their outputs of health. As discussed in Chapter 4, in institutional economics these organisational or institutional considerations can be extended further to incorporate the idea of institutions as rules, and social rules in particular.

One important consideration in this context is that these features make a communitarian paradigm for health and in turn for health economics more amenable to considerations of justice and equity. Social institutions can be just or unjust, and not only in terms of their outcomes, to which consequentialist theories are necessarily restricted. The emphasis currently in health economics on equity seen in terms of distributive justice (i.e. fairness of outcomes and often equality of the single outcome health) or equity as equal use can be shifted to procedural justice, which allows processes, such as equality of access, to be the focus.

As indicated, viewing public health and health care systems as institutions in the sense of rules opens yet more doors; see Chapter 9.

7.6 Communitarianism, choice, and culture

In economics the question that separates the communitarian most from the liberal is that of the nature and importance of choice. For example Bell (2004: 2) argues that communitarians cast doubt "on the view that choice is intrinsically valuable, that a certain moral principle or communal attachment is more valuable simply because it has been chosen following deliberation among alternatives by an individual subject".

Bell (2004: 4) makes the point that "the valorization of greed in the Thatcher/Reagan era justified the extension of instrumental considerations governing relationships in the market place into spheres previously informed by a sense of uncalculated reciprocity and civil obligation". One can clearly include health and health care in these spheres, which were not previously but are now seen as being able to be governed by the forces of the market place. There has been in the last 30 years or so a move to commodify health care, with increasing tendencies to see health care as a market good, and a willingness to accept privatisation as the way to deliver health care well—where "well" is seen in terms of market efficiency, with equity disappearing from view. While it would be an exaggeration to suggest that health *per se* has become a private good (it is not a good at all if that is defined as something that can be traded), nonetheless, the way that health is increasingly seen in public policy places it more and more at the door of individual responsibility.

Along with this tendency there is a perhaps inevitable shift politically, with governments becoming more loath to interfere with market forces. Obesity is seen as a market failure that is to be corrected by either strengthening the market—giving people better information about the poor health effects of certain forms of consumption (i.e. correcting demand)—or by lecturing companies that produce unhealthy foods about the error of their ways (i.e. supply side alterations). The idea that the selling of and the consumption of unhealthy foods is part of the success of the market (Jan and Mooney 2006) is not accepted, so that limiting advertising of unhealthy foods to children is not seen as part of the job of government, at least not of neo-liberal governments.

There is an important issue here that differentiates liberalism in the market place from communitarianism. Liberalism and certainly neo-liberalism in the market place is about freedom of individual choice, with the added assumption that individuals are willing and able to exercise consumer sovereignty. Indeed, there is a moral goodness about such individual choice. This can be split into two parts: first, the notion that through choice of revealed preferences (i.e. studying individuals' choices in the market place) allows us to judge what their preferences and strengths of preferences are; and, second, the fact that this choice is individual choice.

Setting choice in a more social cultural context, Taylor (1992: 47) writes:

The crucial point here is this: since the free individual can only maintain his identity within a society/culture of a certain kind, he has to be concerned about the shape of this society/culture as a whole. He cannot ... be concerned purely with his individual choices and the associations formed from such choices to the neglect of the matrix in which such choices can be open or closed, rich or meagre. It is important to him that certain activities and institutions flourish in society. It is even of importance to him what the moral tone of the whole society is ... because freedom and individual diversity can only flourish in a society where there is a general recognition of their worth. If realizing our freedom partly depends on the society and culture in which we live, then we exercise a fuller freedom if we can help determine the shape of this society and culture.

There are thus social aspects of communitarianism that the liberal, free marketeer will choose to ignore. The concepts of freedom are different and even more different when we encounter the neo-liberalism of the market place. Freedom to choose for the individual dominates the philosophy of the latter. Oddly, as Taylor hints at, freedom is not consciously or overtly valued in the market place, in the sense that it is not seen as being in need of protection. Rather it is taken for granted, as a given. The market delivers freedom. This is close to being a mantra, a fundamental belief, and as with most fundamental beliefs, it is not open to question, it is not even subject to questioning (Evans 1984). In a fully fledged market, one individual freely exchanges with another individual, and they only freely choose to do so if each believes that they will thereby be better off.

The shaping of the neo-liberal economy follows from this two person exchange, as the whole economy can be seen as simply a large number of such two person exchanges, each of which is entered into freely (Haworth 1994). In recent years in the wake of, *inter alia*, Thatcher's famous statement that there is no such thing as society, the economy and society have become, in neo-liberal speech, synonymous and the word "citizen" is obsolescent, as the consumer becomes all that the individual is seen to be. The shaping of society, for those who still believe in such an entity, can in turn be left to the market, and individuals do not have to be concerned about it. The invisible hand is writ yet larger than Adam Smith could ever have envisaged.

Communitarians, on the other hand, are very much concerned with the shaping of society. They do not believe that this can be left to individuals *qua* individuals. It is citizens as products of the society or community who shape and, importantly, who are shaped by the society or community. Community identity and individual identity are interlocked and interdependent. There is a dualism here that is critical to the whole basis of communitarianism.

There are of course different forms of public cooperation in any economy. The difference with respect to communitarianism might be seen as one of degree, but, more accurately, as one of considerable substance—as Boswell (1990: 11) argues. It is a question of "appropriate beliefs". He suggests:

To regard public co-operation in the economy as an instrument or mechanism produces ... little support for it and even some confusion. Rather, the most effective cultural and attitudinal nurture for public co-operation comes from a deeper source. It springs from a conviction that public co-operation forms part of a wider search for community which has value in itself, indeed supreme value; from an assignation of top priority, in its own right, to the quality of interpersonal and intergroup relationships.

7.7 Conclusion

This chapter has looked at the nature of communitarianism, initially from a primarily philosophical perspective, but then moving to more of an economics stance. It has been suggested that it is useful to juxtapose communitarianism and liberalism.

Linked to Anderson's expressive theory of Chapter 6, this analysis of communitarianism points the way to the consideration of a new paradigm in health economics. It is to this that we turn in the next chapter.

References

Adams, V. (1999) Equity of the ineffable: cultural and political constraints in ethnomedicine as a health problem in contemporary Tibet. WP Series No. 99.05, Harvard Center for Population and Development Studies, Cambridge, MA.

—— (2004) Equity of the ineffable: cultural and political constraints on ethnomedicine as a health problem in contemporary Tibet, in S. A. Anand, F. Peter and A. Sen (eds.), *Public Health, Ethics and Equity*. Oxford: Oxford University Press.

Anderson, E. (1993) *Values in Ethics and Economics*. Cambridge, MA: Harvard University Press.

Avineri, S. (1972) *Hegel's Theory of the Modern State*. Cambridge: Cambridge University Press.

—— de-Shalit, A. (eds.) (1992) *Communitarianism and Individualism*. Oxford: Oxford University Press.

Barry, B. (1995) *Justice as Impartiality*. Oxford: Clarendon Press.

Baum, F. (2008) *The New Public Health*. Melbourne: Oxford University Press.

Bell, D. (2004) Communitarianism. Available at: http://plato.stanford.edu/entries/communitarianism (accessed 20 Dec. 2007).

Boswell, J. (1990) *Community and the Economy: The Theory of Public Cooperation*. London: Routledge.

Chua, A. (2003) *World on Fire*. New York: Doubleday.

Dworkin, R. (1977) *Taking Rights Seriously*. Cambridge, MA: Harvard University Press.

—— (1989) Liberal community, *California Law Review*, 77(3): 479–504.

Etzioni, A. (1993) *The Spirit of Community: The Reinvention of American Society*. New York: Simon and Schuster.

Evans, R. G. (1984) *Strained Mercy: The Economics of Canadian Health Care*. Toronto: Butterworth.

Friedman, M. (2003) *Autonomy, Gender, and Politics*. Oxford: Oxford University Press.

Gutman, A. (1992) Communitarian critics of liberalism, in S. Avineri and A. de-Shalit (eds.), *Communitarianism and Individualism*. Oxford: Oxford University Press.

Habermas, J. (1984) *The Theory of Communicative Action. Vol. 1. Reason and the Rationalization of Society* (trans. T. McCarthy). Boston, MA: Beacon Press.

Haworth, A. (1994) *Anti-Libertarianism*. London: Routledge.

Houston, S. (2004) The past, the present, the future of Aboriginal health policy. PhD thesis, Curtin University, Perth.

Jan, S. and Mooney, G. (2006) Childhood obesity, values and the market, *International Journal of Pediatric Obesity*, 1(3): 131–2.

Kymlicka, W. (1992) Liberal individualism and liberal neutrality, in S. Avineri and A. de-Shalit (eds.), *Communitarianism and Individualism*. Oxford: Oxford University Press.

Larmore, C. (1987) *Patterns of Moral Complexity*. Cambridge: Cambridge University Press.

Macintyre, A. (1985) *After Virtue*, 2nd edn. London: Duckworth.

Margolis, H. (1982) *Selfishness, Altruism and Rationality*. Cambridge: Cambridge University Press.

Marshall, T. H. (1950) *Citizenship and Social Class and Other Essays*. Cambridge: Cambridge University Press.

McPherson, C. B. (1977) *The Life and Times of Liberal Democracy*. Oxford: Oxford University Press.

Mooney, G. (2004) *Economics, Medicine and Health Care*. London: Prentice Hall.

—— (2001) Communitarianism and health economics, in J. Davis (ed.), *The Social Economics of Health Care*. London: Routledge.

Rawls, J. (1971) *A Theory of Justice*. Oxford: Oxford University Press.

Ross, P. (2002) Socialist communitarianism: a Marxist normative political theory? Available at: www.psa.ac.uk/journals/pdf/5/2002/ross.pdf (accessed 12 Dec. 2007).

Rothstein, B. (1998) *Just Institutions Matter*. Cambridge: Cambridge University Press.

Sagoff, M. (1986) Values and preferences, *Ethics*, 96: 301–16.

Salvaris, M. (2000) Political citizenship, in W. Hudson and J. Kane (eds.), *Rethinking Australian Citizenship*. Cambridge: Cambridge University Press.

Sandel, M. (1984) The procedural republic and the unencumbered self, *Political Theory*, 12(1): 81–96.

—— (1992) The procedural republic and the unencumbered self, in S. Avineri and A. de-Shalit (eds.), *Communitarianism and Individualism*. Oxford: Oxford University Press.

Sen, A. (1992) *Inequality Re-examined*. Oxford: Clarendon Press.

Senate Legal and Constitutional References Committee (1995) *Trick or Treaty? Commonwealth Power to Make and Implement Treaties*. Available at: www.aph. gov.au/Senate/committee/legcon_ctte/completed_inquiries/pre1996/treaty/report/index.htm (accessed 18 Nov. 2007).

Sugden, R. (1981) *The Political Economy of Public Choice*. Oxford: Martin Robertson.

Sullivan, W. (1986) *Reconstructing Public Philosophy*. Berkeley: University of California Press.

Taylor, C. (1992) Atomism, in S. Avineri and A. de-Shalit (eds.), *Communitarianism and Individualism*. Oxford: Oxford University Press.

Terrill, R. (1974) *R. H. Tawney and His Times: Socialism and Fellowship*. Cambridge, MA: Harvard University Press.

Wilkinson, R. (2005) *The Impact of Inequality*. London: Routledge.

Wiseman, V. (1997) Caring: the neglected health outcome? or input? *Health Policy*, 39(1): 43–53.

——(2003) Citizenship and social choice: implications for the elicitation and aggregation of citizens' preferences for the allocation of health care resources. PhD thesis, Curtin University, Perth.

8

Communitarian Claims

8.1 Introduction

The concerns expressed in earlier chapters about the state of much of current health economics lead to the need for a reconsideration of a number of facets of health, health care, health policy, and health economics. A refocusing is required, for example with respect to the use and application of epidemiology, with its sole concern being health and the measurement of health, to make it more of a servant to health policy than to lead it. While social epidemiology has grown in recent years, it still remains very much the junior partner alongside clinical epidemiology. It is social epidemiology that is most relevant to the new paradigm.

Issues around social agency with respect to both health care systems and public health need to be explored much more. This will involve examining the broader social role of health care systems as institutions, in the sense not just of organisations but of institutions as forming part of the fabric of society. Lucy Gilson (2003: 1464), for example, sees the central role of the state as being "to manage the processes through which the meaning of the health system to society, and so its contribution to broader society value, is established". The question then arises as to whether any debate around managing these processes is about health policy or social policy. There is no way to disentangle this in any complete sense. Health policy is of course about health (but not necessarily that alone), but the health care system is about both health and social policy. Gilson (2003) sees a central challenge for health systems as being "to review the purposes and institutions of democracy which allow citizens to participate in the creation of a society, enabling each to develop as a person but also to contribute to the good of the community as a whole" (in Ranson and

Stewart 1998: 257). That points to a wider concern for what is in essence social policy. I would endorse Gilson's view.

Such a focus for health care systems and public health means devising ways to involve the community as a community in formulating the values that should underpin these social institutions.

On this front there is a responsibility to change the focus of much of the work of the various disciplines that come under the umbrella of health sciences—medical sociology, health management, anthropology, and health promotion. The key focus of this book, however, is health economics: the prime concern is for a different paradigm for health economics. What is critical in this new paradigm is, in a sense, old. It is the specification of a relevant social welfare function (or as Kemp and Asimakopulos 1952 called it more than half a century ago, a "constitution") for health services and public health.

This chapter builds on the previous two chapters. The expressive theory of Anderson (1993) and the ideas discussed in Chapter 6 on reflective and group preferences, together with the communitarianism of Chapter 7, are used to provide a base for communitarian claims.

8.2 The new paradigm

With respect to the allocation of health care resources, it is proposed that there is a need for a dual level approach: one that is personal, but nested within a community one. One is at the level of individual desire for own health. Additionally, however, there is likely to be a need to include other non-health benefits, both outcomes and perhaps also some processes, which affect individuals' utility.

The community level is concerned with the social principles or values on which health care systems and public health are to be based, which was called a "constitution" in Chapter 7 (with further elaboration on this idea in the next chapter). This section draws on Mooney 1998.

At this community level the individual now is a citizen rather than a patient. He or she may be concerned to have his or her voice heard with respect to the "setting of the stage" for others (primarily the policy makers) to play out the process of health policy planning. He or she may want to be more involved than that and be a part of that planning process. There are parallels here with the notion of procedural as compared to distributive justice. Citizens set the procedural rules together with the structures or principles on which to base the social welfare function or the maximand for health care and public health. Others determine, within these, how to operationalise the desired outcomes

The roles of the individual as patient and the individual as citizen may seem to conflict. Lomas (1997: 105) suggests "in our role as taxpayer we may oppose increased funding, while in our role of patient we may demand new and expensive services". The two roles are not necessarily mutually exclusive. What an individual *qua* individual brings to his or her role as citizen may be in part shaped by his or her experience as an individual patient. The individual patient A is being asked to look only to his or her own interests, to maximise his or her own utility. That can involve a caring externality where individual A's efforts to maximise his or her own utility may be affected by some gain or loss in utility of individual B. Note it is not B's utility that is considered here, but the impact on A's utility of any change in B's utility.

At the citizen level the individual is being asked to adopt a different perspective, one where he or she is thinking more of his or her identity as a member of a community. The emphasis is on community welfare maximisation.

This chapter examines this latter community focus, which can be interpreted as the principal–agent relationship at a social level. Citizens are not well placed to form judgements about the benefits and costs of different types and forms of health care or public health, either in relation to specific interventions or to health care systems or public health organisations. They may then want to rely on health care decision makers, policy makers, or "bureaucrats" to help to make decisions for them about the merits of different procedures, interventions, and organisational structures.

Citizens, however, care about the principles on which both the health care system and public health are based (see the Appendix to Chapter 9). Yet these principles are often neglected, not just by health economists but by health policy makers. The epidemiological imperative of health maximisation that so much of current health economics endorses means that different systems and organisations of health care and public health are judged on the basis of this maximand alone. At the same time, in adopting a wider view there is a danger of missing or fudging the target and allowing various irrelevant arguments to creep into the maximand, which will, additionally, provide opportunities for decision makers within the system (especially clinicians) to seek to defend inefficient practices on the basis of non-health outcomes and/or process variables that are not endorsed by the community at large. Citizens have a direct interest in the efficiency of the system; consequently that system needs to be accountable to them. For this to happen, decision making must be transparent, in particular with respect to the values used. What is included as the set of principles or the constitution on which a health care system is to be based, should be determined by the community served by the health care system. The values underlying public health should be those of the people whose health is being promoted. If informed citizens, however, want consequentialism, that is just as acceptable in this paradigm as if they do not. The need is to have citizens establish the constitution on which the paradigm is to be based.

On the issue of dual-preferences, Cribb (2005: 59–60) worries that

there are some fundamental tensions between patient empowerment and community empowerment. The public at large, as citizens of the health polity, should have some say in shaping and regulating the institutional regimes of healthcare. But these democratically authorized regimes will, in turn, shape the potential opportunities for, and constraints upon, patient empowerment... The limits of patient power are set, to some extent by the reasoned preferences of the public [which] will, on occasions put the patient as patient in conflict with the patient as citizen.

This concern misses two key points. First, while citizens can "shape the potential opportunities for, and constraints upon, patient empowerment", given the simple logic of resource constraints, some such shaping has to be done anyway, by someone and according to some set of values or principles. The question then is who is best to do this shaping, not whether it is a good thing. Second, it is possible that the value sets of patients and citizens may overlap on occasion, but this is most unlikely. Citizens are to set the principles for the health care system. Patients then decide on their use of that system. Of course, patients may find that what they want, they cannot have, because it is not made available as a result of the principles set by the citizens. While the choice set available to the patients may be different than if it were determined by the doctors, politicians, bureaucrats, or some mix of these, it is not the case that the shift will be from an unconstrained choice set to a constrained choice set. The choice set is inevitably constrained, only differently.

Thus what is proposed as the basis for a new paradigm in health economics is that citizens first set the principles on which social agents are to act, but thereafter they let the agents proceed with policy making. Only when it becomes apparent that the principles are not being adhered to will the citizens become directly involved again at this level. This might be to revisit the principles or, more fundamentally, to demand that their principles be adhered to, or as a last resort that the agents be replaced. The citizens are also potential or actual patients, and as such they are setting the rules for resource allocation in health systems that will have a direct bearing on what services they are able to receive.

These ideas are very much akin to the concept of the formulation of a "constitution" in the 1950s from Kemp and Asimakopulos (1952: 196). Further, in the economics debate at that time with regard to the nature of social choice and of the social welfare function, we find Bergson (1954: 242) writing as follows: "the problem is to counsel not citizens generally but public officials... [The official's] one aim in life is to implement the values of other citizens *as given by some rule of collective decision making*" (emphasis added).

Two potentially important caveats need to be registered here. First, there will almost certainly have to be some efforts made to educate the citizenry such that the setting of the constitution is done on an informed basis. Second, in depending on such factors as the homogeneity of the society, the extent of social solidarity, etc., there is a risk that minority groups will not have their claims adequately recognised by the majority. The question of whether to allow this within the constitution needs to be debated and indeed resolved.

Opponents of the approach proposed will argue, for example, that Hitler was elected democratically. That is true. The paradigm proposed here does not guarantee the rights of minorities.

What it does do is seek to ensure that there is a debate about the set of principles underlying this paradigm. In contrast, such a debate and any recognition of the need for it are not present in current health economics. Neither the new paradigm nor the old guarantees in any absolute sense the rights of minorities. But faced with a choice between a society where there was scope for informed debate by citizens in some deliberative democratic manner and a society where such scope did not exist (my own country of Australia is an example of the latter), I for one would choose the former.

8.3 Levels of preference

What is required to pursue the above proposal is to determine how different levels or "orders" of preference might be elicited. Three levels of preference (or utility) functions are proposed. It might be better to think of these in more neutral language as "interests functions" to avoid criticisms from those economists who might want to restrict the concept of a utility function more than is intended in this chapter—since (i) usually utility functions are based solely on consequences and not "processes" or "actions"; and (ii) the notion of multiple utility functions in the same individual has come in for considerable criticism from some economists (see Brennan 1993).

Nonetheless the idea of multiple utility functions is seen as a useful analytical device, as exemplified in Chapter 7 in Margolis's fair shares model (Margolis 1982). Let me expand on that, but now more specifically in the context of health care.*

The relevance of Margolis's model for health care systems lies in the fact that such systems sit on a spectrum that stretches from the individualistic, market orientated, part-of-the-reward-system type of organisation through to a paternalistic, equitable, needs-based organisation. What Margolis's model does is to allow us to see these different systems in the dimensions of group participation utility and selfish utility, this latter being the standard selfish individualistic outcomes-based utility. Thus, to the extent that a society is composed of individuals who find their equilibrium between selfish utility and group participation to be very much at the selfish utility/low participation end, then it will be the market orientated system of health care that will dominate. If individuals are of the type that is keen to participate and play down selfish utility, then the UK's NHS type system will more likely dominate. While there are other explanations for the NHS (see for example Culyer 1976), the point is simply that, as Titmuss (1970) argued, even if he did not use the language of communitarianism, an NHS type system is more likely to find a home in a more communitarian society.

Relevant to this concept of Margolis's participation utility is that nearly 40 years ago Titmuss (1970) published his book *The Gift Relationship*, which showed that supplying blood through a process of voluntary donation (as occurs in the UK) was more effective and almost certainly more efficient than the commercial process used in the United States. While the empirical evidence seemed to support him on this front, it was the wider aspects of his book (subtitled *From Human Blood to Social Policy*) that provoked greater controversy and that made it a classic. Titmuss (1970: 224) wrote: "Altruism in giving to a stranger does not begin and end with blood donations. It may touch every aspect of life...it is likely that a decline in the spirit of altruism in one sphere of human activities will be

---

* This section draws on Mooney, G. (2004) *Economics, Medicine and Health Care*, 3rd edn. Reprinted with kind permission of Pearson Education.

accompanied by similar changes in attitudes, motives and relationships elsewhere."

It was from this sentiment that he went on to describe the establishment of the UK's NHS in the following terms (Titmuss 1970: 225): "The most unsordid act of British social policy in the twentieth century has allowed and encouraged sentiments of altruism, reciprocity and social duty to express themselves; to be made explicit and identifiable in measurable patterns of behaviour by all social groups and classes."

Despite his protestation, it is clear that Titmuss saw the UK's NHS as a morally superior form of organisation of health care, not primarily because of the health it delivers but because of what it does to promote, first, altruism and, second, a greater sense of community. Whatever one's views are on whether to support Titmuss in these conjectures, in terms of justifying the NHS it would be unfortunate if we had to rely solely on the argument that, whatever its merits in terms of health, it was better at delivering altruism. Where does this leave Margolis? It is likely that Margolis would endorse the idea that the NHS represents a means whereby the *community* can pass to a single entity the responsibility for the community's health. In standard health economics the notion of the caring externality has some parallels with the idea of group utility. However, Margolis's participation is preferred, in that the evidence supports the view that the NHS's equity goal is couched in terms of access rather than of health or, indeed, of health care consumption. Access for the group is essentially what Margolis is about: beyond that utilisation and health involve selfish utility resources, a point which appears to be at least implicitly accepted in NHS policy.

On the basis of this discussion, a key factor that in practice separates out different health care systems, especially public and private, is equity, defined most often in terms of equality of access. That is not to say that arguments around efficiency are then redundant in such choices, but they are less clear cut. Measuring efficiency and thereby demonstrating differences in degrees of efficiency are problematical. The goals of public and private health care are also likely to be different.

Where participation altruism *à la* Margolis (1982) is strong, and there is a relatively homogeneous set of preferences, then "communitarian" (see Chapter 7) would be how to describe such a society. The health care system is then likely to be at the more publicly funded end of the spectrum. Where there is broad satisfaction with the existing distribution of wealth, concern for individual utility is of prime interest to the citizens of a country, and freedom of choice fosters heterogeneity of preferences, more market orientated health care systems will tend to prevail. It is not a complete explanation by any means, but looking at Denmark, on the one hand, and the United States, on the other, which are very different societies in terms of individualism, would provide some empirical support for this explanation of why health care financing systems differ.

In the context of multiple utility (or interests) functions, it is useful to think of Frankfurt's first and second orders of preferences (Frankfurt 1971) and to develop a third order as well. The first approximates rather loosely to some notion of impulse or desire; the second is more about what individuals want from their preferences when they have had time to reflect on them, perhaps considering the issue of what sort of individuals they want to be. Let us call these "reflective preferences". As noted in the previous chapter, these may be different, not only in being reflective, but also in terms of the object of the preferences. This is, *inter alia*, because reflection comes at a cost: time is needed for reflecting. There are possibilities, for example, of thinking in terms of the "returns to reflection". (There seems little point in reflecting too long on whether to buy a chocolate bar, but we might want to dwell a little longer on our preferences regarding our chocolate dependency.)

This notion of different orders of preferences is anathema to many economists, but it is likely to be more readily accepted by other disciplines. The reason for highlighting the notion is a belief that it is neither helpful nor appropriate to try to place all preferences on the same measuring rod, especially (as is commonly done in economics) on a goods-based utility function. Trade-offs still have to be made and that is the key merit of a single measuring rod. My point is that some trade-offs are at different levels than others—the choices that individual consumers make are from different choice sets than those that citizens choose from. As individual day to day consumers we do have to choose between more or better carrots and more or better beer. As more reflective individuals we might want to make life style choices about better health. The essence of this point is that it is not possible to argue that happiness lies at the end of a chocolate bar, but it might be beneficial to consider more broadly diet and nutrition.

As indicated in Chapter 7, there is some discussion and evidence in the health economics literature about the importance of reflection on preferences. Also relevant here is the debate between Lutz (1993) and Brennan (1989 and 1993) in which Lutz sets out various arguments in favour of multiple utility functions. Brennan, in response, suggests that there is little if anything that multiple utility functions can achieve that can not be achieved through single utility functions. It is argued here that such devices are potentially useful if only for the sake of allowing consideration analytically of different orders of preferences along the lines proposed by Frankfurt (1971).

People will choose differently depending on what hat they are asked to wear. In a study in South Australia, for example, people who were asked to make choices first as individuals and then as citizens made different choices (Mooney and Jan 2000).

From a communitarian stance (and not directly from Frankfurt 1971), there is a need to consider additionally what might be termed "third order preferences", but which, following the discussion in Chapter 7, I will call "communitarian preferences". These relate to issues that are more distant from the individual *qua* individual but which nonetheless are important to the individual *as a citizen*. As citizens of our country we might want our community to make choices about international food policy, food subsidies, etc. As global citizens we might want our country to make choices about overseas aid and how generous it might be. These might be interpreted in terms of Sen's "realised agency success", where agency refers to the capacity for autonomous decision making and action by the individual. As indicated previously, this might include broad social concerns—the concerns attributable to citizens—the examples given by Sen (1992: 56) being "the independence of her country or the prosperity of her community".

Thus communitarian preferences are related to the question of what sort of society citizens want, including what sort of social institutions they want and what sort of principles they want these social institutions, such as health care systems, to be based upon. It may also be possible to interpret communitarian preferences as being the equivalent at a social level of Sen's capabilities and functionings, which he considers only at the individual level (even if his discussion is set out in an at least quasi-communitarian context). Such communitarian capabilities are discussed in Chapter 10.

There are trade-offs at all these levels, and there are eventually trade-offs between these levels. Often, however, the trade-offs at the different levels are made by different people or by people seeing themselves as different identities—day to day consumers; more reflective consumers; national citizens; or global citizens. Coping with just one level can be difficult; coping with all of them simultaneously as is implied in welfarism is problematical. Implicit in the communitarian claims approach is an acceptance that there are different levels of trade-off; that acknowledging this is important; and that finding a way to deal with it is required. That is what is claimed for the communitarian claims approach.

Sen recognises that individuals are different in terms of their abilities to convert commodities into ways of providing themselves with well being so that even if goods were allocated equally across different individuals, this would not necessarily lead to equal well being or utility. An individual's functionings are "what he or she manages to do or to be" (Sen 1993: 31). "Capabilities" are about freedoms or opportunities to choose. Thus capabilities represent the freedoms that an individual has in terms of the range of functionings that the individual faces by way of choice.

Functionings are what are achieved from some range of capabilities; they are realised capabilities. It is also *not* assumed by Sen that the individual will necessarily choose to maximise his or her own well being as he allows for other possible motives for choice (such as obligations to others).

Sen makes the related but separate point that the utility tradition suffers from two problems: one he calls "physical-condition neglect" and the other, "valuation neglect". A person who suffers from physical condition neglect (for example he or she is undernourished) "can still be high up in the scale of happiness or desire-fulfilment if he or she has learned to have 'realistic' desires and to take pleasure in small mercies" (Sen 1985: 23). Further, he claims (Sen 1985: 149), with respect to valuation neglect: "Valuing is not the same thing as desiring and the strength of desire is influenced by considerations of realism in one's circumstances." He argues (Sen 1992: 149) that "an overdependence on what people 'manage to desire' is one of the limiting aspects of utilitarian ethics, which is particularly neglectful of the claims of those who are too subdued or broken to have the courage to desire much".

What this discussion of orders or levels of preferences suggests more generally is that it is possible and potentially helpful to depart from the standard notion of economics of single order preferences. While (following Frankfurt 1971) the separation of the first and second orders is a useful one, particularly germane to the thrust of the paradigm set out in this chapter is the third order developed here, the so-called "communitarian preferences". It is these that relate back to Arrow's concept of "social choice rules" (Arrow 1951) and to the notion of communitarian claims developed in the next section.

8.4 Communitarian claims

Broome (1991: 61) has proposed: "To take account of fairness we must start by dividing the reasons why a person should get a good into two classes: 'claims' and other reasons. By a claim to the good I mean a duty owed to the candidate herself that she should have it." He continues: "Claims ... are the object of fairness."

I have previously suggested moving Broome's concept of claims to make it more relevant to the discussion here in the following ways.* First, it is proposed that "communitarian claims" be a sub-set of claims more generally where this sub-set is the responsibility of the community to meet or address. Thus the duty in the case of communitarian claims is a duty owed by the community.

The terminology of "communitarian claims" as opposed to community claims is deliberate. As indicated in Chapter 7, communitarianism (see for example Walzer 1983; Sandel 1984; Avineri and de-Shalit 1992) recognises that individuals are not free floating atoms but that their identities are embedded in some or other community or communities. It also recognises that being active in a community is good in itself and is not just instrumental. Hence being part of the process of determining claims is good in itself. Claims can help to inform decisions in health care not only about equity but also about efficiency in the sense of what it is that the community wants its health services to be about and hence what it wants health service resources to be efficiently deployed to achieve. They can assist in determining the allocation of resources to and within public health. This is a clear recognition that institutions such as health care, but also education, are valued not only for producing some narrowly defined outcomes, such as health gain and educational human capital gain. They can be valued for other outcomes in health (e.g. information), in processes (e.g. caring), or in institutions *per se* that contribute to the decency of a society (such as a tax-based universal health care system).

Claims at this level are labelled "communitarian claims" reflecting the fact that it is the community who has the task of deciding what constitute claims, the duty to allocate claims, and to decide on the relative strengths of different claims. There is value in being part of the process of arbitrating over claims. An atomistic, individualistic society will be slow to recognise that the community does have a duty with respect to meeting such claims. The more embedded individuals are in a community and the greater the recognition of such embeddedness, the stronger will be communitarian claims in that community.

---

* This section draws on and was reprinted from *Social Science & Medicine*, 47(9), Mooney, G., "Communitarian claims" as an ethical basis for allocating health care resources, pp. 1171–80, ©1998, with kind permission of Elsevier.

The strength of a claim is not a function of an individual's ability to manage to feel harmed. Harms and the strengths of these harms are for the society to judge. Strictly, with respect to claims, the bad feelings arising for the person harmed are only relevant insofar as the society deems them to be relevant. They are a matter for "community conscience" (Mooney and Jan 1997: 85).

The question then arises as to whether efficiency can also be handled through claims. Efficiency is about the use of resources to achieve some maximand or socially specified objective, often set in terms of a social welfare function (but also, in this case, with some concerns for equity). Yet economics has failed to reach a consensus about how to define that social welfare function. Given the need to consider on what bases to allocate resources, if the individualistically based social welfare function (according to, for example, Jeremy Bentham) is abandoned, might it not be argued that communitarian claims could provide an alternative?

There are parallels between claims and rights. Claims can be seen as a sub-set of rights. Thus Almond (1991) suggests that there are four forms of rights: claims and other rights relating to powers, liberties, and immunities. With respect to the particular use of the term "claims" in this book, the following distinguishing features are identified which make communitarian claims somewhat different, even if perhaps they remain a sub-set of rights.

The word "claim" is perhaps an unfortunate one in this context, as in everyday usage it tends to require an active role for the person who is to benefit from the claim. "I claim" and "you claim" is standard usage where this is a shorthand for "I claim on my behalf" and "you claim on your behalf". Here we *the community* determine how resources are allocated on the basis of how we *the community* determine, first, what constitute claims—what are deemed relevant criteria for allocating health care resources—and, second, how we *the community* see various different groups' or individuals' strengths of claims for the resources involved. It is *our* preferences, the community's preferences, for *their* claims (i.e. the various groups' claims), that determine how the resources are allocated. It is we *the community* who also decide what is relevant in identifying and weighting claims in terms of the characteristics of the different potential recipient groups and the community as a whole (Mooney and Russell 2003).

Communitarian claims are neither welfarist nor extra-welfarist. They allow the society or the community to decide who shall have access to what quantities of resources for what purposes. They accept that resources are limited and provide a community determined mechanism for their allocation to competing groups. They are thus about community provision. *At this level* there is no need strictly for the groups to be active in claiming "their" resources. There is also no implied absolute right of any individual to consume any service. There cannot be any absolute right given the acceptance within the concept of claims of the scarcity of resources. The claim establishes the legitimacy of that service for that individual (or more likely for a group into which that individual falls). The extent to which that service, in practice, is provided will in turn hinge on the community's judgement of the strengths of claims involved and the resources available.

The actual *consumption* of the resources, however, remains determined by how an individual values the options with which he or she is then faced. As indicated in the last chapter with the Margolis's (1982) fair shares model, there may be a "loop" here, such that if certain groups, in some sense or other that the community seeks to favour, do not use or misuse the resources made available to them, this may influence the community in assessing claims and strengths of claims next time round. This "outcome" may be unsatisfactory or inadequate for some in the public health discipline who seek to maximise health. The question then is where does that objective come from. If it is not from individuals or the community then what legitimacy does it have?

To sum up this discussion of claims and rights: first, the notion of claims is interpreted as being more relative and less absolute than rights are often portrayed. Second, communitarian claims, as indicated, fall to the community to exercise their duty over. Third, claims do not have to be "demanded" by the individual who has the claims (and while this is true of some rights as well, it is one way of identifying this sub-set of rights). Fourth, communitarian claims are clearly community-based while many rights are more individualistically based.

8.5 Communitarian claims and the objectives of health care

Vanberg (1994) makes the case for having some structure in organisations which results in what he calls "rule-following" (p. 7). He argues (Vanberg 1994: 292):

even if interpersonal comparisons of utility were possible and an aggregate social welfare measure could be constructed, the essential question remains whether the respective individuals would like, and would voluntarily choose, to live in a social community in which policy decisions were to be based on a Benthamite social welfare rule. Such [a] social welfare rule would have to be considered as one among a number of potential alternative rules for political decision making and...it would have to be subjected to the same test as all its potential rivals, the test of voluntary agreement on the part of the individuals involved.

He continues (Vanberg 1994: 7): "An adequate theory of rules and institutions cannot really be developed on the basis of a purely formal 'logic of choice'. It requires a theory of behaviour that has empirical content and that accounts for the element of *rule-following* in human conduct" (emphasis in original).

The adoption of the concept of claims and the use of communitarian claims in an institutional framework for health care are proposed. Relevant to this is Vanberg's notion above of "rule-following in human conduct" and which is prevalent in the work of Simons (e.g. Simons 1964) and Williamson (e.g. Williamson 1975) often construed in terms of "rules of thumb", "bounded rationality", "information impactedness", etc., sometimes emerging in the principal–agent relationship in health care at the individual doctor/individual patient level but now, this book proposes, needing to be extended to considerations of such a relationship at a more social level. Vanberg, however, goes further than Simons or Williamson in that he argues for rules being the object of social valuation.

With respect to the objectives of health care as a social institution, the basis of rule-following for the "agents" (here the policy makers and politicians charged with running the system) might be social judgements on what constitute claims and strengths of claims over health service resources. In a market system, claims are based primarily on individuals' incomes and wealth, and in turn on willingness to pay (which will be a function of ability to pay). As discussed earlier, there has tended to be an assumption that the allocation of public health care resources is and should be based *solely* on health status gains, with an underlying presumption that, however these claims are manifested, the result will be the maximisation of the health of the population.

The community to be served by the health service is not consulted with respect to what social choice rule it wants to govern the allocation of health care resources. The community may, of course, choose to do this according to a standard concept of health need. What communitarian claims allow is to test with the community what the basis of that social choice rule is to be rather than, as with health needs, assuming or presuming it.

It is also the case that within health economics there has been debate about how best to measure health with most health economists siding with the QALY and only a minority with the Healthy Year Equivalent (HYE). (For more detail see for example Culyer and Wagstaff 1995; Gafni and Birch 1997.) The technical details of that debate are not immediately relevant to the discussion here but there are value elements to it, social issues around the valuation of health, that are.

HYEs measure health profiles over time, while QALYs measure health states, which are then summed over a relevant time period. These are quite likely to give different results. Which is to be preferred on what grounds led to a heated debate in the health economics literature in the 1990s. What is germane in the context of this section of this chapter is that many health economists felt confident to take part in both the debate about the value issues and the debate about the technical issues. I can find no suggestion in the literature on that QALY/HYE debate on the value issue being put back to the community whose health is at stake. There is a tendency for health economists to overstep ourselves and become involved in value issues that are more legitimately the province of the community to be served by the health care system or of the people whose population health is at issue.

Which arguments are "to count" in resource allocation decision making is to be determined *by the community*. Where the key challenge of this chapter lies is principally in arguing against the standard assumption in health economics that assessments at the individual patient level can be aggregated to some macro goal for health services, as it is, for example, in statements about health maximisation. The new paradigm argues that it is better to see the direction of this relationship as being from the macro to the micro. If the informed community adopts a set of principles, the community's constitution, which seeks to bring other outcomes or processes, such as reassurance or respect for patient autonomy, or caring into priority setting, or to include non-unitary weightings of health gains into priority setting, then the ranking of priorities that might have emerged from, say, a QALY league table or any other priority setting approach based purely on health on the benefit side is likely to change. The decision on what is in or out is in the hands of the informed community.

The implication of the "rules" underlying current needs-based planning is that the basis for a claim to resources—and usually the only basis—is either the prospect of health status gains or the addressing of health needs, and that the strength of claims to these resources is a direct function of either the capacity to create health gains or the size of the health problem.

Nothing else counts. Yet there is evidence (see for example Nord et al. 1995) that there is more than health present and more than some simple health maximisation goal. The results of citizens' juries in Australia (see the Appendix to Chapter 9) show that citizens in aggregate want more than simply health from their health services. Concerns about self-induction of disease and some aspects of moral hazard also suggest otherwise. Proponents of euthanasia would question the monopoly of health gains in any health service maximand. Evidence from Williams (1997) on "the fair innings" notion of health gains challenges the unitary weighting of health gains, as does work by Nord (1994) and my own work with others (Mooney et al. 1995). In turn this research raises doubts about the social choice rule being the maximisation of health gains, independently of any consideration of who the recipients are and the prospects of weighting of the health gains.

Strictly, benefit maximisation or health maximisation says nothing about who gets the benefits or whose health is improved. Here is the treating-people-as-vessels-to-be-filled-with-utility (or health) criticism that has been aimed at utilitarianism.

The new paradigm involves the notion of a third party, in this case the community, determining what claims are and their relative strengths. As Broome (1991) indicates, people do not have to feel bad to have been harmed and as a result of harm to exercise claims. With communitarian claims, it is for society or the community to recognise these claims and to determine their strengths. This fits well (as indicated earlier) with Sen's concerns about some individuals having an inability to manage to desire (Sen 1992). These people clearly get penalised within a utility-based framework but not necessarily within a needs-based framework and even less likely within a communitarian-claims-based framework.

8.6 Bases for communitarian claims beyond "simple" need

A possible example of a communitarian claim beyond "simple" need (where "simple" need is defined as being the extent of the health problem or the capacity to benefit in health terms only and where all health gains are weighted equally no matter who gets them) is the rule of rescue. Let us assume that the intent is to maximise health gains with the available resources. For patients close to death there might then be efforts made to stop them clutching at ineffective care. Thus van de Ven (1996) points out that the Dutch government argues that there might be a need for a government to protect the population from spending money on what might well be futile care.

Yet this very same phenomenon might be seen from a social standpoint as the rule of rescue, in essence that if someone is about to "fall over a cliff" (to death or permanent disability, say), society may want to do something, indeed to be seen to be doing something, to prevent this from happening, even if it is "ineffective" in terms of health gains. Alternatively, it is possible to argue that the measure of effectiveness needs to be widened to include something more than health. Or that we need to look at what constitutes a good or decent society, including whether it is prepared to stand by and say, "let them fall over the cliff". Or that we ask the community whether people who are about to "fall over the cliff" have claims on health care resources, and if so what the strengths of such claims are, as compared, say, to those who have a treatable (at relatively low cost) disease.

Also relevant to what constitute claims is that, insofar as existing health state is treated as a basis for claims on health care resources, two nominally equal health states will not necessarily attract the same strength of claim. That strength may vary depending on why the health state arose in the first place. Thus the strength of claims on health care resources of two chronic bronchitis sufferers may differ if, for example, one sufferer's condition was induced by cigarette smoking and the other's not.

Such an example can, however, be seen as potentially naive. One reader of a draft argued: What if the smoker were born into a family of smokers, raised in penury, and abused as a child? The answer is simple under a regime of communitarian claims. Any or all of these factors may be deemed relevant as bases for claims beyond the smoking *per se*. Without these claims and operating only on the basis of health status as need, none of these factors would be judged relevant. They might still not be judged so, depending on the community's assessment, but at least the community are given the chance to decide whether these factors are relevant to resource allocation. The alternative, as in current health economics, is to argue that all that is relevant is health status, as in health need.

This suggests that, while it may well be the case that the existing health state is a marker for strength of claims, there will be variations around that depending on other factors related to the reasons why the health state occurred in the first place. The same sorts of issues arise here when one queries the goal of equal health, as I attempted to indicate with Steve Jan (Mooney and Jan 1997) in looking at a variation on the theme by Varian (1974) on "wealth fairness" in what we termed "health fairness".

Varian suggests equality of incomes is not necessarily just. Such "wealth fairness" might translate into "health fairness", which would not be equated with equality of health. "Some people put more effort into being healthy, for example through a sensible diet, the consumption of which may be less enjoyable than that of an unhealthy diet. Others eat 'what they like' even if it is less healthy; some people jog; some hang glide" (Mooney and Jan 1997: 82). With Steve Jan, I proposed that the sorts of factors that might be included in judging claims and their strengths would be "the extent of self-induction of disease, the perceived social responsibility for inequalities in a society, guilt (in the case of Aborigines), different cultural values in a multi-cultural society, 'blame', etc." (Mooney and Jan 1997: 82)

We can speculate about other bases for communitarian claims. For example, in a country like Australia, remoteness is likely to be seen as relevant, but perhaps distinguishing between remote communities of origin and remote communities of choice. Whatever the case, if the notion of "claims" were to be accepted, then there would be the need for a research programme to look at what the bases and strengths of different claims on health care resources might be. However, the sorts of factors that might form a basis for claims are: age, SES, current health status, Aboriginality, timing, and distribution, English speaking versus people with a non-English speaking background, rural/urban, availability of alternatives, with dependents/without dependents, whether recipients are "contributors" or "drains" on society, etc. These are presented simply to exemplify what might emerge if a more detailed assessment of communitarian claims were pursued.

While this section has concentrated on claims to health care resources, the ideas can be readily extended to public health where more than health outcomes are likely to be valued. As discussed for example in section 4.5, "preparedness" may well be a part of what a community values from the investment in public health. Community reassurance is also likely to be present. Weightings of claims in public health may follow a similar pattern as in health care but with more emphasis on risks of bad or adverse events.

8.7 Conclusion

Where does this leave an epidemiologically driven concept of health maximisation versus some more broadly based maximand in health care as a basis for decision making about health care resource allocation?

Culyer and Evans (1996) cite evidence at the macro level in the UK and Canada, essentially statements of intent from governments about the goals of their respective health care systems, in support of the view that health services are about health only. In the context of discussions about the overall allocation of society's resources for education, transport, health, etc., then it is difficult to disagree with this view. *At this level* the "claim" by a health service is that it promotes the health of the community it serves. If we sought to establish, as proposed in this chapter, the basis of claims *at this level* then it is likely that this view from Culyer and Evans would prevail. If, however, we then move the discussion to consider the question at the level of "given these resources for health care, what as a society do we want done with them?" or in the language of this chapter "what are the bases for communitarian claims on these health care resources for different citizens?", then there is likely to be considerable debate about the extent to which the basis for claims *at this level* will relate only to health and even greater debate about whether it is about health maximisation with no differential weighting of health gains to different recipients. Would a community really want to ignore respect for patient autonomy? Or respect for patients' dignity? Would it be a matter of indifference in Australia, for example, in its valuation of health gains for Aborigines and non-Aborigines? (This question has been answered in a citizens' jury but the results have not yet been published. The citizens were prepared to weight health gains to Aboriginal people at about 1.5 times as high as those to non-Aboriginal people.)

The notion of communitarian claims in this chapter may also, if picked up more generally, have yet another advantage. It might serve to maintain enthusiasm among policy makers for trying to establish community values or preferences. There has in recent years been a growing desire to consult the public and to try to obtain community values about health care priorities. While this has been done in a multitude of ways, there has been all too little follow through into policy. That needs to change. The vehicle of communitarian claims can allow that to happen.

Finally, it is apparent that there are problems in advancing the concept of claims and retaining the ability to measure and to quantify within whatever "constitution" emerges. We cannot do so adequately at present in the restricted confines of need, health status, etc. Adopting the expressive theory of Anderson (1993) from Chapter 6 together with the concept of communitarian claims would make these problems of measurement yet more difficult.

On this Sen argues that measurement can be taken too far and he seeks to guard against "over" completeness. "'Waiting for toto' may not be a cunning strategy in a practical exercise" (Sen 1992: 49). He suggests that "the nature of interpersonal comparisons of well-being...as a discipline may admit incompleteness as a regular part of the...exercise...An approach that can rank the well-being of every person against that of every other in a straightforward way...may well be at odds with the nature of these ideas."

8.8 Epilogue

I am aware of only one attempt (Hall et al. 2006) to critique the approach of communitarian claims. I believe it is useful for me to comment on that critique as it may help to clarify some aspects of the new paradigm. That is the point of this epilogue. (Recently Davis and McMaster (2007) have also drawn on communitarian ideas, but then gone down the road of rights. That is clearly a potentially useful but different approach.)

In discussing my earlier writings on communitarian claims, Hall and colleagues argue:

While welfarism could be rescued by sufficiently broadening what is considered allowable in individual preferences, this is not pursued by...communitarianism... Sen remains committed to the individual as the source of values and to tolerance of heterogeneity in preferences. In contrast...communitarianism derive[s] from other sources for values.

They also state:

the community determines which claims are recognised, and the strength of those claims. This community preference takes precedence over the individual's perception of those claims or any harm resulting from them. In communitarianism too, the decision-makers have an influential role as they act as community agents who interpret the rules or principles set by communities for health care resource allocation; in addition they also can determine when majority views hold sway and when other principles take precedence.

There are a number of misunderstandings here. The idea that welfarism just needs a bit of broadening in terms of "what is allowable in individual preferences" ignores the (to me) fundamental point that the individual in welfarism and the individual in communitarianism see the world through different lenses. The former is an individual who takes his or her identity from a focus on being an individual: yes, there can be externalities but these are still observed by an individual *qua* individual. The individual in communitarianism is a member of a community and his or her identity as a community member whose attitudes and preferences are moulded by being embedded in a community. It is not solely a question of what is included in preferences; the question of *how* preferences are formed is different in the two cases. How the world is viewed is different. Take commitment: Sen's commitment is counter-preferential; it cannot be accommodated in welfarism; in communitarianism, commitment can be to the community and can be accommodated by making the maximand that of the community rather than of the individual.

To make the statement that communitarianism derives "from other sources of values" as if there were somehow other sources of values than those of people is again based on a misunderstanding. Individuals are not only and not always individuals *qua* individuals, they are also sometimes members of a community (perhaps of several). There is a need to recognise this community focus in at least certain instances. This point is made in my 1998 paper (Mooney 1998), which is a part of the body of my writing on communitarianism that these authors draw upon in their critique. There I stated:

it is proposed that there is a need for a dual level approach, a personal one nested within a community one ... One is the level of individual desire for own health where the (now) relatively standard models ... are probably acceptable for the weighing of health gains. The other, second level is concerned with the basis on which these sorts of choices are made.

So at the first level we have the individual as an individual, at the second the individual as a citizen. There is no other source of values than people. It is possible to get individuals to express preferences at these two different levels.

Third, there is no basis for the statement that the decision makers "can determine when majority views hold sway and when other principles take precedence". Hall and her colleagues are *almost* right to argue that the decision makers do "have an influential role as they act as community agents". "Important", however, might be a better descriptor than "influential". Their influence is only as agents for the citizens. It is the role of the public official, as the welfare economist Bergson (and mentioned earlier in this chapter) famously described it more than half a century ago (Bergson 1954: 242). "[The public official's] one aim in life is to implement the values of other citizens" and Bergson added "as given by some rule of collective decision making" (which is what I describe elsewhere in this book as "the constitution").

There is, however, no sense in which the decision makers are charged with forming judgements about where and when "majority views" are to be replaced with others. Neither is it the case in communitarianism, as is claimed, that "decision-makers have a powerful position as they can determine the weightings to be given to different values expressed, or even override majority views on ethical stands". The decision makers are agents on behalf of the community; they are not there to choose whether they want to accept community preferences or to "over-ride majority views". Again it is Bergson's point that for decision makers in the communitarian approach, their "one aim in life is to implement the values of other citizens".

Hall et al. criticise the communitarian approach for being dependent on "the benevolence and wisdom of decision-makers in allocating resources". It is dependent on their wisdom—but I see nothing problematical with that. It is not dependent on their benevolence unless by this it is meant that they seek as community agents to honour what the community preferences reveal, and if they do not, then they will be held accountable to the community.

These authors also argue that communitarianism excludes non-consequentialist forms of utility. This is incorrect. They come to this view because of the following statement in Mooney (1998): "In particular, it is argued that decision makers should not be allowed to defend inefficient treatment on the basis of non-health outcomes, or process variables." They go on: "This seems to imply QALY maximization as a proximate social welfare goal."

Now there is a problem here. Certainly, by allowing "non-health outcomes or process variables", there is a risk that decision makers might try to use these to "defend inefficient treatment". In no sense is that intended to exclude these other sources of utility. I am arguing only that we need to guard against attempts by decision makers to bring in variables purely to seek to defend inefficient treatments. Then to attempt to argue, as Hall and her colleagues do, that this would allow "QALY maximization as a proximate social welfare goal" is a *non sequitur*. It is especially so because in that same article, in defence of including process utility, I ask: "Would a community really want to ignore respect for patient autonomy? for patients' dignity?" Again in that same article I wrote (Mooney 1998: 1175): "These communitarian preferences are related to the question of what sort of society citizens want, including what sort of social institutions they want and what sort of rules or principles they want to govern these social institutions, such as health care systems." Later (in a chapter with Elizabeth Russell and drawn on by these authors in building their critique), we

165

wrote (Mooney and Russell 2003: 215): "At a citizen level...one may be interested in much broader issues such as accessibility to health care generally for different groups as a function of, for example, what is seen as a decent society." This is now very far removed from consequentialism, even further from QALY maximisation, and is much more akin to Anderson's expressive theory.

The authors do then concede that "more recently, the notion of health being the sole contributor to the social welfare function has been rejected in favour of more research on what constitutes claims in different settings (Mooney 2005, p. 253)". That was always my position.

The final point where I will challenge these authors' critique is where they write that the communitarian approach

requires decision-makers to collect and process several levels of data that include individual health status (e.g., QALYs), weighted health status incorporating reflective values, the nature and extent of communitarian claims, the weights to be attached to competing claims and the weight to be given to health maximization as against claims. It is not clear how these various levels of preference ordering can or should be combined to satisfy the communitarian objective.

Again, they miss the point that there *are* different levels of decision making. Individual health status and health maximisation remain at the level—the only level—that welfarism and extra-welfarism deal with. Apart from that, decision makers do have to get to grips with some community engagement process to assess "the nature and extent of communitarian claims". But that is all. There is no need additionally to determine the "weights to be attached to competing claims". That has already been done in assessing "the nature and extent of communitarian claims". And there is no need additionally to weight "health maximisation against claims". If health is there as a claim—and it is most likely that it is—then again this issue is subsumed within communitarian claims. To repeat: there are different levels of decision making. Once that is accepted, the question of sorting out or combining "these various levels of preference ordering" is a non-issue.

References

Almond, B. (1991) Rights, in P. Singer (ed.), *A Companion to Ethics*. Oxford: Blackwell.

Anderson, E. (1993) *Value in Ethics and Economics*. Cambridge, MA: Harvard University Press.

Arrow, K. (1951) *Social Choice and Individual Values*. New York: John Wiley.

Avineri, S. and de-Shalit, A. (1992) Introduction, in S. Avineri and A. de-Shalit (eds.), *Communitarianism and Individualism*. Oxford: Oxford University Press.

Bergson, A. (1954) On the concept of social welfare, *Quarterly Journal of Economics*, 68: 233–52.

Brennan, T. J. (1989) A methodological assessment of multiple utility frameworks, *Economics and Philosophy*, 5: 189–208.

—— (1993) The futility of multiple utility, *Economics and Philosophy*, 9: 155–64.

Broome, J. (1991) *Weighing Goods*. Oxford: Blackwell.

Cribb, A. (2005) *Health and the Good Society*. Oxford: Oxford University Press.

Culyer, A. J. (1976) *Need and the NHS*. Oxford: Martin Robertson.

—— Evans, R. G. (1996) Mark Pauly on welfare economics: normative rabbits from positive hats, *Journal of Health Economics*, 15(2): 243–52.

—— Wagstaff, A. (1995) QALYs versus HYEs: a reply to Gafni, Birch and Mehrez, *Journal of Health Economics*, 14: 39–45.

Davis, J. B. and McMaster, R. (2007) The individual in mainstream health economics: a case of persona non-grata, *Health Care Analysis*, 15: 195–210.

Frankfurt, H. (1971) Freedom of the will and the concept of a person, *Journal of Philosophy*, 68: 5–20.

Gafni, A. and Birch, S. (1997) QALYs and HYEs: spotting the differences, *Journal of Health Economics*, 16: 601–8.

Gilson (2003) Trust and health care as a social institution, *Social Science and Medicine*, 6(67): 1452–68.

Hall, J., Gafni, A. and Birch, S. (2006) Health economics critiques of welfarism and their compatibility with Sen's capabilities approach. CHERE Working Paper 2006/16, CHERE, University of Technology Sydney, Sydney.

Kemp, M. C. and Asimakopulos, A. (1952) A note on "social welfare functions" and cardinal utility, *Canadian Journal of Economics and Political Science*, 18: 195–200.

Lomas, J. (1997) Reluctant rationers: public input to health care priorities, *Journal of Health Services Research and Policy*, 2(2): 1–8.

Lutz, M. A. (1993) The utility of multiple utility: a comment on Brennan, *Economics and Philosophy*, 9: 145–54.

Margolis, H. (1982) *Selfishness, Altruism and Rationality*. Cambridge: Cambridge University Press.

Mooney, G. (1994) *Key Issues in Health Economics*. Hemel Hempstead: Simon and Schuster.

—— (1998) Communitarianism and health (care) economics, in M. L. Barer, T. E. Getzen and G. L. Stoddart (eds.), *Quality and Inequality: What Care, Whose Costs, Whither Quality?* London: Wiley.

—— (2005) Communitarian claims and community capabilities: furthering priority setting? *Social Science and Medicine*, 60(20): 247–55.

Mooney, G. and Jan, S. (1997) Vertical equity: weighting outcomes? or establishing procedures? *Health Policy*, 39(1): 79–88.

Mooney, G. and Jan, S. Wiseman V (1995) Examining preferences for health gains, *Health Care Analysis*, 3: 261–5.

—— —— (2000) The use of conjoint analysis to elicit community preferences in public health research: a case study of hospital services in South Australia, *Australian and New Zealand Journal of Public Health*, 24: 64–70.

——Russell, E. (2003) Equity in health care: the need for a new paradigm?, in A. Scott, A. Maynard and R. Elliott (eds.), *Advances in Health Economics*. Chichester: Wiley.

Nord, E. (1994) The person trade-off approach to valuing health care programmes, *Medical Decision Making*, 15: 201–8.

——Richardson, J., Street, A., Kuhse, H. and Singer, P. (1995) Maximising health benefits vs egalitarianism: an Australian survey of health issues, *Social Science and Medicine*, 41: 1429–37.

Ranson, S. and Stewart, J. (1998) Citizenship in the public domain for trust in civil society, in A. Coulson (ed.), *Trust and Contracts: Relationships in Local Government, Health and Public Services*. Bristol: The Polity Press.

Sandel, M. (1984) The procedural republic and the unencumbered self, *Political Theory*, 12: 81–96.

Sen, A. (1985) *Commodities and Capabilities*. Amsterdam: North Holland.

——(1992) *Inequality Re-examined*. Oxford: Clarendon Press.

——(1993) Capability and well-being, in M. Nussbaum and A. Sen (eds.), *The Quality of Life*. Oxford: Clarendon Press.

Simons, H. (1964) On the concept of organizational goals, *Administrative Science Quarterly*, 9: 1–22.

Titmuss, R. (1970) *The Gift Relationship: From Human Blood to Social Policy*. London: New Press.

Torrance, G. (1986) Measurement of health state utilities for economic appraisal, *Journal of Health Economics*, 5: 1–30.

Vanberg, V. J. (1994) *Rules and Choice in Economics*. London: Routledge.

Varian, H. (1974) Equity, envy and efficiency, *Journal of Economic Theory*, 9: 63–91.

van de Ven, W. P. M. M. (1996) Market-oriented health care reforms: trends and future options, *Social Science and Medicine*, 43(5): 655–66.

Walzer, M. (1983) *Spheres of Justice*. Oxford: Blackwell.

Williams, A. (1997) Intergenerational equity: an exploration of the "fair innings" argument, *Health Economics*, 6(2): 117–32.

Williamson, O. (1975) *Markets and Hierarchies*. New York: Free Press.

Part III

Some implications of the new paradigm

9

A future health policy: nationally and internationally

9.1 Introduction

In the wake of the development of the new paradigm in Part II, there is a need to examine how public health and health care might be better delivered. This chapter considers these issues generally, both at a national level and globally. It also looks at health policy globally, going beyond considerations of formal health *care* policy. It examines how to overcome some of the problems created by neo-liberalism. In doing so it uses the model of a national health policy as developed by Navarro (2007) but modifying this to a more global level. This is based on an interpretation of Hegel's ideas of institutions (Muller 2003) but now taken at a global level. Additionally, it argues for eschewing not just neo-liberalism but any hegemonic system, suggesting that the links between culture and health point to the need to preserve the diversity of cultures across the globe. This is best achieved by allowing different cultures to be supported by appropriate economic structures.

The other chapters in Part III deal with more specific issues. Chapter 10 considers priority setting and Chapter 11, equity. In Chapter 12 a range of other specific issues are addressed, including for example the implications of the new paradigm for economic evaluation and for the economics of public health in general.

9.2 Constitution in health

Vanberg (1994: 127) argues:

What gives the [goal] paradigm its apparent plausibility is probably the fact that it is for us the natural and unquestioned way of interpreting the actions of an individual human actor. Just as we take it for granted that a person's actions can be understood in terms of his or her goals we are inclined to suppose that organised collective action can equally be understood in terms of goals pursued by such action. Yet, whatever may be said about the fruitfulness of the goal paradigm in the study of individual human behaviour... it is of questionable value when applied to organized collective action... The seemingly solid agreement on the relevance of the concept [in the relevant literature] appears to become meaningless as more serious efforts are made to specify its content... Advocates of the 'goal paradigm' seem to face a dilemma: they insist that the concept of an organizational goal is indispensable, but are unable to define clearly the concept without reifying the organization.

When the question of what health services are about is posed at a more micro level—with respect to treatments, screening, diagnosis, etc.—it becomes yet clearer that there is more to health services than health. Treatments often require that patients are treated with dignity, that their autonomy is respected, that they are informed. More of those screened get benefits from information and reassurance than through changes in mortality and morbidity. Diagnosis *per se* does nothing for health status. These are not just instrumental variables en route to a greater good—they are a part of the good (or bad) that health services deliver.

The paradigm that has been developed recognises anew that health services are a social organisation, and that health services and public health are there to serve the population. It is the values of the community that then drive these social institutions.

There is an ongoing debate over what role the general public should play in health care planning. Sceptics of public involvement (for example Torgerson and Gosden 2000) have expressed concerns over the limited interests and expertise of the public. Advocates (such as the Australian Health Reform Alliance, see: www.healthreform.org.au/) have argued that, regardless of the problems involved, it is ultimately society's resources that are being allocated and therefore society's preferences that should count.

To get the citizenry heavily involved in health care planning is just not practical. Athenian democracy has its appeal, but the opportunity costs are just too high. We need to devise and adopt a set of principles for social choice—a "constitution"—for health services along the lines of those fathers of welfare economics—Adam Bergson (1954) and Kenneth Arrow (1963). The paradigm suggests that this is best done by the informed citizenry.

The idea of stepping back and thinking through the principles on which societies seek to build their health services is a simple one. Questions of the appropriateness of economics in health care of evidence bases and of health outcomes measurement—all potentially laudable—cannot satisfactorily or comprehensively be addressed until there is clarity on the values that do and should drive the health care system. This set of values has to come from the community.

What is possible is to bring public preferences into health service decision making without all the complexities and costs of Athenian democracy. This involves using the community voice to establish the values that should underpin it and leave the "experts" to operationalise the constitution.

9.3 Valuing institutions

On institutional concerns about health care Blaauw et al. (2003) write (p. 3) "the dominant discourse in health systems research and health sector reform still reflects a preoccupation with the infrastructure, technology and economics of health systems rather than its human and social dimensions, the 'hardware' of health systems rather than the 'software'". They argue (Scott 1995):

the health systems literature has tended to overlook the everyday organisational reality of health systems [and they propose that] there are useful insights to be gained from the field of organisational and institutional studies, which has long viewed organisations as social and cultural systems rather than simple production systems.

Blaauw et al. (pp. 39–40) suggest: "Health systems are complex social systems. This seemingly obvious observation is curiously absent in much of the current discourse about health systems and health sector reform." They claim that this is in part due to the "economic biases of the field" (p. 39). They go on to say that

[b]ecause health systems are social systems, health system researchers and reformers need to pay much more attention to social theory... It is necessary, not only to pay more attention to the socio-cultural dimension of health systems, but also to ensure that existing interventions do not undermine the development of more humanistic approaches. Our understanding of the complex social world of health systems is limited and fragmented. Current perspectives rely on simplistic assumptions about human behaviour but we lack the methodological tools to develop more complex insights.

They argue that there is a need to "focus on priorities such as developing shared goals, promoting organisational values, creating supportive work environments, influencing informal social networks, building trust, and improving organisational learning". They accept that "[p]ractical health system researchers and reformers may be sceptical that such an approach is too complex or too normative".

These authors thus get us part of the way to valuing health care systems *per se* even if they do not go far enough in seeing health care as a social institution.

Looking to health services as social institutions and not commodities means that they become more akin to social services, where the inputs are not simply the resources of the health services but involve also the resources of the citizens. This is most obvious at the level of the patient and his or her carers in the community. But citizens can also be involved as a resource in health care in the sense of the time and effort they take in offering their informed preferences for the procedural foundations of health care, i.e. the constitution for health care.

Freedman (2005) argues that too infrequently is the issue of a health care system as a social institution addressed or taken into account in health policy making. She makes this point in the specific context of the Millennium Development Goals (MDGs), arguing (p. 1) that the way that the goals are framed

invites a technocratic, largely top-down approach with a familiar sequence of steps: determine the primary causes of the MDG diseases/conditions; measure the incidence and prevalence; identify the medical interventions to prevent or treat these causes; determine the most cost-effective delivery systems for those interventions; calculate the costs; advocate for "political will" to get the job done.

More fundamentally still and very much in line with the new paradigm, Freedman writes (p. 3):

Human rights activists have long understood the political arms of the state—prisons, judicial systems and police forces—to have the power to exclude, abuse and silence. But rarely are social and economic rights and the social institutions on which they depend approached with the same understanding. This must change.

Crucially she adds: "Health systems are part of the very fabric of social and civic life."

Freedman (p. 3) suggests that

the health system is not simply a mechanical structure to deliver technical interventions the way a post office delivers a letter. Rather, health systems are core social institutions. They function at the interface between people and the structures of power that shape their broader society. Neglect, abuse and exclusion by the health system is part of the very experience of being poor. Conversely, health claims, legitimate claims of entitlement to the services and other conditions necessary to promote health, are assets of citizens in a democratic society... Health actions, the choices and means that enable individuals and communities to control their health, to participate as agents—not victims—in shaping their own life circumstances are important for individual capabilities and the enjoyment of individual rights.

Gilson (2003: 1461) supports this view, arguing that health systems "are not only producers of health and health care, but they are also purveyors of a wider set of societal norms and values". They are thus social institutions in the sense that they help to mould and are moulded by the nature of the society in which they operate. There is a two-way interaction between the health care sector and the population, and not the unidirectional emphasis that health policy and health economics tends to assume or adopt. The health services are technocratic organisations which are there to serve the health of the people. But they are more than this. They are also social institutions, a part of the social fabric and with the capacity to be major players in influencing the nature of society. Thus they need to take their place alongside other major institutions such as the education sector, corporations, the courts, and the public service. How people react to and respect these institutions can in turn influence the make-up of society and have an effect on individuals' perceptions of their position in society. These are, in Freedman's words (p. 5), "more fundamentally social, culturally embedded, politically-contingent institutions".

According to the new paradigm, the health care system thus has a value of its own independent of or at least additional to what it produces by way of outputs, such as improved health to individuals. This value takes the following forms: a social institution that contributes to the health of the population as a whole and not just the individual's health; a social institution that by being accessible to all, contributes to the idea of living in and helping to build a caring society (a form of social option value); and a social institution that, in being amenable to the preferences of citizens, enhances democracy. These features together we may place under the heading of "building social decency".

Let me give an example. If a primary care organisation wishes to set up some strategic planning exercise, this will most often be goals focused. It may lead to no more than a description of how decisions are to be made. Often this process ignores the issue of establishing the foundation of principles on which that planning is to be based. Debate about what the values base might be may well be bypassed.

Instead, if there is a recognition of the need for a constitution on which to plan the functionings of the organisation, that in turn requires discussion on to how this is to be done and according to whose values. Again many answers might be given to these questions, but the key point is that, having asked these questions, they now need to be answered. If there is a further recognition of the idea of health services as social institutions, this will point in the direction of using community values. Again if there is an acknowledgement that the players who are around for the long haul are the community who are served by these services, then citizens are the people who are most likely to provide, in the words of Jan (2002: 271), long term "credible commitment" to the social institution that is health care.

9.4 Mackintosh and Navarro on health care institutions

Maureen Mackintosh is one of the very few health economists who have set health care systems in a somewhat different context from the norm. She writes (2001: 175): "Current debate in the literature focuses on the impact of health care systems on health outcomes and on the impact of social inequality on health outcomes . . . It does not pay anything like the same attention to the direct interaction between social inequality and healthcare systems themselves."

She set out to consider this issue (p. 175), analysing

health care systems as a core element of social inequality in any society, in the sense that unequal legitimate claims upon a health care system, and unequal experiences of seeking care, are important elements of poverty and social inequality in people's experience. It argues that health care systems, as social institutions, are built out of the existing social structure, and carry inequalities within them. However, health care systems are *also*, and at the same time, a key site for contestation of existing inequality: they offer a representation back to us of our societies' capacities for care, and a public space for reworking those capacities.

Mackintosh (2001: 185) goes further and endorses the use of a form of "claims" that I have previously advocated (Mooney 1998). She writes:

In unequal societies, some people's claims will be denied legitimacy, and some legitimated claims are likely to remain unfulfilled. Decision making responds to institutionalized understandings of priorities and principles and also on institutional experiences of active claiming. Hence the culture and operation of the health care system (as a whole, public and private) *is* the way in which claims are established, legitimated, and denied or fulfilled by "society".

She suggests that "the implication is that health care claims are relational; they are shaped by the norms and experiences governing patients; relations to providers" (Mackintosh 2001: 185).

This use of claims is, however, somewhat different from that advocated in the paradigm in Chapter 8. It misses the point about *society* setting the basis of claims and the strengths of claims. Mackintosh's conclusion, however, remains valid—that, to be achieved, this is dependent on the "culture and operation of the health care system".

It is of note that Mackintosh finishes her paper by looking at what appears to me to be very much a constitution for health care, although she does not call it that.

Some of the elements of Mackintosh's "constitution" are as follows (p. 187):

- accepting the relational nature of health care
- strengthening the capacity of the poor to make claims
- establish some principled universal commitments...as a basis for claims
- consider both medical treatments and also care and respect for patients, when formulating universal principles
- decide what inequalities to live with within the system and be open about them

Mackintosh suggests (p. 188): "Health care systems...help to create a more individualist or a more mutual society, they polarize or string links of solidarity across divides. Ethical and redistributive commitments in health care are both a set of principles and an institutional construction in the form of a set of working understandings."

While Mackintosh explores these ideas of "ethical and redistributive commitments" and rehearses the idea of claims, she does not tie these two elements together. This is best achieved, first, by recognising that claims of a communitarian kind are set by the community; they are not based on individuals' or sub-groups' claims for themselves. The communitarian claims are thus a way of getting beyond the polarization that can occur in any society, where claims are based on market power (primarily income and wealth), and that in turn implies accepting values based on willingness to pay, despite the fact that the valuation base will inevitably be affected by ability to pay. Mackintosh seems to leave open the question of where the "ethical and redistributive commitments" come from, whereas communitarian claims specifically identify that source as being the community or the society. That does not mean that these claims will necessarily be based in solidarity or that their exercise must lead to a more solidaristic society. The chances, however, of both must be enhanced.

As an example of pursuing the notion of community values driving health care, Mackintosh (p. 186) refers to the work of Londono and Frenk (1997) who point to the need for a health care package in Latin American health care systems which is "a social commitment based on citizenship principles" (p. 27), and argue that it should be "a key focus for social mobilisation and participation, promoted and encouraged by the public sector". Significantly Mackintosh adds: "Most health sector reform models ignore this analytical link between 'universal' commitments and the promotion of activism in claiming care". She argues that this link must draw on a "conceptualization of health systems in terms of the relationships between populations and institutions" (in Londono and Frenk 1997: 1).

In Navarro's discussion of these issues, he develops a "national health policy" (Navarro 2007: 1). In the language of this book this amounts to interpreting health policy (and with it the health care system and public health) as social institutions. He sets these out as three major components of a national health policy. They are as follows (Navarro 2007: 3): "the first includes interventions aimed at establishing, maintaining, and strengthening the political, economic, social and cultural *structural determinants of good health.*" Navarro argues that these are the most important elements in any public health policy, noting at the same time that, despite this, they are seldom mentioned in this context. He argues (p. 3) "countries with lower class, race, and gender inequalities in standards of living also have better levels of health for the whole population". This points to the need to embrace policies aimed at reducing inequalities in any national health policy. More fundamentally, it acknowledges that a national health policy as a social institution must address issues of power. It is not just a social institution, but also a political institution.

Navarro's second form of intervention is *"lifestyle determinants"*. These include "public policies aimed at individuals and focused on changes in individual behaviour and life style". He suggests that these are what are very often most visible in national health policy, perhaps because they are perceived by policy makers to be more manageable. They can also be interpreted as the responsibility of individuals rather than of public institutions "that are primarily responsible for the structural determinants". He adds (p. 4) that this is "one reason why conservative and liberal governments... tend to emphasize this second type of intervention over the first". Health policy is replete with examples of "blaming the victim" for his or her obesity, smoking, or diabetes. Too seldom are structural issues around the marketing strategies of those companies who, for example market fast foods, brought under scrutiny. (See for example Jan and Mooney 2006.)

The last type of intervention (p. 4) is what Navarro calls "*socializing and empowering determinants*" which "establish the relationship between the individual and the collective responsibilities for creating the conditions to ensure good health". These he suggests "would include the encouragement of individuals to become involved in collective efforts to improve the structural determinants of health, such as reducing the social inequalities in our societies or eliminating the conditions of oppression, discrimination, exploitation, or marginalisation that produce disease".

The underlying principles of these three forms of intervention can easily be revealed. The first is based on the principle of social support for the promotion and maintenance of good health; the second, on improved individual behaviour; and the third, on the principle of the promotion of solidarity. This clearly takes health policy well beyond the confines of the health care system and is more closely aligned with the health economics paradigm that is developing in this book.

9.5 Global health economics

The proposed strategy in this book involves moving away from the notion of *any* hegemonic economic system. The nature of a society is primarily determined by the economic means and ownership of production. In the best traditions of the social determinants of health and in the interests of protecting the diversity of cultures across the globe, cultures in which people can feel comfortable, flourish, and be healthy, there is a need to develop greater heterogeneity of economic systems.

Economic systems are ideological and cultural phenomena. They largely determine the nature of the society. If some "alien" economic system is imposed on a country, it then becomes difficult for that country to maintain and retain its culture. Protecting local cultures means protecting local economic systems. Thus diversity of cultures is best promoted by diversity of economic systems.

The maintenance of culture is an important social determinant of health. Without diversity in economic systems of the ownership and the means of production, cultural identity will struggle to survive locally or nationally. There is good evidence, again in Indigenous societies, that loss and destruction of cultures can lead to health problems.

Currently some community-based economic systems do exist. These need to be assessed to determine whether, with suitable cultural adjustment, they may provide lessons for other societies or communities where neo-liberalism has taken over. Some of these alternative models operate at the level of the nation state, such as in Cuba and the Scandinavian countries. Others are more local, such as the communitarianism of the Mondragon cooperative economy in the Basque region of Spain, which is based on mutuality and sharing (see: www.mondragon.mcc.es/ing/index.asp); the state of Kerala in India, which has a communist past and more egalitarian present; and the Grameen micro credit banking system in the Indian sub-continent, where credit is seen as a human right (Grameen 2004). It is significant that, for example, Cuba and Kerala have remarkably good population health despite their relative poverty. This appears to be a function of both their health care systems and the natures of their societies, in which many of the positive determinants of health, but especially relative income equality, are present and fostered politically.

Continuing this theme, Navarro (2000) shows that in the European Union it has been possible for some governments, primarily the Scandinavians, to "throw off" the ties of neo-liberal globalisation and follow their own chosen road. Nation states can still function well in the global economy without adopting neo-liberal policies. And the health of the Scandinavians within their so called "Scandinavian solidarity" is generally very good.

What is crucial, however, in Navarro's analysis is that, where this alternative road has been followed, there have been correspondingly strong social institutions that have provided the necessary framework to allow this. He indicates that among these institutions "a key element is the existence of a social pact between employers and unions and the government" and where a central part of that pact is a commitment to "full-employment and expansionist policies".

This theme was addressed by Drèze and Sen (1989) in their book on hunger. They argue that avoiding hunger requires analysis, not just of food intake but also the access that people have to such facilities as health care and clean water. While again it would be possible to see these purely in resource terms or to "commodify" them, the argument returns to the need to have or to create the social institutions to underpin these other aspects, and to allow such a philosophy to be the basis for public policy. Again, there is the emphasis from Drèze and Sen on social institutions.

What is potentially problematical with respect to this road to avoiding the neo-liberal excesses of globalisation is that many poor countries have weak social institutions. The strengthening of these forms a major part of the paradigm presented in this book. For the moment, however, the links between market economics, globalisation, increased poverty, and worsening distribution of income are such that the very *recognition* that there is a way out is important. Where there needs to be more attention is in the building of solid democratic institutions where, *inter alia*, strong unions are not only present but are accepted as key players in pacts with government and industry in deciding how the resources of a country are to be used.

At a global level, there needs to be a much greater recognition of a world community autonomy where the rich will allow the weaker nations of the world to have genuine autonomy in their own affairs. There is too little social compassion at an international level. In any ideological competition, a caring globalisation must put human freedom and development above economic market forces.

Thus the current goals of globalisation lead to resource allocation, income and power in individual countries being dominated by the laws of the neo-classical market place. This in turn is most likely to result in the continuing neglect of the standard of living of the world's poorest. The freedom that Sen (1999) recognises in his analysis of human rather than economic development is a way forward. The emphasis on building strong democratic institutions can mean that the benefits from globalisation can be both obtained and distributed fairly and across all, especially given an emphasis on vertical equity with positive, pro-poor policies. But this is not enough, as Navarro (2002) brings out in his critique of Sen. There is a need for a shift, in essence in power, to ensure more involvement of societies, citizens, and communities. Navarro (2000) shows that redistributional policies for income, employment, and services are the keys to improved health status for populations, especially for those most disadvantaged. This is more likely to happen with more democratic control over the means of production.

The opening up of trade on a fair basis rather than on a free basis can provide, not just positive economic growth, but also economic welfare. The major argument against totally free trade is that it leaves power in the hands of powerful markets and the powerful liaisons within markets. The weak, i.e. the poor, are then sidelined. Handled carefully, with due care being taken over distributional issues and with an emphasis on reducing unemployment, global forces can reduce poverty. The key would seem to lie, however, not in global forces *per se* but in ensuring that individual countries have the relevant social and political infrastructures and institutions to allow distributional issues to be addressed rather than being left to the vagaries of the market place. This requires a major shift in the organisation and philosophy of world trade and in turn a different form of governance than the WTO has exhibited to date.

There is a need to embrace what is perhaps best described as "community autonomy", where members of a community are able to combine, in some appropriate way and at a community level, their concept of freedom of choice *as a community*. Such autonomy can apply to a village community, a club, a professional body, a country, or even the world community. It is supported, as indicated earlier, by the Hegelian concept of freedom, where social institutions play a pivotal role. Such community autonomy stands juxtaposed to its individual, neo-liberal counterpart in today's market economy. Community autonomy assumes both a coalition of those willing to act and, just as importantly, a coalition of those unwilling to be acted upon.

Raffer and Singer (1996: 14) note:

There is...a need for a new relationship between the richer and the poorer countries...The richer countries feel like unwilling dispensers of favour imposing strict discipline as conditions for their favours...while the poorer countries feel they do not really own the policies imposed on them but they are beggars who cannot be choosers.

These authors suggest that the "right way forward is...by way of development contracts, genuine contracts in which both sides make clearly defined and voluntarily entered commitments, and remain in continuing consultation to adjust the contract in the light of unforeseen new circumstances. Conditionality must become a two-way business."

Raffer and Singer suggest (p. 248) that to have their proposals implemented requires an "independent panel of arbitrators". They see such a body as being "composed of independent experts selected by the UN General Assembly...It could dispose of funds raised by international taxation to finance measures against poverty." They make no mention, however, of a place for the voice of the public, neither do they give any indication of what values or principles their panel might adopt. They suggest that this body "could use indices such as the Human Development Index as the basis on which to judge" progress and how to allocate the resources at its disposal.

Such a proposal is be to lauded, but there is no indication given as to how it might come about. The idea of global communitarian claims would fill this void.

When global health is examined, what is immediately striking is the very large differences in health status between rich and poor countries. These echo differences within countries between rich and poor, but are still more marked. There is a need to ensure that consideration of the rich country versus poor country divide does not obscure the rich people versus poor people divide. While it is somewhat simplistic, when social determinants of health are considered internationally, poverty and inequality would seem to mask almost every other consideration. Indigenous peoples subject to colonialism might need to be included as a separate category. What is common is that, where people are lacking in power their health suffers.

This suggests that at an international, global level, issues of power again come to the fore and that compassion, this time across countries, is again a necessary ingredient of any policy that is to deal successfully with these major imbalances in power and income. This is Nussbaum's point when she argues (Nussbaum 2001: 403) that compassion can be a force when we reflect "about the duties of rich nations toward poor nations, in promoting both political and economic well-being".

The new paradigm provides a strong argument that whatever applies within nation states in principle in tackling the economics of health will apply (inevitably with some adjustments) at an international, global level. The problems of individualism that plague both health economics and the social determinants of health in individual states are at least as prevalent when the focus moves to the international stage with, at that level, the increasing hegemony of neo-liberalism, as promoted currently by our global institutions.

The paradigm at this level remains the same. There is still a need for a community-based value system for health and health care. Now the community is the global one and the impediments are not only the individualism that permeates decision making at that level in the form of neo-liberalism, but the "social institutions" globally such as the IMF and the World Bank. As identified in Chapter 5, these fail to reflect the wants and demands of people. The membership of these organisations is made up of nation states and governments not representatives of "the people".

To pursue the paradigm shift in health economics at this level needs an abandonment of the dominance of the governments of the G7 and G8 in international affairs; an attempt to reflect better the values of the world citizenry; and an agreed basis for redistributing health care and health promoting resources on some agreed equitable basis. While there can be some trade-offs between equity and efficiency in individual nation states' handling of health, at the global level it is much more likely that efficiency and equity will move together rather than in competition.

What is needed is the proposed paradigm shift at national levels to be applied at the global level, with respect to, first, public health and, second, health care systems. That will mean major changes to "social institutions" at that global level. While these remain driven by national governments and more specifically the national governments of relatively few powerful nations, whose institutions in turn are directed by the laws of the market place and the ideology of neo-liberalism, the prospects for making inroads into the health divide between North and South remain remote.

With respect to health care systems, currently the North are beneficiaries of the neo-liberal freeing up of the movement of labour and attract many health care professionals from the poor South, thereby depleting the latter's health services yet further. Mackintosh (2007: 166) argues for what she calls "restitution". To achieve that, however, there needs to be a concern for social justice, the compassion to consider the very idea of restitution, and the political will to implement it.

These movements are a direct result of the lack of compassion in the North and the lack of market power in the South under economic systems governed by neo-liberalism. The adoption of the paradigm of communitarian claims as described in Chapter 8 can go some way to resolve these difficulties.

The other part of the paradigm that is important is the need to build a communitarian constitution for global health care and global public health. Can this be done? It is already partly done through the People's Health Movement (PHM) and the People's Health Assembly (PHA), which is the global meeting of the PHM. This PHM "is a global coalition of grassroots and health activist organisations dedicated to addressing the burden of preventable disease globally but in particular that carried by developing countries". The goal of the PHM is to re-establish health and equitable development as top priorities in local, national, and international policy making, with comprehensive primary health care as a key strategy to achieve these priorities.

The purposes and orientation of the PHM are spelled out clearly in the People's Charter for Health (see: http://phmovement.org/charter/). "We aim to entrench the right to health as a basic human right ... to tackle the broader determinants of health (globalisation, environmental degradation, violence and war). We see a people-centred health sector with strong popular participation as keys to these goals."

The first six of a total of 24 statements from the Cuenca Agreement of the PHA (see: http://phmovement.org/pha2/papers/cuencadec3.php) read as follows:

1. Health still stands high on the international development agenda and calls for a major push ahead—now!
2. The roots of most health inequities are unchanged: they are social and political.
3. Socially-conditioned health inequalities continue to be an important political issue.
4. The social determinants of health are still not being incorporated into planning in too many countries in the world.
5. The choice of vocabulary these days more and more calls for the use of "social justice" and "right to health" as opposed to "efficiency and cost-effectiveness".
6. Health care interventions targeted at disadvantaged groups still only seek to repair the damage inflicted by social inequity.

The above can be seen as the beginnings of a world constitution on health. There are also various declarations on human rights which could be used to build health and health care constitutions. One example is Article 25 of the Universal Declaration of Human Rights (see: www.unhchr.ch/udhr/lang/eng.htm):

Everyone has the right to a standard of living adequate for the health and well-being of himself and of his family, including food, clothing, housing and medical care and necessary social services, and the right to security in the event of unemployment, sickness, disability, widowhood, old age or other lack of livelihood in circumstances beyond his control.

Other considerations that might be addressed in any constitutions might include the following.

- A recognition that neo-liberalism and the hegemony of neo-liberalism work against the positives in the social determinants of health and lead to increased inequality in societies, loss of social cohesion and social capital, and thereby lower population health.
- A need to oppose the current world situation in which global institutions, such as the World Bank and the WTO, are dominated by Western neo-liberal governments, whose goal is to further the economic national interest of their countries and to promote neo-liberalism in those countries who have not yet embraced it.
- A belief that globally we need new "social" institutions where the voice of world citizenry can be heard and where the power vested in these social institutions reflects that voice.

- The key consideration, however, is that any such constitutions are based on the values of the people, in this case the global community.

Mishra (1999: 118) puts the case for the community collectively to determine the social standards in various fields, but including health. He argues that "membership in a national community which entails reciprocity, interdependence and solidarity presupposes basic rather than minimum standards", suggesting that "it is the role of the polity to guarantee or uphold these basic social standards".

As highlighted in Chapter 5, global public goods for health (Kaul et al. 1999) are not the answer in seeking to address the health problems of the world's poor. The way forward is to build a caring world and, especially, caring governments and caring institutions. This point is made by Sen (2001). He argues that while economic progress can yield health benefits to a population, "much depends on how the income generated by economic growth is used" (p. 343) and even in poor economies "major health improvements can be achieved through using the available resources in a socially productive way" (p. 343). Sen's message is, as ever, optimistic but what it does require is that governments be good, caring, and compassionate, believing that they can be a force in building a better society for the poor and not just facilitators for market forces to hold sway, or mediators for the worst excesses of modern capitalism.

The solution does not lie in allowing the markets to guide the resolution of these issues. Neither does it rest in hoping that GPGH might come to the rescue. Indeed these two—the power of neo-liberalism in world markets at present and the potential futility of GPGH—are linked.

The point is well made by Collard (1978) and can be extended beyond the individual society to which he was referring, to the world society:

a society of egotists would not be prepared to support an "altruistic" social policy. To claim otherwise would be an odd position to take. It would imply that a group of benevolently inclined policy makers was able to hood-wink a community of egotistical voters into accepting altruistic social polices. It has the further implication of comfort to the elite perhaps, that the voters are generally selfish but stupid while their rulers are altruistic and wise. I find this implausible. If a society is truly selfish it can surely be manipulated into adopting non-selfish policies only for short periods: after that it will throw out those rulers who have hood-winked it.

What Collard thus argues is that we need our rulers to encourage us to see the merits of altruism; not just the merits for the poor but for the rich as well.

The notion of a constitution for health, as discussed earlier, would be a base on which to build. That certainly would be novel at a global level. The "community" at the centre of the constitution would be the global community. There would be a value to and in the community *per se*, and a value in being a part of—being embodied in—the community.

9.6 Conclusion

There is a need for a genuine community autonomy, which is the basis for social solidarity and in turn healthy societies. The hopes for that have become tarnished by the spread of market values beyond the market place into so many aspects of our societies. Neo-classical *homo economicus* is not concerned for the community or for compassion.

Instead there is a need for health economists to elicit the preferences of the poor and the dispossessed. Stigler (1971: 132), for example, writes:

Conflicts over fundamental values are at the center of democratic debate. Critics of globalization charge that globalization has been managed in such a way as to take some of the most important issues out of the realm of public discourse within individual countries and into closed international forums, which are far from democratic in the usual sense of the term. With the voices of corporate interests heard so clearly and strongly, and without the checks and balances of democratic processes, it's not surprising that the outcomes seem so objectionable, so distant from what would have emerged had there been a more democratic process. The most daunting challenge in reforming globalization is to make it more democratic; a test of success will be in how well it succeeds in ensuring that these broader values triumph more often over simple corporate interests.

There is a need to accept that the building of community and social cohesion will not just happen, but needs to be fostered. There is a need for compassionate leadership. That is not the responsibility of health economists but we can do more to analyse what a more compassionate world would mean for the health of the planet. Social cohesion is something that health economists can analyse, as Di McIntyre (2007: 194) has done. In looking to determine how health care in Africa might be better delivered, she points to examples "of low-income and middle income countries in other parts of the world that have achieved excellent levels of health status despite constrained economic resources". Her analyses show:

Key elements of their success have been universal coverage of the population with either mandatory health insurance of general tax funded services, where the entire population is entitled to the same service benefits and use the same provider, which are either owned by government or the social security organization.... These systems have both equitable financing incidence, where higher-income groups contribute considerably more of their income to health care funding than lower-income groups, and equitable benefit incidence, where service use is closely linked with need for, or capacity to benefit from, health care.

McIntyre does not analyse compassion, but she does show what the impact of compassion might be through the creation of a more cohesive society where the whole society gets the same health care benefits from the same groups of providers, and where the better off subsidise the worse off. Her target in her analysis is Africa; it might easily, however, be applied to the whole planet.

Addressing the issue of compassionate leadership more directly Martha Nussbaum (1990: 101) writes of the risk that we have "impoverished models of humanity before our leaders' eyes—numbers and dots, taking the place of women and men". She continues: "when one's deliberation fails to endow human beings with their full and complex humanity, it becomes very much easier to contemplate doing terrible things toward them. We want leaders whose hearts and imagination acknowledge the humanity in human beings."

What is missing currently in many deliberations around world poverty and world health is the acceptance of the notion of a global community, where health services and global public health are based on the values of the global citizenry, and, importantly, who are encouraged to see themselves as world citizens and not just, for example, Canadians, Danes, or Egyptians. (This is the basis for a global communitarianism as set out in Chapter 7 and the global communitarian claims of Chapter 8.) There is here the recognition of the need for there to be a more genuinely "world" citizenry voice rather than, as currently, simply national governments who promote the interests of their constituents, i.e. their countries.

Health economists cannot resolve these problems. We can, however, refocus our efforts regarding some of these wider global issues. Building on Anderson's expressive theory can allow health economists to break out of the confines welfarism and extra-welfarism have imposed on us. There is thus a need for us to broaden our focus and revisit the theoretical underpinnings of our discipline.

A9.1 Appendix: Eliciting principles and claims

A9.1.1 *Introduction*

The question of how best to establish community principles and communitarian claims remains to be determined. As it happens, in recent years there has been increasing interest in involving communities in decision making in health and health care through various forms of "deliberative democracy" (Davies et al. 2006). These usually involve a selection of people, a community, or a group of citizens who are asked about certain issues.

I have experimented with citizens' juries (Mooney and Blackwell 2004) as one form of deliberative democracy that might serve as a vehicle for the purposes of setting principles and establishing communitarian claims. These bring a random selection of citizens together, give them good information and a chance to quiz experts, and thereafter allow them to discuss and reflect on certain questions, against a background of resource constraints.

The examples below are presented to indicate more the sort of results that have emerged, rather than to suggest that this is necessarily the best way to tackle these issues.

It is also important at a broader level not to lose sight of the issue that has been raised at times in this book about citizen engagement in social institutions and building such social institutions—the idea of fostering democracy and democratic governance. While this can be restricted to being instrumental, the idea that this might be seen as a valued benefit of the process is acknowledged by some writers (see for example Kashefi and Mort 2004) who argue for this as an outcome, consequence, or benefit in its own right. Kashefi and Mort warn against some of the problems of settling for instrumentality. "Incidental" consultations are deeply mistrusted and can be seen as "social control disguised as democratic emancipation" or "simply...ways of deflecting criticisms of mainstream (un) democratic practice". These same authors express concern at "the heavy reliance by health and social care agencies on the extractive, incidental outputs of the consultation industry" (Glasner 2001: 44). Certainly, there are risks associated with public consultation. It can result in a cynical response in attempting to build democratic governance, and this author has experienced such cynicism in facilitating citizens' juries, albeit from a small minority of jurists. Most of these groups enthusiastically endorse the process and express positive feelings (even delight!) at being involved, some very readily arguing that such deliberative processes ought to be extended to other areas of social life. Beyond the anecdotal, however, research is needed to show that citizens do value their health care system and public health as social institutions. This in a sense is self-evident, but it does need to be supported with good quantified evidence regarding the nature and extent of this value.

Citizens' juries have their genesis in the UK (see for example Davies et al. 2006), but more recently the author has been involved in facilitating six of these in Australia (see for example Mooney and Blackwell 2004). This first hand experience has been partly responsible for my being persuaded, not only that communitarian claims are in principle the way to provide the constitutions for health care and public health, but that citizens are well able to provide these values. Certainly, there is much work to be done in determining just how best to establish communitarian claims and their weightings, but the early soundings—essentially pilot studies—suggest that such an approach can be made practical.

What is sought is to establish which values drive citizens' wants from these social institutions. There are thus three key objectives. First, there is the desire to establish which factors citizens want to be taken into account when scarce resources for health care and public health are being allocated. These might be simply and only health or health need. They might be more concerned about addressing problems thereby focusing on health needs, such as sickness, rather than about looking to see what difference the resources might make, i.e. their capacity to benefit. They may seek resources for particular issues, conditions, or disease—for those suffering from mental illness, for example.

Second, there are issues around equity where the citizens seek to determine what they mean by equity, for example whether to opt for equal access for equal need, equal health and horizontal or vertical equity. Weights also need to be attached to different characteristics, such as for vertical equity for benefits to, say, poor people. They have to decide which people merit having above average weights and why. Is this solely about disadvantage, and who in their view would be identified as being disadvantaged—the poor, the elderly, Aboriginal people, those who are mentally ill?—the definition of who they considered to be vulnerable would be for the citizens to decide. They would need to decide which groups in this context were most disadvantaged and if this identification would lead to yet greater weights to be attached to any benefits to them?

Third, there may be considerations around organisational issues, such as the existing balance in resource use between, say, prevention and cure; between the community and hospitals; and between curative and palliative care. There may also be other organisational issues that would merit additional funding, such as seeking to ensure efficiency and transparency in decision making; providing adequate information to the public on what services are available and when; and ensuring there are safeguards in place to promote quality of care.

To propose that the community get more involved in health service decision making is not new. The WHO (1954), more than half a century ago, proposed a move to have citizens' values drive health service decision making. That idea has been around since then (see for example the World Federation of Public Health Associations in 1984—Vuori 1984: and more recently the Romanow Commission in Canada—Romanow 2002).

A9.1.2 *Two examples of eliciting principles and claims*

A9.1.2.1 A CITIZENS' JURY'S PRINCIPLES

A group of citizens was randomly selected from the electoral roll from the health service area concerned, the South West Area Health Service (SWAHS) in Western Australia. Of these initially 30 people expressed interest in being on the jury. These were then whittled down to 13, in trying to ensure a good mix of age, gender, and geographical location. The purpose of the jury was to allow the SWAHS to tap into the community's preferences for the set of principles they wanted to underpin SWAHS' decision making.

The jury were asked to consider themselves from the standpoint of being citizens of the South West—rather than from any specific town in the area and without bringing their own personal issues with them. They were told that what they came up with would be used as the values foundations on which SWAHS would plan in future.

They were then presented with information by "experts" (senior health service staff) on the health of the people in the area and relevant demographics; the services currently available; the resources available and their current deployment; safety and quality issues; and the organisational and other constraints that the health service faced. They were also given the opportunity to quiz the experts who presented the information.

Thereafter they were given time to reflect and discuss as a group what principles and values they wanted to underpin the decision making of SWAHS. Finally they came up with a list of the following set of principles.

THE PRINCIPLES

Fairness

The principle on which the citizens placed most weight was fairness (equity). They defined this as equal access for equal need, where equal access involved equal opportunity to use health services. The barriers to using health services were many, including financial cost, distance, racism, etc. Equal access was where people perceived the barriers they faced to be equally high; need was taken to be capacity to benefit (i.e. how much good can be done?) and disadvantaged people were to be weighted more highly (e.g. higher weighted health gains for Aboriginal people).

In general, they had a particular concern for the most disadvantaged, especially the health of Aboriginal people.

At the same time the jury acknowledged the "trade off" or competition between equity and efficiency.

Efficiency

Efficiency was seen by the jury in two ways: first, in terms of doing things as well but more cheaply, or doing more with the same resources; and, second, it was about doing as much good as possible (benefit maximisation) with the resources available.

The citizens were of a view that the second type of efficiency needed greater emphasis, i.e. there should be more consideration given to priority setting across different programmes. For example should the health service spend more on maternity care even if that meant less on care to the elderly?

With one notable exception, they were not inclined to argue for higher priorities/increased spending for certain specific areas. They did want to ensure that such priority setting was done explicitly. The exception was in services for the mentally ill.

Where they wanted to make savings, if these had to be made, was through hospital rationalisation. They believed that the existing deployment of resources to and in hospitals and emergency departments was inefficient and asked that SWAHS examine ways to rationalise these. They suggested, for example, that some of the hospital buildings might be converted into aged care facilities or to provide services for the mentally ill.

Trust with respect to safety

A third set of principles related to quality, safety, and risk management. In this context their strategy was one of trust. They trusted SWAHS to "take care of" these issues on behalf of the community.

Prevention

The next principle was prevention. They wanted a higher priority given to prevention but were concerned with the "value added". By this they meant that, where other organisations (e.g. the Cancer Council, Heart Foundation) were already involved in prevention, SWAHS should avoid duplication and concentrate on the kinds of prevention that would not otherwise be pursued.

In discussing health promotion within the context of prevention they saw the objective as being about promoting informed choices about health issues.

Self-sufficiency

The area was such that some patients went to Perth, the capital city of WA and two to three hours' drive away. On the principle of whether SWAHS should aim for greater self-sufficiency in treating patients, the jury had no strong views but felt that total self-sufficiency did not make sense. The extent of self-sufficiency must and should vary according to the condition.

Holistic care

The jury expressed concerns about "body parts" medicine and saw an increasing role for holistic health.

Transparency and accountability

The citizens supported transparency in decision making in SWAHS as demonstrated in the holding of the citizens' jury.

Community values

Finally, they endorsed the principle of the community establishing the principles and values on which SWAHS should base its decision making.

A9.1.2.2 A CITIZENS' JURY'S CLAIMS

A citizens' jury was held for the Perth Primary Care Network (PPCN), which is a "Division of General Practice", i.e. a geographically based primary care network that is primarily GP focused and that can influence GPs in how they practice. The jury consisted of 17 members: 14 drawn randomly from the relevant electoral registers; two were selected Aboriginal people; and one was a selected youth. The jury were addressed by experts and had the opportunity to question them on any issue they wished.

This jury was asked to consider claims on resources and to set the principles on which they wanted the PPCN to operate. It was put to the jury that, in thinking about factors that they might take into account in deciding how to allocate any additional monies which might be available to the PPCN, the idea of such factors might usefully be seen as the bases of "claims" on resources. The question to them was, then: what characteristic of a group of people might justify them receiving more than average resources? Thus someone having blue eyes was unlikely to affect the weighting of that person's claims on the network's resources—but their poor health might.

A full list of the initial bases of claims (in no particular order) is as follows:

- Poor health
- Having had a raw deal
- Being poor
- Living in rural areas
- Being elderly
- Being a child
- Aboriginality
- Being overweight/obese
- Being part of vulnerable/marginalised groups
- Having poor access
- Ability to give feedback to the community
- Being unemployed
- Being mentally ill
- Having a chronic disease
- Prevention/health promotion

There are thus many bases for claims. The key ones were:

- Poor health
- Being marginalised/vulnerable, especially noted were Aboriginal people and mentally ill people
- Having poor access for a range of reasons, but especially through issues of poverty and geographical, i.e. living in a rural area

The issues marked as worthy of high claims on resources can be summarised largely as disadvantage, with poverty, Aboriginality, and mental illness being the factors where the PPCN might best devote its energies and resources.

With respect to *strengths* of claims, poverty emerged as the strongest claim, ahead of both poor health and Aboriginality. The aggregation of claims was not possible but the strength of claims of the poor, being Aboriginal, and being in poor health would clearly be high.

Strengths of claims were also elicited. For poor people (average household income of A$30,000 per annum) compared to the rich (average $100,000 per annum) the weight was over 4. For poor health (life expectancy of 60 years) versus better health (life expectancy of 80 years) the ratio was 2:1. For Aboriginal versus non-Aboriginal, the ratio was just under 2:1. Additional "strengths of claims" established were: 2:1 for children to adults; 1.5:1 elderly to non-elderly adults; and 1:1 for men to women.

For this jury the set of principles included:

Accessibility

This was an important principle on two fronts—availability of GPs by time of day and day of week.

Equity

This was also a major principle and was seen as best described as equal access regardless of ability to pay, defined broadly.

Universality

While universality (of access) might have been included under equity, the jury saw it as sufficiently important to list as a separate principle.

Quality of service

The principle of high quality was readily agreed. Components included more holistic care, but linked to the idea of a duty of care on the part of the doctor to the patient as a whole; GPs running on time; better referral systems, especially for mental illness; and improved doctor–patient relationship, with greater transparency on a number of fronts, particularly (a) influence of pharmaceutical companies on GPs' practice; and (b) greater shared decision making in general but also, for example, on choice of specialist that patient is referred to. The jury also established a principle of greater sensitivity and responsiveness to patients' wishes by GPs.

Emphasis on lifestyle

The principle of emphasis on lifestyle was very real but was tempered by a recognition that the network's budget was small and GPs in general could not be expected to do everything. Therefore these issues might be better addressed elsewhere in the health system. This was a conclusion reached with some reluctance and represented a change of heart along the way.

Value for money/efficiency

The principle of value for money was endorsed for the PPCN.

Transparency of and accountability in decision making

These two related principles focused on transparency and accountability with respect to the patient–doctor encounter. They were discussed against a background of a concern regarding the extent to which the patient could always trust the doctor to do what was in the patient's best interests, these interests being defined or, as a minimum, agreed upon by the patient. Examples of lack of trust were raised in the context of the pressures doctors face from pharmaceutical companies and the lack of transparency where a GP chooses to refer a patient to a particular specialist without adequate explanation as to whether and why that specialist is the best for that patient.

Greater sensitivity on the part of GPs

Again this related to the behaviour of doctors towards their patients and the need for the doctors to be more ready to recognise the inequality in the relationship between doctor and patient. In doing so the doctor needed to acknowledge better the sensitive nature of the encounter, and involve the patient more in the decision making process by providing adequate information and respecting patients' desires for autonomy. The Jury wanted to see the PPCN take positive steps to make doctors more aware of the need for such sensitivity, and provide guidance or training as to how the GPs might do better on this front.

References

Anderson, E. (1993) *Value in Ethics and Economics*. Cambridge, MA: Harvard University Press.

Arrow, K. (1963) Uncertainty and the welfare economics of medical care, *American Economic Review*, 53: 941–73.

Avineri, S. (1972) *Hegel's Theory of the Modern State*. Cambridge: Cambridge University Press.

Bergson, A. (1954) On the concept of social welfare, *Quarterly Journal of Economics*, 68: 233–52.

Buchanan, J. and Vanberg, V. (1994) Constitutional choice, rational ignorance and limits of reason, in V. Vanberg (ed.), *Rules and Choice in Economics*. London: Routledge.

Blaauw, D., Gilson, L., Penn-Kanana, L. and Schneider, H. (2003) *Organisational Relationships and the "Software" of Health Systems Reform*. Johannesburg: Centre for Health Policy, University of Witwatersrand.

Collard, D. (1978) *Altruism and Economy*. New York: Oxford University Press.

Davies, C., Wetherell, M. and Barnett, E. (2006) *Citizens at the Centre*. Bristol: Policy Press.

Drèze, J. and Sen, A. (1989) *Hunger and Public Action*. Oxford: Oxford University Press.

Freedman, L. (2005) Achieving the MDGs: health systems as core social institutions. Available at: http://ipsnews.net/indepth/MDGGoal5/MDG5%20Freedman.pdf (accessed 16 Dec. 2007).

Gilson, L. (2003) Trust and the development of health care as a social institution, *Social Science and Medicine*, 56: 1453–68.

Glasner, P. (2001) Rights or rituals? Why juries can do more harm than good. Participatory Learning and Action Notes No. 40. London: IIED.

Grameen (2004) *Grameen Banking for the Poor*. Available at: www.grameen-info.org (accessed 27 Jun. 2007).

Jan, S. (2002) Institutionalist perspectives on the economics of health and health care. Unpublished PhD thesis, Sydney University, Sydney.

—— (2003) A perspective on the analysis of credible commitment and myopia in health sector decision making, *Health Policy* 63(3): 269–78.

—— Mooney, G. (2006) Childhood obesity, values and the market, *International Journal of Pediatric Obesity*, 1(3): 131–2.

Kashefi, E. and Mort, M. (2004) Grounded citizens' juries, *Health Expectations*, 7: 1–13.

Kaul, I., Grunberg, I. and Stern, M. A. (1999) Defining global public goods, in I. Kaul, I. Grunberg and M. A. Stern (eds.), *Global Public Goods: International Cooperation in the 21st Century*. New York: Oxford University Press.

Londono, J.-L. and Frenk, J. (1997) Structured pluralism: towards an innovative model for health system reform in Latin America, *Health Policy*, 41: 1–36.

Mackintosh, M. (2001) Do health care systems contribute to inequalities?, in D. Leon and G. Walt (eds.), *Poverty Inequality and Health*. Oxford: Oxford University Press.

——(2007) International migration and extreme health inequality: robust arguments and institutions for international redistribution in health care, in D. McIntyre and G. Mooney (eds.), *The Economics of Health Equity*. Cambridge: Cambridge University Press.

McIntyre, D. (2007) Pay the piper and call the tune: changing health care financing mechanisms to address public–private health service mix inequities, in D. McIntyre and G. Mooney (eds.), *The Economics of Health Equity*. Cambridge: Cambridge University Press.

Mishra R. (1999) *Globalization and the Welfare State*. Cheltenham: Edward Elgar.

Mondragon (2004) A better way to go to work? Available at: www.justpeace.org/mondragon.htm (accessed 20 Dec. 2007).

Mooney, G. (1998) Communitarian claims as an ethical basis for allocating health care resources, *Social Science and Medicine*, 47(9): 1171–80.

——(200) Communitarian claims and community capabilities: furthering priority setting? *Social Science and Medicine*, 60(20): 247–55.

——Blackwell, S. (2004) Whose health service is it anyway? *Medical Journal of Australia*, 180: 76–8.

Muller, J. Z. (2003) *The Mind and the Market: Capitalism in Western Thought*. New York: Anchor Books.

Navarro, V. (2000) Are pro-welfare state and full-employment policies possible in the era of globalization? *International Journal of Health Services*, 30(2): 231–51.

——(2002) Development and quality of life: a critique of Amartya Sen's Development as Freedom, in V. Navarro (ed.), *The Political Economy of Social Inequalities*. New York: Baywood.

——(2007) What is a national health policy? *International Journal of Health Services*, 37(1): 1–14.

Nussbaum, M. (1990) *Love's Knowledge*. Oxford: Oxford University Press.

——(2001) *Upheavals of Thought*. Cambridge: Cambridge University Press.

Raffer, K. and Singer, H. (1996) *The Foreign Aid Business: Economic Assistance and Development*. Cheltenham: Edward Elgar.

Romanow, R. J. (2002) *Building on Values: The Future of Healthcare in Canada*. Available at: www.hc-sc.gc.ca/english/care/romanow/hcc0086.html (accessed 22 Dec. 2007).

Scott, W. R. (1995) *Institutions and Organizations*. Thousand Oaks: Sage.

Sen, A. (1999) *Development as Freedom*. Oxford: Oxford University Press.

——(2001) Economic progress in health, in D. Leon and G. Walt (eds.), *Poverty Inequality and Health: An International Perspective*. Oxford: Oxford Medical Publications.

Stigler, G. J. (1971). The theory of economic regulation, *Bell Journal of Economics and Management Science*, 2(1): 3–21.

Vanberg, V. (1994) *Rules and Choice in Economics*. London: Routledge.

Vuori, H. (1984) Overview—community participation in primary healthcare: a means or end? IV. International Congress of the World Federation of Public Health Associations, *Public Health Review*, 12: 331–9.

WHO (World Health Organization) (1954) *Report of the Expert Committee on the Health Education of the Public*, Technical Report Series No. 89. Geneva: WHO.

10

Priority Setting Under the New Paradigm

10.1 Introduction

Two areas where the new paradigm might be applied to advantage are set out in this chapter and the next: priority setting and equity. The new paradigm has the advantage of being based on community values, with the question of the principles or constitution that is to underpin any setting of priorities to be established by the community served. It is built on Anderson's expressive theory which as Chapter 6 highlighted is much less restrictive in what it can contain than the consequentialism of either welfarism or extra-welfarism, and it uses the idea of communitarian claims to allow the community to decide on priorities for, in this case, health care resources. Being based on community values, the problems associated with the lack of credible commitment (Jan 2003a) are better handled than using conventional priority setting, such credibility arising where the "incentive to keep to the commitment is just as strong at the time it is due to be carried out as it was when originally made" (Jan 2003a: 271). That should help to overcome some of the failures there have been in the past in the results from priority setting exercises not being implemented.

The new paradigm has the merit of being able to reflect Sen's concept of capabilities but, importantly, extending these from the listing of individual capabilities, which Nussbuam provides, to a community level.

This provides a more acceptable value base for both public and policy makers, it alters the distribution of property rights and increases the probability that recommendations from priority setting exercises such as with programme budgeting and marginal analysis (PBMA) will be implemented.

This chapter draws on Mooney (2005).*

10.2 Some problems with PBMA

Jan (2000) has exposed a number of problems in getting acceptance of economic analysis in health care and in particular of priority setting. He identifies as a major issue the lack of "credible commitment" (Jan 2003a), specifically in the application of PBMA. He states (p. 272):

when individual managers have reason to doubt the veracity of submissions provided by other managers, the potential exists for such exercises to break down. In this institutional environment, each program manager is unable to commit credibly to providing an accurate evaluation. This situation results from the conflict between individual objectives of each manager to maximise his/her budget and the expectation that each manager will promote broader organisational objectives by providing, in good faith, information that might then be used to cut his/her budget.

Elsewhere Jan (2003b: 20) suggests: "The challenge, in practice . . . lies in altering the setting to one that is more conducive to implementation." The difficulty with this is that "in many instances there is no reason why public sector managers and decision makers have an interest in organisational efficiency".

One way of overcoming these problems is to bring in the community who do have an interest in organisational efficiency and who are potentially present for the long term. They have an interest in the efficiency not only of the organisation (for which they are likely to be paying through taxes or insurance premiums) but also of the way in which resources then get allocated. They can also, should they see fit to endorse the principle, be the judge of what form of equity they wish to see pursued, and what relative weight they wish attached to it vis-à-vis efficiency. They can thus set the principles or constitution, as discussed in Chapter 9. This separates the question of the setting of values/principles from the roles of decision makers within the service, thereby reducing for these decision makers the barriers to committing credibly to both the goals of the service and the process of priority setting. The community are, from Chapter 3, section 3.5, Robinson's functionaries.

---

* Reprinted from *Social Science & Medicine*, 60(2), Mooney, G., Communitarian claims and community capabilities: further priority setting?, pp. 247–55, ©2005, with kind permission of Elsevier.

Thus bringing in the community and their values gives these actors influence over decision making that will decrease the problems of lack of credible commitment, and in turn strengthen the desire to promote efficiency and equity as health service principles for priority setting. To the extent that the community is one that is cohesive, seeks to build social solidarity, values its social institutions, and in turn values the community as a community—in essence is communitarian as set out in Chapter 7 (Avineri and de-Shalit, 1992)—so the prospects for such strengthening of the principles and priorities of health services are yet further enhanced.

There are potentially different perspectives from which preferences can be elicited in health care. Three of these—personal, social, and socially inclusive personal—have been highlighted previously in the health economics literature (Dolan et al. 2003). These authors, however, did not examine the communitarian perspective. The closest they come to this is their third perspective, which involves an individual being asked "to consider her own self-interests as well as the interests of others" (p. 547). Crucial in the context of the new paradigm is that the individual is asked *qua individual*. The community *qua community* is not asked. Further, the questions these authors seek to pose relate only to the value of treatment. No attempt is made to look at the value attached to either the decision making process that surrounds treatment or the social institution that is the health service. The communitarian approach would, first, ask the community *qua* community; second, it would ask about the value of the decision making processes and of the institution *per se*; third, it would ask about the principles with which the community want to underpin their health service; and, fourth, it would ask these questions while suggesting that respondents be guided by what they see as "communitarian claims". The source of value and the scope of valuing with this new paradigm are quite different from those adopted in conventional priority setting exercises by health economists.

The emphasis too is on setting priorities according to the informed and ideally reflective preferences of the community. Here the question of how best to do this is not gone into in any detail, although the example of citizens' juries in the previous chapter is one way of doing so. It is worthy of note, however, that in a citizens' jury that I facilitated (see Chapter 9 subsection A9.1.2.1) not only were a group of randomly selected citizens, who had been given good information, well able to reach a consensus about priorities, but they did so in a logical and well reasoned way. They chose, for example, to improve equity, especially for Aboriginal people; they gave high priority to services for people who were mentally ill; and they wanted more resources to go to prevention of illness and public health, but only to those areas within that broad category that were not being served well by other agencies. They readily agreed that to pay for these increases they would forego acute and emergency services in some small hospitals.

In another citizens' jury the members gave high priority to a primary health care service that would provide information about access to services. It may be that this was driven by some desire to improve outcomes, but it may also be that allowing such non-consequentialist considerations to be eligible as "claims" would allow the community to include values that might otherwise be missed.

10.3 Communitarianism and priority setting

This section seeks to address the issue that represents a major criticism of welfarism (but less so of extra-welfarism), i.e. the separation of desires from values. It is suggested that this is best done on the basis of communitarianism and communitarian claims, as outlined in earlier chapters. It is worth quoting Sen at length on his distinction between welfarism and what he advocates (Sen 1985: 22):

The limitations of the utility-based approach to well-being and advantage are particularly serious when we are concerned with interpersonal ranking rather than with comparisons of alternative possibilities for the same person. It is not implausible to think that if a person desires life A over life B and is happier with A than with B, then the well-being of the person is greater with A than with B. On the other hand, consider the person (call him 1) who has learned not to have overambitious desires and who is easily pleased. Take a case in which he is much more deprived in terms of food, clothing, shelter, medical attention, etc., than person 2 (raised in more buoyant circumstances), and is nevertheless happier than 2 and has more desires fulfilled. It is not at all obvious that 1 must be seen as having a higher level of well-being than 2, though both the perspectives of happiness and desire-fulfilment will recommend that ranking.

Sen argues that, what he calls the utility tradition, and it is also true of welfarism, suffers from two problems: that of "physical-condition neglect" and that of "valuation neglect". A person who suffers from physical condition neglect (for example he or she is disabled) "can still be high up in the scale of happiness or desire-fulfilment if he or she has learned to have 'realistic' desires and to take pleasure in small mercies" (Sen 1985: 23). Thus a person confined to a wheelchair may value his or her health state more highly than those in society generally. Any intervention that results in the person having perfect health will then be valued less highly by that individual than the rest of society generally. In other words, living with the disability may have blunted the person's ability to "manage to desire".

Further Sen (1992: 149) claims, with respect to his second point (i.e. valuation neglect): "Valuing is not the same thing as desiring, and the strength of desire is influenced by considerations of realism in one's circumstances." He emphasises this point when he adds: "Considerations of 'feasibility' and of 'practical possibility' enter into what we dare to desire and what we are pained not to get." He further argues (p. 149) that "an overdependence on what people 'manage to desire' is one of the limiting aspects of utilitarian ethics, which is particularly neglectful of the claims of those who are too subdued or broken to have the courage to desire much".

Thus Sen's main criticism of welfarism stems from his separation of desires and values, and his concern that some people are unable to desire adequately. The question that then needs to be addressed is, if analysts cannot rely on what individuals manage to desire, what values are to be adopted.

This is central to the question of priority setting in health care. If some individuals do not manage to desire good health or at least not adequately, then one option is to respect the position they have taken. Another is somehow to "compensate" for the "inadequate" values that emerge from such individuals.

The standard response of economics to this issue is to argue for externalities or merit goods. Other individuals, on the basis of caring, might be prepared to contribute to improving the health of the individual who does not manage to desire a higher or "adequate" level of health. This might, for example, lead to such individuals having their health care consumption subsidised by others, thereby *ceteris paribus* increasing those individuals' levels of consumption. Another would be if the individual recognised his or her deficiencies with respect to "managing to desire" and indicated that he or she would be prepared to forego consumer sovereignty and let others influence or even determine his or her health care consumption. This can happen anyway within the context of the doctor acting as an agent for a patient. The conventional explanation for this behaviour in the health economics literature lies, however, in the ill informed patient giving way to the judgement of the better informed doctor. The explanation for the existence of agency tends not to rest in any deficiency on the part of the patient in "managing to desire".

With respect to Sen's concerns about deficiencies in "managing to desire", another solution—and one which, if Sen does not actually canvas, is not excluded by him—is that goods for which desires are deficient would be treated as merit goods. Presumably health care could be one such good for at least some individuals in some circumstances.

Sen's concerns about the separation of desires from values is little different in nature from the separation that economists have made, going back at least as far as Mill (1909) in the nineteenth century, between value in exchange and value in use. Where the concern is with resource allocation, with some constraints on resource availability, there is a distinction, not only between value in use and value in exchange, but also between desires and values. The question then is, in what circumstances should the separation of desires from values be considered to be a problem?

With respect to the separation of desires from values, Birch and Donaldson (2003: 1131) write that for people who have "not . . . known anything other than poverty" their expectations will "always [have been] expressed within the constraints of existing opportunities". They continue:

As a result we can either move towards relaxing these constraints to uncover expectations free of the chains of poverty, or have some other body decide what their expectations "should be". Non-[welfare economics] approaches [and they include the communitarian claims approach as one of these] to valuations seem to see the latter as a proxy for the former.

This is not the case for communitarian claims. It is a strength of this approach of communitarian claims that it does not do what Birch and Donaldson (2003) suggest. Thus

we *the community* determine how resources are allocated on the basis of how we *the community* see various different groups' or individuals' strengths of claims. It is *our* preferences, the community's preferences, for *their* claims, the various groups' claims, that determine how the resources are allocated (Mooney and Russell 2003: 217; emphasis in original).

It is also necessary to recognise that what has been said immediately above relates to the allocation of resources and overcomes *inter alia* the problems of lack of ability to desire adequately at that level. The decision about the actual consumption of the services provided by the resources, however, remains in the hands of the potential users.

Thus to reiterate what has been emphasised in Part II of this book: the community or the society as a whole determines how resources are allocated to different groups in the society. The different groups then decide according to their preferences what services they wish to set up and the members of each group, as individuals or as a group, decide what services they wish to consume. The problems (or inappropriate solutions) that concern Birch and Donaldson are thus avoided.

The agency of Sen can fit into the communitarian school of philosophy. That is not to say that Sen is a communitarian. But I can see nothing in his work that rules out his agency being interpreted in communitarian terms. Individuals value being in a society in that they can participate in that society and have interests in the fulfilment of the society's goals. Communitarianism recognises, not just the existence of the community, but involvement in the community as a "good". It goes beyond the traditional consequentialism of classical utilitarianism, welfarism, and extra-welfarism, but would be at home in Anderson's (1993) expressive theory.

10.4 Community capabilities—and compassion

Here Sen's notion of capabilities is moved from its individual base to a community setting. It is also helpful to link the potential for such community capabilities to some concept of compassion. First, compassion is examined in the context of public life and public institutions. Much of what is written here draws on the work of Nussbaum (2001).

Societies or communities, as with individuals, can be differentiated according to how compassionate they are (Sen 2001). The same is true of institutions. Yet most work on compassion relates to individuals. Nussbaum (2001) extends this emotion to public life. She asks (2001: 401): "how can the public culture of a liberal democracy cultivate appropriate compassion, and how far should it rely on this admittedly fallible and imperfect motive?"

Nussbaum (2001: 405) wants compassionate institutions, but at the same time she indicates that this is a two way street: "compassionate individuals construct institutions that embody what they imagine; and institutions, in turn, influence the development of compassion in individuals... institutions teach citizens definite conceptions of the basic goods, responsibility, and appropriate concern, which will inform any compassion that they learn."

There is a need according to Nussbaum for an education in compassion as part of good citizenship. She argues (p. 426) that "every society employs and teaches ideals of citizenship, and of good civic judgment, in many ways".

Capabilities are taken further by Nussbaum in terms of detail than they are by Sen. She lists these "central human capabilities" as (Nussbaum 2001: 427):

- Life
- Bodily health
- Bodily integrity
- Senses, imagination, and thought
- Emotions
- Practical reason
- Affiliation
- Other species
- Play
- Control over one's environment (both material and political).

Anand (2005) also draws on Nussbaum's list of capabilities. I agree with his suggestion that these individual capabilities can be useful in examining resource allocation issues in health care. He discusses how there may be "variations in the desired levels of functionings...with age". He adds, importantly I believe, that society would have to agree "that the acceptable levels of functioning were dependent on age and other factors" before these could be used in influencing which treatments are allocated to whom.

Anand thus does bring in the community at that level, but I think a much more powerful route is to move to what I am calling "community capabilities". Thus what is of particular interest here is whether it is possible to take Nussbaum's list and convert it to a list of what might be termed "central *community* capabilities". In principle there is no reason why this cannot be done. Not all of Nussbaum's human capabilities will translate directly to the community level. These would be about opportunities for *community* functioning. A possible list might include the following:

- Preservation of community life
- A healthy community
- Reciprocity within the community and between communities
- Sharing of joys and sorrows, responsibilities and rights
- Just distributions of whatever it is that the community wants, in accordance with the community's concept of justice
- Democracy and institutions that reflect and/or are built upon community preferences.

Community capabilities will almost certainly affect individual capabilities and vice versa. Democratic institutions will have an impact at the individual level on issues of affiliation. Control over one's environment in Nussbaum's list of individual capabilities will affect the ability to preserve community life.

Such community capabilities can form the basis for the principles or the constitution (see Chapter 9) for which citizens might opt. In turn they can assist in ascertaining what constitutes benefit in any PBMA exercise, not only in outcomes, but also in the very process of establishing a priority setting system. They only partly relate directly to health. Yet if credible commitment is to be fostered in priority setting, there is a need to build an institutional frame to allow that to happen.

This set of community capabilities will allow this shift in property rights to the community over decision making about resource allocation, essentially priority setting. That shift can also provide the basis for increasing the probability that recommendations from PBMA exercises will be implemented.

10.5 Whither priority setting?

In the light of the above, a new base is proposed here, built on PBMA, for priority setting in health care. The approach, using the ideas of Anderson, Sen, Nussbaum, and communitarianism, will work better the more a health service is set in a society that can be described as communitarian rather than individualistic. Such a health service would ideally be seen as a socially just institution. It would normally be publicly funded. Its "constitution" would be based on communitarian values. It is likely to have an equity goal of equal access for equal need, but with an allowance made perhaps for vertical equity. Whatever the details, these criteria would be representative of the values of the community and the extent of existing inequalities and of solidarity within that community. Priority setting would be according to communitarian claims with respect to both what constitute claims and the strengths of different claims.

Crucially this process addresses rather than ignores the problems related to the inability to "manage to desire". As Sen (1992) notes, the idea that resource distribution should be based on individuals' abilities to feel harmed or to desire is one of the most limiting aspects of welfarism. It is also the case that arbitration by the community is not just instrumental but bestows benefit in itself. Clearly there are benefits to those who have claims; but there are also benefits to those who arbitrate over claims, i.e. the community at large.

What will constitute claims remains to be determined. Whatever they might be, the bases of the claims are unlikely to be the same in all communities and may change over time. In priority setting, in addition to overcoming Sen's concerns about individuals' inability to manage to desire, it can also deal with the situation where there are different concepts of health, as there are between, for example, Aboriginal and non-Aboriginal Australians. Other forms of priority setting are usually based on some common concept of health (such as most obviously with QALY league tables).

This approach can be built into PBMA. It has the merit that, if so desired, it can reflect Sen's concept of capabilities (but extending that to a community level); it avoids the often consequentialist basis of a conventional welfarist framework; and it allows community values as opposed to individual values to come to the fore. It thus shifts the property rights over values to the community, which is better placed to deal with these issues as it is likely to be around longer and be more concerned about organisational efficiency than the more conventional decision makers. It alters the decision making context highlighted as problematical by Mitton and Donaldson (2003). It also boosts the prospects for credible commitment, the lack of which is identified by Jan (2003a and b) as a problem in getting recommendations from priority setting exercises implemented in practice.

References

Anand, P. (2005) Capabilities and health, *Journal of Medical Ethics*, 31: 299–303. Available at: http://jme.bmj.com/cgi/content/full/31/5/299 (accessed 21 Dec. 2007).

Anderson, E. (1993) *Values in Ethics and Economics*. Cambridge, MA: Harvard University Press.

Avineri, S. and de-Shalit, A. (1992) Introduction, in S. Avineri and A. de-Shalit (eds.), *Communitarianism and Individualism*. Oxford: Oxford University Press.

Birch, S. and Donaldson, C. (2003) Valuing the benefits and costs of health care programmes: where's the 'extra' in extra-welfarism? *Social Science and Medicine*, 56(5): 1121–34.

Dolan, P., Olsen, J. A., Menzel, P. and Richardson, J. (2003) An inquiry into the different perspectives that can be used when eliciting preferences in health, *Health Economics*, 12(7): 545–52.

Jan, S. (2000) Institutional considerations in priority setting: transactions cost perspective on PBMA, *Health Economics*, 9: 631–41.

—— (2003a) A perspective on the analysis of credible commitment and myopia in health sector decision making, *Health Policy*, 63(3): 269–78.

—— (2003b) Why does economic analysis not get implemented more? Towards a greater understanding of the rules of the game and the costs of decision making, *Applied Health Economics and Health Policy*, 2(1): 17–24.

Mill, J. S. (1909) *Principles of Political Economy*. London: Longman Green.

Mitton, C. and Donaldson, C. (2003) Setting priorities and allocating resources in health regions: lessons from a project evaluating programme budgeting and marginal analysis (PBMA), *Health Policy*, 64(3): 335–48.

Mooney, G. (1998) Communitarian claims as an ethical basis for allocating health care resources, *Social Science and Medicine*, 47(9): 1171–80.

—— (2001) Communitarianism and health economics, in J. Davis (ed.), *The Social Economics of Health Care*. London: Routledge.

—— (2005) Communitarian claims and community capabilities: furthering priority setting? *Social Science and Medicine*, 60(20): 247–55.

—— Russell, E. (2003) Equity in health care: the need for a new economics paradigm?, in A. Scott, A. Maynard and R. Elliott (eds.), *Advances in Health Economics*. London: Allen and Unwin.

Nussbaum, M. (2001) *Upheavals of Thought*. Cambridge: Cambridge University Press.

Ryan, M. (1999) Using conjoint analysis to take account of patient preferences and go beyond health outcomes: an application to in vitro fertilisation, *Social Science and Medicine*, 48: 535–46.

Sen, A. (1985) *Commodities and Capabilities*. Amsterdam: North Holland.

—— (1992) *Inequality Re-examined*. Oxford: Clarendon Press.

—— (2001) Economic progress and health, in D. Leon and G. Walt (eds.), *Poverty Inequality and Health*. Oxford: Oxford University Press.

11

Equity under the New Paradigm

11.1 Introduction

In health economics, access (as in equity policies) seems to defy any sort of precise definition. As raised in Chapter 2, this is for two reasons. First, the obsession with quantification in economics has meant that too often "use" has been substituted for "access". In turn this has taken the pressure off trying to research into access *per se*. Second, what is meant by access (as with health and health need) is in part culturally determined. It is not just that barriers will be different for different cultural groupings, but the construct of access may well be as well.

This chapter examines equity in different conceptual and policy settings, arguing for the abandonment of a universal construct of access, and a universal construct of equity more generally. The need for culturally particular constructs will be emphasised and exemplified in the specific context of Aboriginal access to health care, where cultural barriers including institutional racism and lack of cultural security/safety are major impediments to access.

In the next section, using the paradigm of Chapter 8, different constructs of equity are discussed. Thereafter certain cultural issues related to equity are set out, first, in a case study for Aboriginal people and then more generally. Section 11.4 looks at equity in the context of the culture of poverty and the culture of corruption. In section 11.5 a possible way forward to pursuing equity when dealing with access as a cultural concept is discussed, before a short conclusion is made.

11.2 Defining equity with reference to cultures

Following the paradigm of communitarian claims, it is argued that the relevant citizens of the community which a health service serves are best placed to judge the access barriers they face and their relative heights. A useful definition of equity and access established by a citizens' jury in Perth is used to exemplify this point. This incorporates the idea of potential patients' perceptions of the heights of barriers, need as capacity to benefit, and vertical equity.

The question of how best to define equity in health care is one that health economists have tended to avoid or treat rather superficially. In part this is because there has been an obsession in health economics generally with quantification, which has meant that, rather than grapple with equity in terms of "access", the much more quantifiable "use" has been used in analyses of equity. There are many health economics studies that look at equity in terms of equal use for equal need. Yet to my knowledge no country defines equity in health care in such terms. For health economists to do so is analytical laziness.

This emphasis on using "use" is furthered by the desires health economists have had (see for example Wagstaff and van Doorslaer 2000) to compare equity across different countries, some of which may be quite different culturally. This in turn has pushed us to try to make the concept of equity comparable across different cultures and societies. And this then means seeking something that is measurable on a comparable basis across different systems—hence the adoption of use in measures of equity.

There is a problem here. It is partly philosophical, partly cultural, partly Western arrogance, reflected in Adams' concerns (as discussed earlier in Chapter 7, section 7.5) about what she describes as a lack of "equity of epistemology" (Adams 1999). This can be interpreted in this context as a criticism of the hegemony of Western knowledge and ideas. Why would the Iranians conceive of equity as the same construct as the Indians? Why would the Brazilians be expected to perceive the same barriers to getting to health services as the British? Why would we expect any barrier that both the Sami (the Indigenous people of northern Scandinavia) and the Swedes face to be perceived as having the same height? And since equity is just one possible goal of any health service, why might we assume that the relative weight attached to it as compared, for example, with efficiency would be the same for the Colombians and the Canadians? International analyses containing these kinds of assumptions represent a use of health economists' resources that is of doubtful value. The opportunity cost involved in seeking to compare what is incomparable is great. The fact that, even if we succeeded, the value of the enterprise might be so little, suggests a need for a different approach.

More generally, there has been a slowness in health economics to recognise that the values different societies and different cultures attach to health, health need, access, and equity are likely to vary from one society or even social or cultural grouping to another.

Yet more fundamentally, the *constructs* of health and access are likely to vary culturally. This makes for difficulties in analysing each of them, especially across different social groupings. Equal access for equal (health) need is difficult to operationalise when there is neither a common construct of health nor a common construct of access.

In the new paradigm, culture with respect to equity is seen in two ways. First, culture is a social phenomenon that results in equity and access being viewed differently from society to society. There is also no universal construct. Second, culture in the context of the social determinants of health is seen in a positive light on the basis that in general people are "comfortable" in their own cultures and such comfort is health inducing. The destruction of culture, for example in many indigenous societies, can lead and has led to ill-health.

This is not to argue that all aspects of every culture have a positive effect on health but, in this new paradigm, overall, maintaining and protecting diversity of culture are seen as positive. That is in sharp contrast to a paper from the Department for International Development (DFID) (2007) where culture is interpreted largely in negative terms. There it is argued that countries "face major challenges in dealing with: high burdens of disease; weak health systems; poorly co-ordinated international support; and sometimes traditions or cultures which oppose key actions which will improve health". That last point may be true, but the role of culture as a positive social determinant of health seems to be absent, as is the need to think of access in cultural terms (DFID 2007: 4).

Part of the problem in protecting and maintaining the diversity of cultures arises at a global level. As indicated previously in Chapter 5, the global elitism and universalism of the WHO came through in their *World Health Report 2000* (WHO 2000) where they, i.e. the WHO, decided what equity was to be, that it should be the same everywhere, and that the same weight should be attached to it everywhere. That view would be and is sustained by most health economics. It is challenged by this new paradigm.

In many cases the neo-liberal ideology of the World Bank has inhibited countries in seeking to pursue equity goals. For example Homedes and Ugalde (2005: 94) write: "So far Costa Ricans have resisted the [World Bank's] pressures to dismantle one of the most equitable and efficient health systems in LA." Chile, under Allende until the military coup of 1973, had universal health care coverage with finance from central government. It was at that time seen as one of the most equitable health services in the region. In the wake of implementing neo-liberal World Bank reforms, the Chilean Ministry of Health itself admitted to the fact that the system became "extremely inequitable" (see Homedes and Ugalde 2005: 89). As a result, since 2003 Chile has sought to build a more equitable, more culturally relevant health service.

As previously discussed in Chapter 5, section 5.4.3, the effect of Western neo-liberal ideology in destroying local cultures is apparent in the account from Mander (1996) on the introduction of TV in the societies of the Dene Indians and the Inuit in the Arctic. Such societies that were originally communitarian in nature, when challenged by neo-liberalism, are faced with an unequal struggle. As Mander (1996: 352) states: "the effect has been to glamorise behaviours and values that are poisonous to life up here. Our traditions have a lot to do with survival. Community co-operation, sharing, and non materialism are the only ways that people can live here." Such Indigenous societies can seek to promote their health better and have more hope to flourish according to their own values if the communitarian claims paradigm could operate on a global stage.

Protecting culture and maintaining the diversity of culture matters. It is seen in this paradigm as fundamental to the pursuit of equitable access to health care. This is ignored in current health economics.

11.3 Whose values for equity?

The question of whose values are to count in assessments and concepts of equity and access is central to definitions and objectives. To date most definitions have come from health policy makers or health economists. Following the paradigm of Chapter 8, the stance taken in this chapter is that equity and access are best seen in communitarian terms, through the eyes of the *potential* users and the taxpayers, i.e. the citizens. Once equity is endorsed in terms of opportunity to use, and especially if we go on to accept the notion of freedom to use as proposed by Thiede et al. (2007), it would then be necessary to look to the community for the values that are to underpin constructs of equity and access. It is the community who must form judgements about the extent of the hindrances or disincentives that currently deter them from using services and it is they who must judge how important it is to address differing barriers and differing heights of barriers to the use of health care.

An example of citizens judging what they mean by equity was elicited from the preferences of a community in a citizens' jury in Perth (Mooney and Blackwell 2004). In the context of this chapter this exemplifies the idea of citizens' values underpinning constructs of equity and in doing so opens the door to different social groupings of citizens having a say as to their perceptions of equity and access.

The citizens' definition was as follows:

Equal access for equal need, where equality of access means that two or more groups face barriers of the same height and where the judgement of the heights is made by each group for their own group; where need is defined as capacity to benefit; and where nominally equal benefits may be weighted according to social preferences such that the benefits to more disadvantaged groups may have a higher weight attached to them than those to the better off.

A number of issues arise from this definition with respect to equity. The idea of the barriers and the heights of the barriers being based on the perceptions of the citizens is important in itself. If we are taking access to mean opportunity to use or freedom to use, it is immediately apparent that it is the potential users' perspectives of what constitutes both a barrier and its height that *must* be sought in assessing access and differential access. Two population groups, each facing a fee of $50; a Western style (white) health service; a male gynaecologist; and a travel distance of 100 kms, will not perceive the barriers to be the same height if one is Aboriginal—without a car, poor, and culturally averse to a gynaecologist being male—and the other white, with a car, rich, and has no problem with the fact that the gynaecologist is male.

Second, the citizens endorsed the idea of "capacity to benefit" rather than need due to the severity of sickness, which is the more usual health economists' basis for equity formulations and formulae, as in for example RAWP (DHSS 1976) and its descendants. This capacity to benefit approach means that equity is driven by a concern to improve rather than a concern to address problems. The latter leaves open the possibility of equity policy leading to either ineffective policy, where health care resources do not or can not reduce some problem (for example where there is no effective treatment), or to policies where the use of health care resources may be inefficient. To adopt this capacity to benefit approach also means that judgements are required about what is meant by benefit and how best benefit can be achieved. The latter may well involve primarily technical judgements to be made by, say, doctors, where benefit involves health. The former, however, involves value judgements about what constitutes benefit, in essence raising the social question of what the benefits of health care are. Again it is argued that this question has to be answered by the community that the health service serves. The new paradigm can allow for that. The issue is not addressed in conventional health economics studies. Since normally need as represented by severity of sickness is assumed to be the basis of equity formulations, the question of how to define benefit is not asked. It is assumed to be solely health.

Certainly in considering *capacity* to benefit, it is likely to be the case that technical judgements will be needed to assess capacity. How much health improvement might result from investing in this programme for increased residential care of the elderly, for example, or increased screening of youth for HIV/AIDS? Such questions will require technical inputs from, say, epidemiologists and medical staff. It is to be noted, however, that in moving away from the idea that health is the only benefit means that other experts may be needed to assist in judging capacity to benefit. In the two examples here it may be that citizens include relief for carers as a type of benefit in the former case and reduced anxiety or increased safe sexual activity in the latter. The simple point is that in allowing citizens to judge what the forms of benefit are that they want from health care, the door is opened for the inclusion of benefits that are not normally the province of epidemiologists or medical staff. Other experts such as sociologists, anthropologists, and psychologists may have a role to play in assessing capacity to benefit.

The fact that different social groupings within the same society may have different constructs of benefits or weight the same constructs differently would be problematical if attempts were to be made within the current health economics paradigm to deal with this issue. This is because equity in health economics is most often construed in terms of equal access *for equal need* or equal use *for equal need*, where equal need is defined as equal *health* need. If that definition were replaced by one that allowed different social groupings to define health (and hence health need) differently and to have different preferences for what they mean by benefits (and hence need more generally) then the equity construct of equal use or access *for equal need* would not be sustainable. The notion of equal need could not apply.

The new paradigm using communitarian claims gets over this problem. Need is replaced by capacity to benefit, which is accepted as being a subjective construct that may vary from one social grouping to another. The community as a whole has to weigh up the claims of one group as compared to another's, even when one group's potential for claims is set in different terms to the other's. Thus the claims of Aboriginal people would be set in terms of (at least in part) their more holistic, communitarian construct of health; non-Aboriginal people, in terms of a primarily

Western, more individualistic construct of health. Aboriginal people might place more weight on involvement in decision making on the nature of the health system. Non-Aboriginal people might weight this but to a lesser extent. Again Aboriginal people might argue that the impact of land dispossession is a basis for a claim on health care resources. The community as a whole, Aboriginal and non-Aboriginal together, would then have to decide which of these various factors—Aboriginal health, non-Aboriginal health, involvement in decision making, and the impact of land dispossession—should constitute the basis of a claim and what strength (or weight) should be attached to each claim for each group. That might be a difficult task, but it can be done (see the Appendix to Chapter 9) and needs to be done. Current health economics gets round these issues by adopting a universal definition of equity and thereby ignoring the dilemma of different groupings' different constructs and values for equity.

The perspective of this new paradigm is that of Anderson's as indicated in Chapter 6. To reiterate, Anderson's (1993: 2) theory differs from the standard health economics approach because it

regards the plurality of evaluative perspectives in a more epistemological vein . . . It focuses on the *irreducibly* numerous, intersecting ways people's social positions—of wider scope than the individual, but narrower than all of humanity (as of gender, race, ethnicity, class, and so forth)—affect their points of view.

This approach, which is endorsed in the paradigm set out in this book, adopts a view that "instead of seeking one point of view that has authority over all the rest, it views the authority of different points of view in pragmatic terms".

11.4 Cultural issues

One of the key considerations with respect to equity and access is that these have to be to some greater or lesser extent value-based. Such value bases will often vary from society to society and from culture to culture, perhaps between rich and poor. Cultural variations are discussed in this section.

11.4.1 *A case study*

In Australia, while it is recognized that Aboriginal people have very poor health status and poor access to health and other services, little has been done to establish or elicit the principles that might underlie or drive "culturally secure" health services.*

The greatest barrier for Aboriginal people in attending health services is the fact that most are in their eyes culturally alienating. Access for this cultural grouping takes on a different meaning from that of the rest of Australian society. This problem can be overcome by ensuring that services are "culturally secure". Houston (2004: 15) has defined this as

a commitment that the construct and provision of services offered by the health system will not compromise the legitimate cultural rights, views, values and expectations of Aboriginal people. It is a recognition, appreciation and response to the impact of cultural diversity on the utilisation and provision of effective clinical care, public health and health systems administration. The practical implication of cultural security is that the administrative, clinical and other service domains of the health system are systematically reviewed to ensure that their operation appropriately incorporates culture in their delivery.

For Aboriginal people, no rational, culturally secure, health plan or strategy can be adequately pursued without establishing the Aboriginal value base for the social and cultural institution of health services that they want. As a simple example, quality adjusted life years (QALYs) measure only a Western construct of health and cannot accommodate the much more holistic Aboriginal construct of health. The "solution" here, however, is, not to argue for "Aboriginal QALYs", but to accept that some very different measure is needed. Further, and using this same example, the value base of QALYs (as is true of nearly all current Western health policy) is the values of individuals. The communitarian values of Aboriginal culture, as Houston (2004) emphasises, are not present.

Thus critical in any Aboriginal health strategy, and more specifically in the development of policies regarding equity, is the need to recognise two features of Aboriginal culture: the "holism" with respect to both health and services, and the communitarianism rather than individualism on which Aboriginal culture seeks to exist.

It is of note in this context that most of the resource allocation formulae that health economists have devised or support in health care can be traced back to the RAWP formula for England in 1976 (DHSS 1976). For example the Resource Development Formula in New South Wales (NSW

---

* This section draws on Mooney, G. and Houston, S. (2004) Weighted capacity to benefit plus MESH infrastructure: an alternative approach to resource allocation, *Applied Health Economics and Health Policy*, 3(1): 29–33. By kind permission of Wolters Kluwer Health.

Health Department 1996) is a grandchild of that RAWP approach, as is the Arbuthnott Report in Scotland (Scottish Executive Health Department 1999).

While it would be reasonable to expect that a jurisdiction with greater health problems should receive more health care resources, there is little reason to believe that this should be done *pro rata*. Of course, this must depend on the objectives of the exercise and also on the relative productivity of resources in the different jurisdictions. The issue here is the allocation of *health care* resources. Some health problems are more amenable than others to health care interventions. These interventions may be of differing efficiency. Some problems may be better addressed through housing or education or some other social service. There are difficulties in assuming that the marginal productivity of health care resources is, in any sense, a function of the size of the health problem; and there are even greater difficulties in assuming that this will be in direct proportion to the size of the problem.

A further difficulty with these formulae relates to issues of measurement. Given the difficulties involved in finding appropriate measures for relative morbidity to determine how sick a community or region is, indices of relative mortality are often used instead. Clearly, there are problems in assuming that morbidity and mortality are in direct proportion. Frequently standardised mortality ratios (SMRs) are used in this context. The assumption here is that, if there is an SMR of 130 (the age and sex adjusted death rate is 30 per cent above average) in a region, then that region, *ceteris paribus*, should receive 30 per cent more resources per capita than is the average. It is not logical to assume that the 30 per cent higher SMR indicates that the problem is 30 per cent greater. We are dealing with two potentially very different scales here, and the relationship between them is most unlikely to be directly proportional. Neither, as indicated and even if it were accepted, could we conclude that this justifies the same proportional increase in resources.

While these issues of measurement create difficulties, the more fundamental criticism is not about measurement, but about the health economics philosophy that underpins the RAWP type approach. It is, in essence, about allocating more resources to bigger problems, rather than, first, identifying what good (or benefit) is sought and, second, trying to maximise that good.

What good is sought from the allocation of health care resources to different jurisdictions? One possibility that is most often endorsed by health economists is to maximise the health of the populations involved.

This is in essence an efficiency goal. However, there may be factors besides health to consider. For example the communities might want, in addition, to be informed of their choices, reassured, treated with dignity, and treated with respect. All of these may contribute to health, but they may also be objectives in their own right, and not simply instrumental to the pursuit of health.

Communities may also have concerns about equity or fairness. Indeed, resource allocation formulae are most often concerned with equity. This may be couched in different terms, for example equality of health, equal access for equal need, or equal use for equal need. The distinction can also be made between horizontal equity (the equal treatment of equals) and vertical equity (which is the unequal but equitable treatment of unequals). While there is considerable debate in the literature as to which particular definition of equity is the most appropriate, the debate is not pursued here, at least not directly. According to the new paradigm spelt out in Chapter 8, however, it is argued that the construct of equity should be determined according to the informed preferences of the community or communities involved, while taking due account of the resource constrained environment in which such decisions have to be made. (See for example Mooney and Blackwell 2004.)

In considering an approach based on the new paradigm, the following questions need to be addressed:

1. In any geographical area/jurisdiction, what is the scope for "doing good" with the health service resources available?
2. Are the decision makers indifferent about the relative importance of doing good to different groups who might vary by, for example, disadvantage or might they want to weight the good to some group(s) higher than that to others?
3. Where some of the difference in the scope to do good (as in 1) is a function of the management, leadership, etc. in that area/jurisdiction, can the allocation formula "compensate" those who are less well off with respect to this form of infrastructure?

Point (1) is about need, but uses for this the concept of "capacity to benefit" (Culyer 2001). It does not look at the question of the size of the problem, as with the standard concept of need. Instead it is concerned with the question of improvement, i.e. doing better, in essence working with whatever concept of good is agreed and, importantly given the new paradigm, by the community. It is likely that a sizeable component of the benefit in this capacity to benefit will be perceived in terms of improved health. However, there is no reason to restrict it to that and there is evidence that the benefits sought by citizens from health care resources can be wider than simply health (Mooney 2000).

How to measure capacity to benefit remains unclear. In my research with others for the Indigenous Funding Inquiry for the Commonwealth Grants Commission (CGC) (CGC 2001), it was argued by key leaders in Aboriginal health in Western Australia that capacity to benefit was greatest where the most efficient interventions lay—in environmental health. It was further argued that the second greatest marginal return was likely to be in social health and, third and last, the return would be lowest in trying to change individual health related behaviour (see Houston 2004). Whether these considerations are transferable to other populations remains to be researched.

The second component involves a weighting factor for capacity to benefit. This reflects the idea of vertical equity, that according to social preferences, the value attached to nominally equal benefits may be different depending on who the recipients are. For example, a society might decree that people who are in poor health should have what are nominally equal benefits weighted more highly compared to those in relatively good health. In the language of the new paradigm, disadvantaged people would be deemed to have greater claims over health care resources. In a formula for allocating resources across different peoples, this weighting would reflect the claims that such relative disadvantage bestowed in different groupings. This might be in terms of income, health, socio-economic status, or education. What should constitute "disadvantage" in this context is best determined according to the informed preferences of the society. It is then for the society to decide, according to their preferences, the relative weights to be attached to the different forms and degrees of disadvantage, i.e the various claims. In Australia, for example, as between Aboriginal and non-Aboriginal benefits of health care, in various surveys weights of between 1.2 and 2.5 have been suggested (Mooney 2000). The more compassionate a society the higher such "disadvantage" weights or strengths of claims will be.

Third, there is what is called "MESH (management, economic, social, and human) infrastructure". This concept arose in recognition of the fact that, in the original manifestation of this approach, not all Aboriginal communities were seen to be equally well placed to take full advantage of the resources allocated to them to build programmes, for example, in diabetic health or in eye disease. In discussion with leading figures in Aboriginal health in Western Australia, they recognised that some more cohesive self-governing communities function better with respect to investing in programmes than do others. MESH involves this idea of social solidarity or cohesiveness with consequent good management, the availability of resources, a socially well functioning community, and good human resources, particularly in terms of leadership skills. Where each of these is present, there is a greater likelihood that programmes on specific health problems will be implemented efficiently. Where some or all of these elements are missing, then resources may well be wasted, or at best used to lesser effect.

In terms of access and equity, the key implications that flow from this case study are as follows. Involving the Aboriginal community in planning for its health and its health services will ensure that services are then directed towards ends that are based on Aboriginal people's preferences, thereby being more likely both to improve accessibility and to maximise the benefit or the good (as they conceive it) from the resources available. It will ensure greater utilisation of such services than if they were imposed on the basis of "outside" values. This process of self-determination will itself help to build self-esteem among Aboriginal people, collectively and culturally, thereby also leading to potentially better health and well being. Thus, the new paradigm supports the idea that eliciting the Aboriginal community preferences for health, health services, and health service equity is the basis on which to build Aboriginal health planning and service delivery.

The South African Health Department has recently endorsed the use of MESH at a district level throughout their health service (National Department of Health 2007). They have also developed an assessment tool that is to be utilised annually to allow them to monitor changes over time in MESH. They state:

The MESH District Assessment Tool comprises of the following four components to assess areas:

- management capacity
- economic / financial conditions
- social cohesion and community participation
- human resources at the district level.

The application of the MESH assessment tool will mean that over time it will be possible to determine what factors lead to increases and decreases in MESH, and thereby provide better targeted investment in primary health care in South Africa.

221

11.4.2 *Other cultural issues*

The new paradigm also allows recognition that differences in culture across countries are reflected in the nature of health care systems. For example, the Scandinavian countries are renowned culturally for their "Scandinavian solidarity". This dates back to the nineteenth century, but it survives and forms the basis, not just of health care systems, but of health in the Scandinavian countries. Holm et al. (1999: 323) write: "Solidarity is a political value often expressed in debates about [the Scandinavians'] kind of health care system. It implies a sense of commitment to a just system of distribution that includes all citizens." It is not then surprising that in Western societies the Scandinavians are recognized as having more equitable health services than many others.

Different religions will have different value bases for health and health care. Aroua indicates that when health is seen through an Islamic perspective "individual health and welfare are closely related to the health and welfare of the whole community" and hence equity and access are seen in community terms. From this perspective access to health care "is a social function based on [a] communitarian solidarity that involves both public and individual responsibility". Such health services are not "lucrative enterprises"; they are a social service "that must be [provided] by government or communitarian resources". Thus this Islamic perspective, which informs health care policy in many countries, is based on a more community focused culture than holds good for many Western societies. Such differences between an Islamic perspective and a Western perspective cannot be accommodated in current health economics.

In examining access in cultural terms, a useful case study lies in the notion of informed consent, which in the literature is almost always interpreted as being based on the choices of individuals, i.e. it is for the individual to give consent or not. Yet such an individualistic basis is not universally agreed, especially in those countries where the idea of community is strong and individual choice and preferences do not rule in the way that they do in most of Western society. Thus Frimpong-Mansoh (2006) writes: "the customary African communitarian practice of requiring community leaders' approval before obtaining the voluntary informed consent of potential research candidates provides a multi-step decision-making procedure for safeguarding and fostering the wellbeing of vulnerable research candidates." Here access has a community perspective that, again, is very different from the individualistic perspective of Western medicine and health care.

A related but different equity issue is raised by Adams (1999) and was introduced in Chapter 7, section 7.5. She writes (p. 3) about the "inequity of epistemology" and the fact that the language and culture of international exchange of ideas around health and equity are so dominated by Western thinking that, for example, "Tibetan medical theories and practices both resist description and quantifiability in a manner acceptable to secularist discourse but may nevertheless remain essential to health." Again a universalist construct of equity as in conventional health economics cannot accommodate this; the new paradigm can.

In the case of China, Adams (p. 18) argues that "it would seem that calls for basic cultural liberties would be fundamental to policy discussions on health equity". She asks: "what does it mean to ensure cultural freedom and to bring cultural concerns into the policy arena at the same time?" She worries that this can lead to health care being "politicised" where this means

privileging one set of political and cultural ideas that are forged through contestation into the position of being (usually temporarily) dominant, whether or not there is consensus. Government policies are in this sense seldom universally consensual, and one could ask whether international agendas can ever be as well.

This last point—the lack of universal consensus—is critical and not just because of the lack of a consensus, but the *appearance* of a consensus imposed by the West is an example of the failure of what she describes as the equity of epistemology. There is a need in the broader context of pursuing equity in health care to acknowledge both the cultural differences that clearly do exist across different societies and, additionally, the likely negative impact on health if these differences are denied or destroyed.

11.5 Other cultures

Two other types of "culture" that exist and are relevant to this discussion of the advantages of the new paradigm in addressing equity concerns in health are the "culture of poverty" and the "culture of corruption". Much of the debate on the idea of the "culture of poverty" is based on the work of Lewis (1966). To him poverty was not to be seen as simply economic deprivation but also as a means of survival of the poor who could in certain instances create a "culture of poverty". One characteristic of this was that people with the culture of poverty "did not participate in or were not integrated by, the major institutions of the larger society" (Welshman 2006: 270). Lewis saw this, not just as some short term shift, but the creation of a longer term culture passed down through generations with such traits as "marginality, helplessness, dependence and inferiority" dominating (Welshman 2006: 271).

There is very substantial debate in the literature about this idea of a culture of poverty. There is no need to rehearse it here. It is enough that such a culture can and does exist. In the specific context of equitable access to health care, its existence for people whose access to care will so often be critical to the success of any equity policy is problematical in any pursuit of a common definition of access. While attempting to account for this in any health economics analysis of equity will be difficult, it is immediately apparent that the standard analysis of health economists simply cannot address this matter. The communitarian claims approach at least has the capacity to do so.

Turning to the culture of corruption in health care, the links between poverty and corruption are very real and obvious. When dealing with access to health care, they can become quite critical.

Corruption in health care is rife in many settings. Savedoff (2007: 1) states:

When resources are stolen from public health systems, patients frequently suffer the consequences, whether through poor quality care and ineffective medications, or simply not getting the services they need. This health impact of corruption and fraud is large enough to appear in population-wide health indicators.

Allin (2006) et al. have examined corruption in health care in the old Soviet Union countries in the form of so called "informal payments". These are very common despite the fact that services are supposed to be zero priced. As they state, these under-the-table payments "can undermine official payment systems, distort the priorities of the health system, reduce access to health services and impede health reforms". They argue: "Informal payments exist for several reasons, including economic ones such as a general scarcity of financial resources in the public system; and socio-cultural ones, such as the lack of trust in government and a culture of tipping." It is evident that access by the poor will suffer most from such "informal payment" mechanisms.

In Bangalore, Sekhar (2000) describes the impact of similar payments there where poor patients pay large sums of "extortionary money" to get care in public sector maternity hospitals. "The average patient in a maternity ward run by the city corporation pays Rs 1089 (approximately $22 US) in bribes to receive adequate medical care. A further 61 per cent of the respondents were forced to pay for medicines, though public policy clearly mandates that they be given free of charge."

Where societies and cultures turn a blind eye to such corruption—where there is an acceptance of the culture of corruption—this is an added concern in any attempts to assess access. This culture of corruption again makes access hard to define across different groupings. It makes equality of access yet more difficult to achieve, especially for the poor who will be hit hardest by the financial payment systems that arise under such corruption. Again the new paradigm seems potentially better placed to address these issues.

11.6 Conclusion

Under the new paradigm the community as a whole determines what constitute the barriers to use, i.e. the access barriers. Some of these (but of course not equally) may apply to all: distance, financial cost, and time of day or week when a facility is open/available. Others may be "sub-group" specific: lack of cultural security for Aboriginal people; racism for coloured people; Islamic values influencing the nature of care sought; or lack of participation in the broader society for the poor. The community's judgement here is based on putting themselves in the position of those faced with these barriers. The adjudged heights are again determined from this stance.

Given judgements about what constitute barriers and their appropriate heights, the community has the basis for assessing access or relative inaccessibility for different groups. What the community does about reducing the variations in relative inaccessibility for different groups is then based on the community's willingness to reduce different barriers—their assessment of the strengths of claims for better access of the different groups.

Thus in a society concerned not to be seen to be racist, wishing to right the wrongs from a colonial past and seeking to protect and support minority cultures, the strength of claims of, for example, Aboriginal people will be high and allocating resources to make health services more culturally secure will be a priority. Where the emphasis in a society is on assimilation by the dominant culture, where egalitarianism takes the form of equality and universal values are promoted as the basis of good citizenship, the strength of claims of Aboriginal people will be lower and the resources allocated to make services to Aboriginal people more access-ible will be fewer.

The actual *use* of services, however, remains determined by how indi-viduals perceive the barriers with which they are then faced and their (the individuals') willingness to surmount them.

There is no easy answer to the question of how to deal with equity once it is accepted that it is a social and cultural phenomenon; that being comfortable in one's own culture is in most instances health enhancing; and that consequently one wants ideally to maintain the diversity of culture both within nations and across different countries. Even in mono-cultural societies (ethnically speaking), there are still issues of di-versity of cultures, at least between the culture of the rich and the culture of the poor. The rooting out of the culture of corruption in certain coun-tries is also necessary for the advancement of better access for the poor and other marginalised and disadvantaged groups.

To make a stand against the increasing hegemony of neo-liberalism is the place to start in building more equitable and more accessible health and health care. That is difficult, but defending local cultures supported by local economies can be a way into this. Mander (1996: 81) has some positive words on this front:

there are movements everywhere which are encouraging and developing the growth of local economies, protecting rural and urban communities and family life . . . communities are also developing alternatives, going back to organic agricul-ture, promoting village self-reliance and rehabilitation of degraded habitats (land and marine) for survival and livelihood.

The task of delivering equity in health care according to some construct or constructs of access is difficult. It has been made unnecessarily so by the neo-liberal stances of the WTO, the IMF, and the World Bank, in which equity has taken a back seat or has been seen to be redundant or irrelevant. The elitism and univeralism of the WHO has further thwarted the equity cause.

As health economists, in analysing access and in turn equity, we have been driven by a desire to reduce values and variables to manageable proportions, which has in turn meant losing some of the meaningfulness of our objective. While it may be messy and awkward, since to date we have had little success with the neat and tidy, Anderson's (2003: 2) pos-ition as laid out in Chapter 6 is to be preferred and with it communitarian claims that "instead of seeking one point of view that has authority over all the rest, [the need is for a position that] views the authority of different points of view in pragmatic terms".

References

Adams, V. (1999) Equity of the ineffable: cultural and political constraints in ethnomedicine as a health problem in contemporary Tibet, Harvard Center for Population and Development Studies, WP Series No. 99.05 April 1999.

Allin, S., Davaki, K. and Mossialos, A. (2006) Paying for "free" health care: the conundrum of informal payments in post-communist Europe. Available at: www.transparency.org/global_priorities/health/service_delivery/informal_payments (accessed 20 Dec. 2007).

Anderson, E. (1993) *Values in Ethics and Economics*. Cambridge, MA: Harvard University Press.

——(2003) Sen, ethics and democracy, *Feminist Economics*. Available at: www-personal.umich.edu/~eandersn/SenEthicsDemocracy.pdf (accessed 12 Dec. 2007).

Aroua, A. Health: an Islamic perspective. Community health in Islamic perspectives. Available at: www.islamset.com/hip/ahmed_aroua.html (accessed 12 Dec. 2007).

CGC (2001) *Indigenous Funding Inquiry*. Canberra: Australian Government.

Culyer, A. J. (2001) Economics and ethics in health care, *Journal of Medical Ethics*, 27: 217–22.

DFID (Department for International Development) (2007) Working together for better health. Available at: www.dfid.gov.uk/pubs/files/health-strategy07.pdf (accessed 12 Nov. 2007).

DHSS (1976) Sharing resources for health in England. Report of the Resource Allocation Working Party (the RAWP Report). London: Her Majesty's Stationary Office.

Frimpong-Mansoh, A. (2006) Culture and voluntary informed consent in African health care systems, *Developing World Ethics*. Available at: www.blackwell-synergy.com/doi/full/10.1111/j.1471–8847.2006.00181.x (accessed 10 Jun. 2007).

Holm, S., Liss, P.-E. and Norheim, O. (1999) Access to health care in the Scandinavian countries: ethical aspects, *Health Care Analysis*, 7: 321–30.

Homedes, N. and Ugalde, A. (2005) Why neo liberal health reforms have failed in Latin America, *Health Policy*, 71: 83–96.

Houston, S. (2004) The past, the present, the future of Aboriginal health policy. Unpublished PhD thesis, Curtin University, Perth.

Lewis, O. (1966) *La Vida: A Puerto Rican Family in the Culture of Poverty*. New York: Random House.

Mander, J. (1996) Technologies of globalization, in J. Mander and E. Goldsmith (eds.), *The Case Against the Global Economy: And for a Turn Toward the Local*. San Francisco: Sierra Books.

Mooney, G. (1998) "Communitarian claims" as an ethical basis for allocating health care resources, *Social Science and Medicine*, 47(9): 1171–80.

——(2000) Vertical equity in health care resource allocation, *Health Care Analysis*, 8: 203–15.

Mooney, G. and Blackwell, S. (2004) Whose health service is it anyway? *Medical Journal of Australia*, 180(2): 76–8.

—— and Houston, S. (2004) Weighted capacity to benefit plus MESH infrastructure: an alternative approach to resource allocation, *Applied Health Economics and Health Policy*, 3(1): 29–33.

—— Russell, E. (2003) Equity in health care: the need for a new paradigm? in A. Scott, A. Maynard and R. Elliott (eds). *Advances in Health Economics*. Chichester: Wiley.

National Department of Health (2007) *Health District Development and Performance Assessment Tools*. Pretoria: National Department of Health.

NSW(New South Wales) Health Department (1996) *Resource Development Formula*. Sydney: NSW Health Department.

Rousseau, J.-J. (1979) *Emile* (trans. A. Bloom). New York: Basic Books.

Oscar, L. (1966) *La Vida: A Puerto Rican Family in the Culture of Poverty—San Juan and New York*. London: Secker and Warburg.

Savedoff, W. D. (2007) Question of the culture of corruption: transparency and corruption in the health sector: a conceptual framework and ideas for action in Latin America and the Caribbean. Health Technical Note No. 03/2007, Sustainable Development Department Inter American Development Bank, Washington, DC.

Scottish Executive Health Department (1999) *The Report of the National Review of Resource Allocation for the NHS in Scotland* (also known as the "Arbuthnott Review"). Edinburgh: Scottish Executive.

Sekhar, S. (2000) Maternity health care for the urban poor in Bangalore: a report card, Public Affairs Centre. Available at: www.pacindia.org (accessed 20 Dec. 2007).

Sen, A. (1993) Positional objectivity, *Philosophy and Public Affairs*, 22: 126–45.

—— (1977) Rational fools: a critique of the behavioral foundations of economic theory, *Philosophy and Public Affairs*, 6(4): 317–44.

Smith, A. (1976) *The Theory of Moral Sentiments*. Oxford: Clarendon Press.

Thiede, M., Akweongo, P. and McIntyre, D. (2007) Exploring the dimensions of equity, in D. McIntyre and G. Mooney (eds.), *The Economics of Health Equity*. Cambridge: Cambridge University Press.

Wagstaff, A. and van Doorslaer, E. (2000) Equity in health care finance and delivery, in A. J. Culyer and J. P. Newhouse (eds.), *Handbook of Health Economics*. Elsevier: Netherlands.

Welshman, J. (2006) Searching for social capital: historical perspectives on health, poverty and culture, *The Journal of the Royal Society for the Promotion of Health*, 126: 268–74.

WHO (World Health Organisation) (2000) *World Health Report 2000*. Geneva: WHO.

12

Some Further Implications for Health Economics and the Economics of Health Policy

12.1 Introduction

In this chapter I want to look at a few more issues both in health economics *per se* and in the economics of health policy, where the adoption of the paradigm of this book might make a difference. The account here has to be rather tentative. Central to the new paradigm is that it is the relevant communities or societies who must set the constitutions for the social institutions of health care and public health. It is thus only possible, in most instances, to speculate as to what these might be.

In the next section I will examine how the new paradigm might affect health economics in the specific context of economic evaluation. Section 12.3 looks at the economics of health care policy. The question of whether the paradigm can work in practice is addressed in section 12.4, before the chapter offers a brief conclusion.

12.2 Economic evaluation

The new paradigm spells the end of cost–utility analysis and QALY league tables. It means, for example, that NICE which is the "QALY league table"-based system of priority setting in the UK will have to rethink how it sets its priorities, which currently is on the basis of a cost per QALY threshold. QALYs and QALY league tables have been largely artificial constructs built out of extra-welfarism for reasons of, at best, analytical and quantitative neatness or, at worst, intellectual laziness. They were in any case never applicable outside of health care economics (see Gerard and Mooney 1993).

The new paradigm requires that the benefit side of the economic evaluation equation embraces more than just health and that the values that are used in setting principles and claims are drawn from the community as a community. It is to be noted too that these values and the emerging claims are unlikely to be constant across different jurisdictions (contrary to what is often implied in QALY league tables).

This new approach to economic evaluation is best described as "community cost–benefit analysis" where the values used are those of the community *qua* community rather than, as in standard cost–benefit analysis (CBA), the aggregation of individual consumers' values. The framework is again drawn from the expressive theory of Anderson (1993), which allows so much more flexibility than any consequentialist theory.

It is not new to propose a broad framework for economic evaluation. Ten years ago the health economist Jerry Hurley (1998: 391) suggested that "there are situations in which health effects appear to dominate, others where utility effects dominate and others where other considerations altogether dominate" (p. 391). He went on:

The challenge is to develop defensible principles to guide analysts through such issues ... The principles employed might reflect, for example, alternative levels of analysis ... the nature of the alternatives under examination ... the nature of the groups affected by the policies under consideration or the ultimate source of benefit ... The point is to let the question drive the analyses rather than simply imposing a pre-determined framework and making the question fit the framework in procrustean fashion.

This stance by Hurley is echoed in the new paradigm. However, Hurley did not go on to indicate how these "defensible principles" were to be derived. The paradigm developed in this book is designed to resolve that issue.

Hurley (p. 392) was also right to argue that

economists and others who conduct evaluative economic analyses must appreciate more deeply that such analyses are inherently exercises in social ethics ... The development of methods for such evaluative economic analyses needs to occur in conversation with the broader literature on social ethics and moral philosophy.

The "social ethics and moral philosophy" adopted here are those of communitarianism.

This leaves "community cost–benefit analysis" with a much greater breadth and degree of openness than either standard cost–benefit analysis or cost–utility analysis. What constitutes benefit is whatever the informed community want it to include, on the basis of the principles and the communitarian claims the community identifies. The claims weighted by the preferences of the citizens represent the bases for determining resource allocation priorities once they have been weighted according to the preferences of the citizens.

Take the example of the possibility of introducing into some health service jurisdiction one of the following (all costing the same): a helicopter ambulance; 80 more coronary artery bypass operations; or 250 more hip replacements. The relevant community, after establishing what principles they want to underpin their health service and what they deem are the relevant claims on health service resources, would be requested to judge which of these options best benefits the community, for example by establishing the community's willingness to pay (probably out of the health service budget, where the opportunity costs of their choices are spelt out to them).

A study by Olsen and Donaldson (1998) went part of the way to assessing these options in "community cost–benefit" terms. They presented these three options with appropriate information about their health effects to a random selection of the relevant community (to citizens as tax payers, albeit also as individual householders) and asked them about their willingness to pay (WTP) in taxation for these programmes.

In designing their study, Olsen and Donaldson were testing out the possibility of some wider concerns (they do not call them claims) that might be relevant to the community in reaching their judgement about the value of the options. They indicate, for example, (p. 2) that the helicopter ambulance "was considered to be a particularly interesting candidate on which to carry out a WTP study". This is because it was thought to have other utility bearing characteristics:

(1) it is a "rescue service" which may reduce anxiety in people in rural areas [who were those most likely to benefit from the service because they could be flown to the hospital in the town]; (2) although few people use or benefit directly from the service, it may have a considerable "option value" derived from knowing that the service is available should use in the future be required; and (3) it contributes to reducing regional inequalities in access.

Thus while the authors did not use the language of principles or claims, their approach is along these same lines. Certainly what they did do is relevant to any future study, which might go further down the road required in adopting the paradigm of this book.

The "community cost–benefit" analysis that is advocated under the new paradigm is very different from cost–utility analysis. It is important to recognise more generally that it is also different from standard cost–benefit analysis, which uses the values of individual consumers rather then those of citizens as members of a community.

Turning now to economic evaluation in public health, the key change that the new paradigm will engender is a greater recognition of the need for more research by health economists in economic evaluation outside of health care. Currently the heavy emphasis on applying economic evaluation to pharmaceuticals amounts to a serious misallocation of scarce health economists' resources. This is in large part the result of the amount of funding available from the industry for such work, but there are ethical issues here that health economists have to consider when choosing to do this work. The question has to be asked, however, whether this funding bias is in the wider interests of the efficient use of societies' resources in the pursuit of population health. It is a question that health economists should be addressing.

Additionally there is the evidence that those clinical trials that are funded by the industry are four times more likely to come up with results that are favourable to the industry. Thus Lexchin et al. (2003) state:

Research sponsored by the drug industry was more likely to produce results favouring the product made by the company sponsoring the research than studies funded by other sources. The results apply across a wide range of disease states, drugs, and drug classes, over at least two decades and regardless of the type of research being assessed—pharmacoeconomic studies, clinical trials, or meta-analyses of clinical trials. The totality of the evidence reported in our meta-analysis of a subset of homogeneous studies suggests that there is some kind of systematic bias to the outcome of published research funded by the pharmaceutical industry.

The evidence presented in the first chapter of this book on the paucity of research on inequality and poverty being published in health economics journals and presented at the most recent iHEA congress is an indictment of the current paradigm in health economics. A major reason for developing this new paradigm is to seek to change this pattern of research interest. While more work is being done today than previously on the economics of the social determinants of health, it is still on a small scale and tends to be on specific issues, such as smoking and obesity. Neglected almost totally are poverty and inequality.

The new paradigm, emphasising health rather than health *care*, is concerned with communities' wants, including those of the global community rather than only individuals' preferences. It has an important focus on neo-liberal globalisation and the impact of neo-liberalism on poverty and inequality and in turn health, and argues for a democratisation of the relevant health and health care institutions, from a local community concerned about its local hospital through to the global community's concerns about the operations of the IMF, the WTO, and the World Bank. The "people's principles", which the paradigm proposes should underlie these social institutions, will almost certainly drive policy in the direction of addressing poverty and inequality as major ill health inducing characteristics of societies, both nationally and globally. Health economists will need to shift our focus.

12.3 The economics of health policy

At a policy level the implications of the new paradigm are many. Let me speculate on just two: first, on financing of health care and, second, on primary health care.

On financing under the new paradigm, the likelihood is that many more countries will opt for more public than private health care. It might mean the serious curtailment of private health care and private health insurance. It is difficult to see that, if there were "democratisation" of health care, citizens would still opt for private health care. Insofar as they do, as patients at present, this is largely the result, not of a desire to be able to exercise choice, but because the private system is seen to be and often is of higher quality. If the public sector can have adequate resources invested in it (in support, it is assumed, of the citizens' claims) then the question of choice over quality becomes redundant, as we find is the case now, for example, in much of Scandinavia today. That region is also testament to the fact that if the middle class can have access to good health care in the public sector, this will result in good health care for all, as the middle class opt and indeed push for quality care in the public sector.

It is relevant to this trend in the public sector to note that there is increasing evidence in a number of countries (for example Australia, see: www.aph.gov.au/library/Pubs/rn/2003–04/04rn57.htm) that citizens in opinion polls are keener to have governments spend more on health services (but not necessarily on other social services) than to have tax cuts. There is, however, little information available on how best the public want that additional money spent, except perhaps that they appear to favour public health care.

Clearly the emphasis on funding of health care varies from country to country. It can readily be argued that this is driven at least in part by the fact that health care systems are social institutions and as such are a reflection of the society in which they exist. Whether they reflect what the citizens *qua* citizens, if well informed, would want in some communitarian sense, however, is not clear. The new paradigm would push analysts (including health economists) to determine this.

What citizens would choose for a health care system is the question that needs to addressed in looking at how the adoption of the paradigm of communitarian claims would affect the funding arrangements. The evidence from Australian citizens' juries (as indicated in Chapter 9) suggests that equity is a major principle at the level of delivery. This again implies public funding, since public services are more likely to deliver equitably.

The countries that currently do well on equity in health care are Scandinavia and Cuba, and these are very much dominated by public spending. Under the new paradigm there will, of course, be no single model that will be adopted by all countries, but the current balance between public and private is most likely to shift in many towards the former.

A second policy level where we can speculate about the likely impact of applying the new paradigm is in primary health care. There are a number of PHC issues that might be handled differently. It is likely, for example, that the community might argue for a shift in the balance of health care resources to primary care.

Another likely change would occur in policy on remuneration systems for GPs. Payments to GPs can be by fee for service, salary, capitation, target payments, or a mix of some or all of these. Different systems can affect how doctors behave and how they treat their patients. As discussed in Chapter 1, closely related in the health economics literature to this issue is the question of supplier induced demand. Remuneration systems at present are almost wholly concerned with payment of doctors, and the extent to which they are used as a tool of health policy is limited.

The new paradigm is likely to place more attention on GP remuneration as an instrument of health care policy. While there can be a number of reasons for this, the key is that there is a need with communitarian claims to think much more about how to get doctors to respond to the sorts of claims that citizens make on their health services, and hence in turn from their doctors. Remuneration systems, given how they can influence doctors' behaviour, become important in the new paradigm in persuading or cajoling doctors to do what the community wants them to do.

While again the principles and claims that different societies will come up with will vary from society to society, we can predict that many communities will want their GPs to be involved, for example, in providing health inducing services, prevention, and public health more generally, acting as agents or gate keepers to specialist and hospital care, being accessible and assisting patients/citizens to gain access to other services, and furthering equity with particular reference to disadvantaged people.

This will almost certainly mean some sort of mix of remuneration systems, with capitation to assist in population health issues, fee for service to "fine tune" the sorts of services GPs provide, and target payments to encourage closer to 100 per cent coverage of some, often preventive, services. It will mean that health economists will need to research more on how to use different mixes of payment to move GPs (and other doctors) to provide what the community has indicated in its principles and claims that it wants from its health care system and in particular from its doctors.

Within the power structure in the political economy of health care there will be a need for general practice or better still primary health care to have more power and status. This is an issue that health economists currently tend to neglect. Yet the power structure in health care is such that hospital clinicians in many countries wield power to such an extent that they can coral more resources than are justified in terms of allocative efficiency. The emphasis in the new paradigm on PHC and hospitals as social institutions to be based on the values of the community can help to alter that power imbalance.

One very likely communitarian claim that is underplayed in primary health care at present is access. The evidence from citizens' juries to date is that primary care needs to devote more of its resources to making citizens more aware of what services are available and how to get to them. Communitarian claims will also likely stretch beyond health care *per se*, in that citizens are less concerned about primary health care than primary care for health. The social determinants of health will thereby become of more significance in the economics of health policy.

The new paradigm points to the need to see public health as a social institution. Currently in most countries there is either no or only a poorly recognised entity or institution of public health. That needs to change. Quite how best to do this will vary from country to country, but there is a case for having separate health and health *care* ministries. Most existing so-called health ministries and departments of health are health *care* institutions.

Health, as in public health, population health, and the social determinants of health, is a holistic construct and needs to be addressed as well as possible by a holistic organisational structure, which stretches across the "whole of government"—a wholistic holistic structure. The tasks of such an organisation would include an overall watch on the social determinants of health and advocating with other government departments for health. It would have a brief to prepare "health impact assessments" of government policies, such as: changes in housing allowances for the poor; tax changes and other policies affecting income distribution; how energy policy and global warming policies might affect the health of the population and especially the disadvantaged; food import policies; work place agreements; industry location policies; employment policies; etc. The work is massive and exciting, especially if all government policies were subject to such a "health impact assessment".

With respect to health promotion in public health, health economics currently performs rather badly, largely because it is too often stuck in the paradigm that involves assuming that health promotion is about health and only health. The new paradigm would involve asking the relevant community what principles they want to have underpinning health promotion, and what claims different groups and activities might have over any health promotion spend. While we can only speculate, it is quite likely that the community will want more than simply health improvement from health promotion and to see claims here in terms more of improved choice and autonomy perhaps as much for communities as individuals.

For example Kickbusch et al. (2005) argue:

To have the capacity to exercise greater control over their health . . . people need information, knowledge and understanding. This gives confidence, a will to assert control and to act. An individual with an adequate level of Health Literacy has basic and elaborated knowledge, competencies and learned abilities to take responsibility for her or his health

where Health Literacy is defined as "the cognitive and social skills and ability of individuals to gain access to, understand and use information in ways which promote and maintain good health" (WHO 1998).

Thus the community may opt for the principle of health promotion as providing information to make healthy choices. What is crucial (and this is missing from the above comment from Kickbusch and her colleagues) is a requirement for the community to have a say in such matters and not have this decided by health promotion "experts". That the new paradigm endorses. It is also for the community to seek health literacy rather than, as Kickbusch suggests, only individuals.

Given the responses from two citizens' juries that I have facilitated, citizens are also likely to want, not just information about health, but about health services so that they can better access existing services. The presence of a "maze" in trying to get to services and the lack of a guide or indeed of knowledge on where to go to get a guide are all issues that "health promotion" under the new paradigm might cover.

The new paradigm, by incorporating concerns for power within a political economy framework, and specifically the power relations that stem from neo-liberalism, also shifts the emphasis of policy in health promotion away from "victim blaming" to aiming policy changes more at the perpetrators. As I have suggested previously together with Steve Jan (Jan and Mooney 2006), in the context of obesity there has been a tendency to try to deal with this public health issue by dealing only with the demand side of the equation, e.g. by taxing fast food to reduce consumption. That may be an answer, but it is not for experts to choose that answer. Instead they should give a series of options to the relevant community with the appropriate information about the costs and effects involved and get them to choose. Certainly among the options there ought to be one or more that look to answers on the supply side of the market, such as taxing heavily the marketing budget of fast food suppliers.

There has been a reluctance on the part of policy makers in this area to consult the community, and also a somewhat "politically correct" view of the market. If the market produces unhealthy food then this is either okay because that is what markets do, or alternatively the reason why markets do this is because markets fail. With respect to the former view, given the ill health effects created then it is clearly not okay. On the latter, the market does not fail. The fact that it serves up unhealthy foods is not a case of market failure. There is nothing in market theory to suggest that any firm should be inhibited from making a profit out of serving ill health (see Jan and Mooney 2006).

More often under the new paradigm there will be a recognition of the need to examine the values underpinning the market, against a background of the constitution that citizens have set for public health. The distribution of property rights, as in the power relations in the market for obesity, needs to be exposed and health promotion policy makers should be prepared, with the aid of health economists, to examine how the structural relations can be altered so that health promotion is based firmly on the community's constitution and its judgements about claims.

In the pharmaceutical industry there is a need for the new paradigm to look beyond the economic evaluation of drugs to the way in which the market for pharmaceuticals operates, the direct marketing to the medical profession, and the power of the large companies in influencing governments and the WTO. There has been remarkably little work done on these issues by health economists. The new paradigm pushes for research to be undertaken by health economists, to investigate the power structures in this market and the influence of these companies on the workings of the WTO and other global institutions.

In public health the influence of corporations is not something that health economists currently address directly, whether it be in food and nutrition policy or with respect to the pharmaceutical industry. Yet the influence of these companies on research on pharmaceuticals is becoming all pervasive. As a result:

There is growing concern about Big Pharma's [the world's major pharmaceutical corporations'] unethical behaviour and lack of transparency. It is increasingly entering into financial arrangements with academic and research institutions that threaten the objectivity and credibility of clinical research...In contracts with academic researchers, the companies may insist on controlling how the research is done and reported, and whether the results will be published. Furthermore, a growing number of clinical trials are being managed by investor-owned businesses that are even more beholden to the drug companies because the companies are their only clients (Global Health Watch 2005: 111).

The influence has become so great that "the highly respected *New England Journal of Medicine* [has dropped] its requirement that authors of review articles of medical studies must not have financial ties to the companies whose medicines were being analysed...[because] the journal could no longer find enough independent experts" (p. 111).

Global Health Watch reports that: "Pharmaceutical companies have also been able to purchase influence in regulatory bodies: half the US Food and Drug Administration's budget for evaluation of new drugs comes from pharmaceutical company user fees, making it dependent on the industry it regulates—an obvious conflict of interest" (p. 112).

Yet health economists currently are almost totally absent from investigating the industry. Their research on pharmaceuticals is focused very firmly on the economic evaluation of pharmaceutical products and to some extent the related issue of pricing.

That would almost certainly change under the new paradigm and for three reasons. First, the new paradigm embraces issues of power in the neo-liberal market place, which can, *inter alia*, restrict access to medicines in many countries and the poor in all countries. Second (and relatedly), the paradigm at a global level will highlight the neo-liberal underpinnings of the WTO (and other global institutions) and their influence in protecting the interests of the major pharmaceutical companies. There will then be at least the chance for health economists to expose the problems created by the structure of the industry operating in neo-liberal markets, and thereby begin a process of helping to reform it. Third, the principles that communities raise in their constitutions, and which the global community will endorse in their principles with respect to the operations of global institution such as the WTO, will almost certainly endorse the need for greater equity, especially between rich and poor. That will turn the spotlight on the inequities in access to the products of the pharmaceutical industry, and in turn the inequities created in health.

12.4 Can the new paradigm work in practice?

In some senses the answer to this question is that it is already working. While not a "text book" example, what is happening in Venezuelan health policy has features that are aligned with the new paradigm. The emphasis in that country is on community participation in decision making, on primary care for health, on public funding, and on promoting the social determinants of health. The Venezuelans have rejected the neo-liberal model, not only in health, but for their economy. In doing so they are part of a trend in South America, which has in the past been subjected to some major structural adjustments imposed by the World Bank and the IMF that, in addition to creating very real economic problems, have resulted in major health problems for the poor.

Thus in Chile, for example, Unger et al. (2008) show how neo-liberal reforms in that country failed to deliver health to the poor. They state: "The Chilean health system underwent a drastic neoliberal reform in the 1980s, with the creation of a dual system: public and private health insurance and public and private provision of health services." They point to the fact that the "private part of the Chilean health system ... is highly inefficient and has decreased solidarity between rich and poor, sick and healthy, and young and old". They conclude:

To present the Chilean reform as a model to be followed by other countries, as has been done by the World Bank and other international bodies, is to disregard the evidence, which tends to show that Chile's relatively successful health care provision has been achieved in spite of the reform, not because of it, or in fact because the intended neoliberal reform could not be implemented as foreseen.

The Venezuelan model is described by Muntaner et al. (2007). It very much involves having a primary care for health model based on community participation in decision making and funded by the public sector. "This integrated model of care emphasizes a holistic approach to health and illness through the coordination of [the primary health care organisation with others] addressing education, food security, public sanitation and employment, among other key social determinants of health" (p. 317). They show that "people lacking potable water who suffer from recurring intestinal infections are not only prescribed the appropriate antibiotics but also encouraged to organize to demand adequate access to clean water" (p. 317). The organisational structure is such that "health teams and patients are supported by Health Committees comprised of [community] residents". It is in this way that the local community residents "exercise their participation in primary health care clinics" (p. 317).

There is no reason, as Muntaner et al. (p. 319) indicate, why this model could not be used in the West. As suggested above, this is not a text book example of what the economics of health policy that could be built on the paradigm of this book might look like but it is an approximate case study of one system, which adheres to a number of the facets of the paradigm. Health economists can learn much from a closer examination of such a case study.

12.5 Conclusion

This and the previous three chapters indicate that the new paradigm can have a major impact on health economics and the economics of health policy. There are many other issues not touched on that will be affected—patient payments, health technology assessment, food and nutrition policy, bilateral trade agreements, etc.

Many changes flow from the adoption of the new paradigm. There is already recognition in some quarters of the problems created by the absence of some aspects of this new paradigm. For example the lack of principles to underpin health care, just one aspect of the paradigm, is highlighted in Australia by Menadue (2007):

It is...impossible to find or even to infer any coherent set of principles in our [Australians'] present health policies, particularly on the issue of health care funding. Some services are provided for free while others receive no government support. Some services are covered by tax-funded insurance, but at the same time there are incentives for people to opt out of sharing and into private insurance. Politicians talk of "universalism" and a "commitment to Medicare" [the social insurance system] while encouraging the development of a two-tier hospital system. Politicians talk about "individual responsibility" while encouraging people to hand responsibility over to health insurance corporations. Governments, particularly Coalition governments, speak vaguely about the virtues of the private sector, but in only a few areas of health care is there a degree of market competition; in general health care has been cosseted from market forces. Labor politicians sing the praises of bulk-billing [GP visits zero-priced at the point of consumption], while supporting high co-payments for pharmaceuticals.

The Nuffield Trust (2007) has recently been teasing out and trying to make more explicit the different principles that might exist in the four different countries—England, Northern Ireland, Scotland, and Wales—that make up the UK. These were set by policy makers and not citizens of the four "communities", but in the context of the paradigm this recognition that the values might differ across these four jurisdictions is a start. Menadue's call for principles (and his are to be based on community values) endorses that part of the new paradigm.

At this time it is inevitable that the details of much that is in this chapter has to be somewhat speculative. As of now we have too little knowledge of what any constitution would look like or what different communities would choose as their claims. We can see, however, that major shifts are needed in health economics and the economics of health policy, both in methodology and focus.

References

Anderson, E. (1993) *Values in Ethics and Economics*. Cambridge, MA: Harvard University Press.

Gerard, K. and Mooney, G. (1993) QALY league tables: handle with care, *Health Economics*, 2: 59–64.

Global Health Watch (2005) An alternative world health report. Available at: www.ghwatch.org/2005report/ghw.pdf (accessed 13 Apr. 2008).

Hurley, J. (1998) Welfarism, extra-welfarism and evaluative economic analysis in the health sector, in M. L. Barer, T. E. Getzen and G. L. Stoddart (eds.), *Health, Health Care and Health Economics*. Wiley: Chichester.

Jan, S. and Mooney, G. (2006) Childhood obesity, values and the market, *International Journal of Pediatric Obesity*, 1(3): 131–2.

Kickbusch, I., Maag, D. and Saan, H. (2005) Enabling healthy choices in modern health societies. Background paper for Parallel Forum F6. Available at: www.ilonakickbusch.com/health-literacy/Gastein_2005.pdf (accessed 12 Apr. 2008).

Lexchin, J., Bero, L. A., Djulbegovic, B. and Clark, O. (2003) Pharmaceutical industry sponsorship and research outcome and quality: systematic review, *British Medical Journal*, 326: 1167–70.

Menadue, J. (2007) Health: the importance of getting principles right. Available at: http://cpd.org.au/user/johnmenadue (accessed 12 Apr. 2008).

Muntaner, C., Guerra Salazar, R. M., Benach, J. and Armada, F. (2007) Venezuela's Barrio Adentro: an alternative to neoliberalism in health care, in V. Navarro (ed.), *Neoliberalism, Globalization and Inequalities: Consequences for Health and Quality of Life*. New York: Baywood.

Nuffield Trust (2007) *Devolving Policy, Diverging Values?* London: The Nuffield Trust.

Olsen, J. A. and Donaldson, C. (1998) Helicopters, hearts and hips: using willingness to pay to set priorities for public sector health care programmes, *Social Science and Medicine*, 46(1): 1–12.

Unger, J. P., DePaepe, P., Cantuarias, G. S. and Herrera, O. A. (2008) Chile's neoliberal health reform: an assessment and a critique, *PLoS Med*, 5(4). Available at: e79doi:10.1371/journal.pmed.0050079

WHO (World Health Organization) (1998) *Health Promotion Glossary*. WHO, Geneva.

Part IV
Conclusion

13

Conclusion

Assessing the recent reforms of the Bulgarian health care system, Daskalova et al. (2005) state:

The professed objectives of the reform were to make the health system and services more efficient and responsible to the patients and to improve their quality on the base of restructuring. Five years after the inception of the reform the evaluations, though not categorical, are largely negative. The analysis of the legislation, practical experience and opinions of both patients and medical personnel surveyed provides a basis to delineate several problem areas that could and must be effectively addressed in dialogue with all concern[ed], especially trade unions...One specific feature of the health reform in Bulgaria is the fact that its implementation has largely been predetermined by the macro-economic objectives established by the international financial institutions, for the funds to be spent on social policy, including health and salaries of the employees in the budget funded sector, have been defined in the agreements signed with these institutions. The model of reforming the system of health was chosen unilaterally by the right-wing government at the time. The social partners and society at large were confronted with the *fait accompli* of a health insurance system model that had not been a subject of any serious public debate. The outcome of restructuring and privatization is declining health status of the population, lack of balance between patient and service provider interests, pronounced commercialization of health care, accent on the market and privatization to the detriment of its social functions, financial instability of the system, lack of motivation, alienation and conflicts between the professional communities and, last but not least, corruption. Unjustified expectations for something better were encouraged in society at large. Yet both patients and health employees have been cheated in their expectations. The reform is now increasingly recognized as a political experiment with the health care system that has not turned out well—that is the view of 70–80% of the respondents in different public opinion polls. Our research also reveals alarming levels of discontent and dissatisfaction among health personnel and the population.

There are many countries where similar stories could be told. Yet as this book has tried to highlight, the extent to which health economists have sought to challenge "the macro-economic objectives established by the international financial institutions" has been very limited. The focus of conventional health economics has been largely on the micro economics of health care. Health economics research around the social determinants of health, especially with respect to global poverty and inequality, has been rather limited. The impact of neo-liberalism, which has done so much to destroy solidarity and a sense of community in so many corners of the globe, has lain almost unexamined by health economists. The influences of the global institutions, and their lack of acknowledgement that they are there to represent the peoples of the world, continue to contribute to the poverty and inequality between "North" and "South". Those influences have, with few exceptions, not been subject to analysis by health economists. Yet the documentation in this book of the failure of the Doha Agreement to make inroads on world poverty; the encouragement of the WHO and of Western governments to poorer countries to embrace the privatisation of health care; the lack of will on the part of the WHO to confront the ideology of neo-liberalism in their Commission on the Macroeconomics of Health; the continuing move to "privatisation" of the WHO; the lack of an institutionalised world voice of the people; the lack of willingness of the WTO to do more to get the pharmaceutical industry to provide cheaper medicines for the poor; the use of "conditionalities" and structural adjustment programmes (SAPs) by the IMF and the World Bank to drive neo-liberalism in the developing world: the implications of these policy instruments for world health need much greater attention from health economists than we have devoted to them in the past.

In evaluating health care interventions, health care systems, and policies to promote population health, there has been little attempt by health economists to look beyond outcomes. Disappointingly, most often such outcomes have been restricted to health. In turn health has been seen as a universalist construct, often imposed on other cultures by the West and/or by Western health economists. The value and importance of the institutions, both as organisations and as sets of rules that deliver the outcomes, have been lost behind the closed thinking of the consequentialism of both welfarism and extra-welfarism. From a standard health economics perspective, health care remains largely a medical institution and its value and role as a social institution have been ignored. For health economists, public health has been too closely aligned with the welfarist and extra-welfarist paradigms we have used in analysing health care. The values that drive health care systems and public health as a social institution have been largely neglected by health economists.

Welfarism and even more so extra-welfarism have the merit of allowing quantification, but that has seemingly become almost an end in itself for health economists. The expressive theory of Anderson, adopted here, does not offer the easy virtue of measurability, but it does have a greater realism in what it can encompass. With health, health care, and public health, which are complex entities that elicit often difficult emotions for patients, health staff, and citizens—and emotional trade-offs—there is clearly a choice for health economists. We can opt for the seeming precision and neatness of quantification, or for something that takes account of the reality of what health, health care, and public health are about. Anderson's expressive theory allows us to get closer to the latter. It is clearly my choice, not just because it supports so much better the communitarianism that I believe can and should underpin health policy, but because we as health economists otherwise risk becoming either redundant or trapped in our rather narrow paradigm, when the major health problems which we might help to ameliorate are elsewhere.

The health issues around world poverty and inequality have largely passed us by. The individualism and other problems for health associated with neo-liberalism (such as inequality) we have chosen to ignore. The health and health inequity problems created or as a minimum exacerbated by the World Bank, the IMF, and the WTO have been of little or no concern to health economists outside of the developing world. Health economics analyses of what reform of these bodies might achieve for global health need to become commonplace on the health economists' future agenda. The WHO's macroeconomic review reads as ideologically neutral, but in effect supports the status quo. As such it does too little to address the problems created by existing political structures. Detailed analyses through political economy are needed. The lack of such research inhibits any serious attempt at redistribution of both power and income in the interests of improving global health.

While agreeing that the market for health care fails, we have done all too little to try to build anew. We have tinkered. Health care remains by and large interpreted as a commodity with its characteristics restricted to just one area, namely health.

When we haven't been able to measure the relevant variables—access in equity policy, the output of hospitals, reduced anxiety through the provision of "after hours" primary care—we have simply measured the measurable—use, cost weighted cases, and health outcomes respectively.

More generally our analyses have been dominated by the desire for quantification and in turn the quantifiable.

There has been an odd lack of concern about the distribution of property rights within health care, and in the wake of that all too little soul searching as to why our analyses have had so little impact. Even more is this the case in public health, where we have made few inroads into the economics of these issues, perhaps because of a lack of imagination in looking for some non-clinical paradigm or perhaps because of a lack of willingness to listen to those whose health is being promoted, i.e. the citizens. And this raises the question: where is the community in our analyses?

This book seeks to place the community centre stage, on the basis that health care systems are social institutions, which ought as such to be driven by the values of the community *qua* community, whether that be a local community, a national community, or a global community. Public health very clearly ought to be driven by the values of the relevant population. Certainly in this book it has only been possible, and even then rather tentatively, to suggest ways of eliciting community values. Much more research must follow. It is in no sense an insurmountable problem. As health economists, we just need to turn our minds to it.

It is not enough, however, to get citizens to reveal their preferences for how they value health and other outcomes and processes. We need them to reveal their informed reflective preferences for what they see as the benefits (or "the good") of health care and of public health. In other words, it is not enough to say, for example, what the preferences are in QALYs for quality of life versus quantity of life, with the analyst predetermining what is in the objective function. It is for the citizens to set "a constitution" for the social institutions of health care and public health.

Joan Robinson's "functionary" (see Chapter 3, section 3.6) can in health care and in public health be played by the informed community or its representatives. Just the how needs to be worked out, and it can be. Health economists should for the future, however, first, accept the need to allow such functionaries into the political economy of health and, second, recognise that we need to be involved in any processes of eliciting community preferences.

On the (admittedly limited, but remarkably consistent) evidence that I have to date from the six inquiries that I have conducted into community values (through citizens' juries), citizens appear to be more compassionate and more concerned for social justice than is currently reflected in many health care systems. Certainly health economists have been active in working at achieving equity, but have become blinkered in their thinking by a concern to measure and to compare. We do have tools that can be used to explain inequity and then to address inequity. We would be better to use these rather than sharpening our measuring skills.

At a cultural level we have indulged in a Western hegemony of thought that has left little room for cultural relativism with respect to health, both individual and population health, and with respect to health care systems. The idea that health, as a construct, is universal underlies too many of our efforts. This is a most odd assumption, which does not stand the test of logic or of evidence. It is born of intellectual laziness. Again the idea that equity might be defined independently of its cultural foundations flies in the face of, not just reason but of cultural sensitivity.

There is a need for a new political economy of health, where Vicente Navarro has trod a rather lonely path for too long. This needs to be very firmly about health and not just health care. It also needs to deal with health care systems and public health as social institutions. Citizens value these institutions, not just for their outcomes.

Political economists of health must analyse the impacts of neo-liberalism on health both within individual countries but also globally. They must also examine the global instruments of neo-liberalism—the World Bank, WHO, WTO, G8, and IMF. The reform of these bodies is urgently needed. It will become more urgent with global warming. Global citizenry is absent from these bodies as are, in terms of any meaningful concept of democracy, many of the governments of the poorer countries of the world.

Would the adoption of a new paradigm in health economics make a difference? Clearly I think it would. I have presented some evidence in earlier chapters that I believe supports my position. But it is for readers to decide, and to aid this decision it is worth repeating the quote from Stigltiz (2003), previously quoted in Chapter 5, section 5.3: "If the issue of [improving] access to AIDS drugs were put to a vote, in either developed or developing countries, the overwhelming majority would never support the position of the pharmaceutical companies." There appears to be a gap between what informed citizens of the world want and what global institutions deliver. There seems also to be a gap between the values of a nation's citizens and what is then provided by way of health care and public health. At its very simplest, this book argues that these gaps need to be investigated more and ways found to address them; that health economists have a role to play (with others) in examining these gaps and seeking ways of filling them; and that the paradigm suggested in this book is one way for health economists to make a contribution to reform.

What has been particularly heartening in researching for this book is to discover that some of my basic concerns and ideas are shared by some esteemed health economist colleagues. They may well not agree with my proposals for reform, but there are some key figures who, as a minimum, share my concerns around the values underpinning many of our current health economics endeavours. I think here in particular of Bob Evans, Lucy Gilson, Steve Jan, Maureen Mackintosh, Di McIntyre, Alan Maynard, Uwe Reinhardt, and Tom Rice.

In challenging the existing health economics paradigm, I am sure that I will have succeeded in inadvertently missing some important contributions to health economics by some of my colleagues. I may well have misrepresented some. I could not and did not write in a manner to "cover my back". My suggestions for the new paradigm are challenging and I am full of hope that others, especially younger colleagues, will pick up the challenge and do better.

Those who may agree with the broad thrust of my new paradigm will, I hope, agree that any revised health economics that emerges from it might well be called "Challenging Health Economics"!

References

Daskalova, N., Tomev, L., Ivanova, V. et al. (2005) Health care reforms and privatization—social and economic consequences case of Bulgaria. Available at: www.gpn.org/research/privatization/priv_bulgaria_engl.pdf (accessed 20 Dec. 2007).

Stigltiz, J. (2003) The global benefits of equality. Available at: www.guardian.co.uk/wto/article/0,,1036367,00.html (accessed 20 Dec. 2007).